Malawi

WORLD BIBLIOGRAPHICAL SERIES

General Editors:
Robert G. Neville (Executive Editor)
John J. Horton

Robert A. Myers   Hans H. Wellisch
Ian Wallace   Ralph Lee Woodward, Jr.

John J. Horton is Deputy Librarian of the University of Bradford and currently Chairman of its Academic Board of Studies in Social Sciences. He has maintained a longstanding interest in the discipline of area studies and its associated bibliographical problems, with special reference to European Studies. In particular he has published in the field of Icelandic and of Yugoslav studies, including the two relevant volumes in the World Bibliographical Series.

Robert A. Myers is Associate Professor of Anthropology in the Division of Social Sciences and Director of Study Abroad Programs at Alfred University, Alfred, New York. He has studied post-colonial island nations of the Caribbean and has spent two years in Nigeria on a Fulbright Lectureship. His interests include international public health, historical anthropology and developing societies. In addition to *Amerindians of the Lesser Antilles: a bibliography* (1981), *A Resource Guide to Dominica, 1493-1986* (1987) and numerous articles, he has compiled the World Bibliographical Series volumes on *Dominica* (1987), *Nigeria* (1989) and *Ghana* (1991).

Ian Wallace is Professor of German at the University of Bath. A graduate of Oxford in French and German, he also studied in Tübingen, Heidelberg and Lausanne before taking teaching posts at universities in the USA, Scotland and England. He specializes in contemporary German affairs, especially literature and culture, on which he has published numerous articles and books. In 1979 he founded the journal *GDR Monitor*, which he continues to edit under its new title *German Monitor*.

Hans H. Wellisch is Professor emeritus at the College of Library and Information Services, University of Maryland. He was President of the American Society of Indexers and was a member of the International Federation for Documentation. He is the author of numerous articles and several books on indexing and abstracting, and has published *The Conversion of Scripts and Indexing and Abstracting: an International Bibliography*, and *Indexing from A to Z*. He also contributes frequently to *Journal of the American Society for Information Science*, *The Indexer* and other professional journals.

Ralph Lee Woodward, Jr. is Professor of History at Tulane University, New Orleans. He is the author of *Central America, a Nation Divided*, 2nd ed. (1985), as well as several monographs and more than seventy scholarly articles on modern Latin America. He has also compiled volumes in the World Bibliographical Series on *Belize* (1980), *El Salvador* (1988), *Guatemala* (Rev. Ed.) (1992) and *Nicaragua* (Rev. Ed.) (1994). Dr. Woodward edited the Central American section of the *Research Guide to Central America and the Caribbean* (1985) and is currently associate editor of Scribner's *Encyclopedia of Latin American History*.

VOLUME 8

Malawi

Second Edition

Samuel Decalo

Compiler

CLIO PRESS
OXFORD, ENGLAND · SANTA BARBARA, CALIFORNIA
DENVER, COLORADO

British Library Cataloguing in Publication Data

Malawi.– 2 Rev. ed. – (World
Bibliographical Series; vol. 8)
I. Decalo, Samuel.   II. Series
016.96897

ISBN 1–85109–238–2

ABC-CLIO Ltd.,
Old Clarendon Ironworks,
35A Great Clarendon Street,
Oxford OX2 6AT, England.

ABC-CLIO Inc.,
130 Cremona Drive,
Santa Barbara,
CA 93116, USA.

Designed by Bernard Crossland.
Typeset by Columns Design and Production Services Ltd., Reading, England.
Printed and bound in Great Britain by Bookcraft (Bath) Ltd., Midsomer Norton.

THE WORLD BIBLIOGRAPHICAL SERIES

This series, which is principally designed for the English speaker, will eventually cover every country (and many of the world's principal regions), each in a separate volume comprising annotated entries on works dealing with its history, geography, economy and politics; and with its people, their culture, customs, religion and social organization. Attention will also be paid to current living conditions – housing, education, newspapers, clothing, etc.– that are all too often ignored in standard bibliographies; and to those particular aspects relevant to individual countries. Each volume seeks to achieve, by use of careful selectivity and critical assessment of the literature, an expression of the country and an appreciation of its nature and national aspirations, to guide the reader towards an understanding of its importance. The keynote of the series is to provide, in a uniform format, an interpretation of each country that will express its culture, its place in the world, and the qualities and background that make it unique. The views expressed in individual volumes, however, are not necessarily those of the publisher.

VOLUMES IN THE SERIES

Contents

Contents

Introduction

Malawi is 525 miles long but only 50-100 miles wide. Eighty per cent of
the territory is land, for the country includes most of the 350-mile-long
Lake Malawi, an extension of the Great Rift Valley and Africa's third-
largest body of water. Out of the Lake's southern extremity and beyond
the country's borders into the Zambezi flows the Shire River. Beneath
Mount Mulanje (at 3,050 metres Central Africa's highest peak), the
Shire is flanked by fertile highlands and estates, and further south by
equally fertile though low-lying land. Despite high rugged ridges in the
north, good rainfall and some of the most fertile soils in Central Africa
make more than half of Malawi's land suitable for cultivation.

Over eight million people live in Malawi, Africa's third most
densely populated state. Although it contains eight major ethnic
groups, Malawi possesses considerable ethno-linguistic uniformity.
The national languagte, Chichewa, is the first language of half the
population and is understood by three-quarters of the people. There
are, however, acute demographic and economic imbalances, exacerbated by President Banda's policies, and these have given cause for
concern. The population is unevenly distributed, with half – including
part of the numerically dominant Chewa – residing in the Southern
Region. That is by far the most developed area, and includes the
country's former capital (Zomba) and its main economic nerve centre
and largest town (Blantyre). The 1975 relocation of Malawi's capital
to Lilongwe (a move which was greatly assisted financially by South
Africa), resulted in a demographic shift towards the Central Region
(Malawi's granary), where 40 per cent of the population resides
(including the other part of the Chewa), and where Banda's home
town, Kasungu, is located. By contrast, the Northern Region has poor
soils and a history of economic neglect. Twelve per cent of the
population live in this undeveloped area and it has traditionally been
little more than a manpower reservoir for the plantations of the south
and for the mines of neighbouring states.

The country is named after the Maravi from whom Malawi's Chewa clans trace their descent. Oral tradition refers to the Maravi originating from Katanga (Zaïre), with the first clans arriving at the southwest shores of the lake between the 13th and the 16th century. There is controversy as to whether a centralized Maravi Empire arose, to encompass parts of Zambia and Mozambique, but internal splits and migrations saw several kingdoms founded in the region. A group that branched westward in the 18th century became the Chewa, while those remaining by the lake became the Nyanja (lakeside people). The latter's dialect, Chinyanja, renamed Chichewa, became Malawi's official language in the mid-1970s. Roughly 80 per cent of the Chewa reside within Malawi where they comprise just over half the population; smaller groups are found in both Zambia and Mozambique. Being farmers, the Chewa lived in decentralized federations of chiefdoms. In the 19th century many fell prey to aggressive new arrivals to the region – the Ngoni from the southwest, and Yao and Swahili slavers from the east.

Among the groups north of the Chewa are the Tumbuka, the Ngonde and the Tonga. The Tumbuka, comprising one-tenth of Malawi's population and the dominant group in the North, are among the oldest indigenous people in the country, originating in Zaïre some time after the Maravi. The Ngonde, found in the extreme northern districts of Karonga and Chitipa (as well as in Tanzania), are the southernmost extension of East Africa's inter-lacustrine ethnic group. Their small but strong kingdom, headed by a sacred leader, succumbed in the 19th century to pressures from slave-raiders from the east, and was rescued only by the arrival of British authority in the region.

Further south, in the Nkhata Bay district, reside the lakeside Tonga. Egalitarian, individualistic, part-Chewa, the Tonga were deeply transformed by the 19th-century arrival in their midst of the Livingstonia Mission of the Free Church of Scotland. Missionary activity and education in the northern districts of colonial Nyasaland had profound effects on the area as a whole. While the positive benefits and negative side-effects of missionary activity are still debated, one result was the development of educational standards, modern skills, and personal aspirations among Northerners who had no productive outlets in the region. Thanks to the superior education provided at Livingstonia, Northerners to this day are better educated than the more indolent Chewa in the South. Nevertheless, geographical isolation, poor soils and the minimal potential of the North assured neglect of the region during the colonial era, and after independence its weaker economic and demographic position, and maverick political orientations, assured its being shut out of the power nexus – despite a preponderance of Northerners in the country's civil service – the 'Northern problem' during the Banda reign. Throughout the colonial era large numbers of Northerners, especially Tonga farmers, school-leavers and missionary-trained apprentices deserted their unproductive lands to seek employment further south, where they were in demand because of their skills and literacy. This outward migration (which had pre-colonial antecedents) was aggravated by the imposition of a colonial hut tax that could be satisfied by salaried labour. The policy was aimed at providing labour for the European estates in southern Nyasaland. (Most Chewa avoided employment since they had fertile land.) In the process the North was depopulated, with 60-75 per cent of working-age males absent at any particular time from their homes, many undertaking the 1,000-kilometre trek south on foot.

Most of the other peoples of Malawi are newcomers who arrived in the 19th century. The Nguni, currently one-tenth of the population and found in several districts especially in the Central Region, are kinsmen of South Africa's Zulu. They arrived in several waves starting in the 1850s, and occupied the cooler highlands suitable for cattle-herding. Aggressive conquerors, they erected hierarchically centralized states. Most Chewa chiefs succumbed peacefully to Nguni overlordship, and progressively 'Chewaianized' the minority Nguni – thus assuring that lasting ethnic animosities were not to develop.

The Muslim Yao are also newcomers, expelled from their original lands in Mozambique. Starting in the 1860s, they arrived first as refugees, but later – having discovered the weakness of the Chewa – as overlords. In contact with trade entrepôts on the Indian Ocean, Yao possession of firearms enabled them to branch off into the slave trade, devastating many southern districts. Comprising 15 per cent of the population, they reside in the districts of Mangochi, Ncheu, Blantyre, Zomba and Chiradzulu. Shunning Christianity (which was, paradoxically, first introduced in their midst), the Yao resisted the entry of British authority in the region. Disliked by the Chewa because of their role in slavery, the Yao still do not play a significant political role in contemporary Malawi.

A number of other slave centres existed in the region, near Karonga and especially at Nkhota Kota. In the latter a Swahili Arab sultanate emerged in the 1840s, and became the largest slave entrepôt in Central Africa, with 10,000 slaves 'processed' annually in the 1870s. It was the predatory devastations of slavers that prompted the plea by David Livingstone for a British protectorate in the region, and that, together with Anglo-Portuguese competition for the interior of East Africa, led to Britain's formal assumption of sovereignty over Nyasaland in 1891.

Finally, one should note the turn-of-the-century migration into the southeast of large numbers of Lomwe, and in the south the more recent arrival of the Sena. Today the Lomwe make up one-fifth of Malawi's people, being the second-largest group after the Chewa. Refugees from brutal Portuguese rule in Mozambique, the Lomwe were at the outset subservient to the Chewa. Being landless, many settled on European estates and became trapped in the exploitative *thangata* system then prevailing. Submitting to gruelling manual labour for low wages, they became the backbone of the plantations. It was Lomwe labour that initially developed, and to this day sustains, the tobacco and tea estates – the foundation of Malawi's post-independence economy. By the 1970s, upwardly mobile Lomwe had moved into the modern workforce and held senior positions in the security forces, where, because of their loyalty and 'immigrant' status, they were utilized by Banda as a neutral bulwark *vis-à-vis* his opposition.

Notwithstanding its heterogeneity, and the frictions resulting from slavery, Malawi is not afflicted by inter-ethnic strife, nor has ethnicity played a seriously disruptive role in political life, and this has permitted the relatively easy establishment of a legitimated nationalist political centre. Nor does it appear to have been hampered by the fact that the country's economic disparities gave rise to powerful regionalist sentiments in the North, anchored in the paucity of employment prospects and services in the area, and aggravated by Banda's anti-Northern biases and the preferential treatment accorded development projects in the South.

Malawi emerged from British colonial rule as one of the world's most underdeveloped countries. Industrial activity was minimal and what little commerce existed was dominated by expatriates (Asian or European) who also staffed every senior administrative and technical post in the country. A narrow range of agricultural products brought in over 95 per cent of the country's meagre export earnings that appeared resilient to expansion. With monumental problems of infrastructure (barely 300 of the country's 6,000 miles of tracks were paved or usable during the rainy season), no resources, a large debt, a minuscule tax-base capable of funding only half the government's recurrent expenses, and social services (such as education and health) largely dispensed by private groups (missionaries), most observers doubted Malawi's viability as an independent entity – a basic consideration behind Britain's 1953 forced merger of the colony into the ill-fated Central African Federation.

Much of Malawi's colonial neglect and continued poverty is a function of the country's scarce exploitable resources, and the costliness of conducting trade with the outside world. Known minerals include deposits such as bauxite in the Mulanje Plateau; glass sands in Mchinji district; sizeable coal deposits in Rumphi; oil-bearing strata beneath the deep lake; and the world's richest monazite deposits (containing rare ores) north of Blantyre. Most, however, are unlikely to be tapped since, problems of infrastructure and logistics apart, prospects are constrained by the costly, unreliable routes to the coast. The principal commercial routes are the railways to Beira and Ncala in Mozambique (which are in a state of disrepair), and the very expensive truck route via Zambia and Zimbabwe to South Africa. Until the mid-1980s Pretoria's support for Renamo's guerrilla activity against Maputo resulted in repeated minings of the railways, making the Mozambique routes hazardous, and so causing major domestic shortages of fuels and other imports, as well as leading to the stockpiling in Malawi of exports awaiting transport. Shipping the country's more valuable exports via South Africa consumed 43 per cent of Malawi's foreign earnings in 1988.

Ultimately, Malawi's sole exploitable resources are its fertile soils and energetic people. Fully 90 per cent of the population engages in agriculture, the majority in the smallholder sector that cultivates four-fifths of the arable land, with maize being the main subsistence crop. Given its fertile soils and adequate rainfall, Malawi is self-sufficient in foodstuffs under normal conditions, and when offered realistic producer prices, Malawi's farmers can produce bumper harvests and hefty surpluses for export. However, although such exports have been important sources of revenue for farmers, the bulk of Malawi's export earnings (82 per cent in 1986) come from three cash crops produced primarily on large plantations.

During the colonial era a pro-European policy allowed settlers to acquire large estates in the south. These included the well-watered lands in the Thyola-Mulanje region, parcelled out to various tea planters, and the Shire Highlands where coffee planters were established as early as the 1880s. The plantations relied on local manpower alienated from the land and compelled to offer their labour in exchange for tenancy rights – the infamous *thangata* system – or on migrant labour from the impoverished North forced to seek paid employment in the South in order to pay their taxes. British colonial policy thus enhanced the outflow of migrant labour, many of whom preferred to seek better-paying jobs outside the colony, with all the disruptive socio-economic consequences this brought in its wake. (The European estates came to be manned by newly arriving Lomwe from Mozambique.) Hundreds of thousands of Malawians sought paid employment outside the colony. So numerous was their presence in the mines of South Africa and the Rhodesias, that Chinyanja was the lingua franca of African townships; and with as many as 270,000 Malawians at any one time working abroad, their annual remittances home ($10 million in 1972) formed a net capital inflow second only to that from Malawi's prime export, tobacco.

Tobacco, tea and sugar account for the bulk of Malawi's export earnings. Tea, one of the first crops to be planted in the south, and since successfully introduced in Nkhata Bay, has become a major foreign-exchange earner, second only to tobacco. With around 35,000 tons a year, Malawi is Africa's second-largest tea exporter. High-quality tobacco is cultivated in the Zomba and Mulanje districts, and more recently in the Kasungu and Lilongwe Plains. Tobacco production assumed phenomenal growth rates after independence, with earnings soaring 600 per cent in 1970-78, and currently accounting for half of Malawi's exports. And in the mid-1970s, sugar, a relatively new crop, displaced groundnuts and cotton to become the country's third-largest export, at times even nudging tea from its second rank. Grown in several locations, large quantities are produced, peaking at 175,920 tons in 1983. Because of the crop's low market price, exports of sugar have been susceptible to adverse changes in transport costs, and are the first to be stockpiled when traffic slows on the railways. Other Malawi crops include cotton, cultivated by the Sena in the Shire Valley (and in the far north), peanuts, and confectionery-quality macadamia nuts.

Although Malawi's economy today bears no resemblance to that of Nyasaland in the past, significant controversy exists about the value of the country's economic advances. At independence few outsiders rated highly Malawi's chances of development – the country was insolvent and half of the recurrent budget needs were being met by British subventions. Malawi confounded sceptics, however, by becoming one of only a few states to attain sustained economic growth and food self-sufficiency. Budgetary balance was rapidly attained, British subsidies were renounced ahead of schedule, and State revenues tripled in the first decade with tight controls on expenditures. Though GDP per capita rose slowly, between 1960 and 1976 Malawi chalked up Africa's third-highest GNP per capita growth rate (4.1 per cent per year), with annual growth averaging 12 per cent during the first decade. But while the infrastructure has been developed, and a powerful export-orientated economy has emerged centred around the plantation sector, the average smallholder has benefited little from these advances, a situation which is at the heart of the controversy about the long-term benefits of Banda's lengthy developmental dictatorship.

The Banda era

Banda was catapulted to power on the back of a tide of nationalism that transformed the Malawi Congress Party into a mass party. The party was the outgrowth of a grouping of seventeen Native Associations founded to promote African interests which, until 1949, had been represented solely by missionaries. It was given a new lease on life with the return from abroad of several young Malawians who laid the basis for a well-organized viable mass movement. All that was missing was a prestigious older father-figure who would provide dynamic leadership, to fuse together the urban, rural, traditional and modern wings of the party and stand up to the British over the Federation issue. In the stagnant Nyasaland of the 1950s there were no candidates for the leadership, but overseas lived Dr Hastings Banda, who had supported the party both financially and through counsel. He had personal contacts with British MPs, the Labour Party and the Church of Scotland – all invaluable pressure points above the colonial administration. Banda appeared to be an ideal interim leader since it was felt that as an established professional (doctor) he could not harbour ambitions that might stand in the way of the succession of the younger clique after his 'task' was concluded.

Born between 1898 and 1902 to a Chewa chief near Kasungu, Banda had entered Livingstonia at the age of 13 to be trained as a teacher. Expelled from an examination, allegedly because of a procedural misunderstanding, he then embarked upon the well-trodden path to the mines of South Africa via Southern Rhodesia, working by day as a clerk/interpreter and studying at night. Sponsored by a missionary group, he went to the United States; after a BA in 1931 (in History and Politics) and an MD in 1937, he then attended Edinburgh University, sponsored by the Nyasaland government and the Church of Scotland, of which he was to become an elder. He set up practice in London, and became a respected doctor. From there he did his utmost to sway the British not to merge Nyasaland with the Rhodesias. In the mid-1950s he was cited in divorce proceedings and uprooted himself to embark on a new, but much less satisfying practice in the Gold Coast. It was during this period in his life that the offer reached him to return after forty years abroad to head the campaign against Federation. Far from being the fulfilled individual the young nationalists assumed they were inviting as their front-man, Banda was at a dead end when he suddenly found himself with an alternative career.

Banda's is a complex personality, and his experiences in Johannesburg's slums and his pride at transforming himself from an unschooled urchin into a respected physician at the hub of the British

Empire, made him vain and intolerant. Despite his long period of acculturation overseas, he remained imbued with a Chewa world-view, and retained a nostalgia for the past, something that struck a responsive chord among rural Malawians also bewildered by the rapidly changing world. All of these facts explain in part Banda's instant popularity and political legitimation when he returned home, as well as the jealousy with which he guarded his political throne.

Banda arrived in Blantyre on 6 July 1958, thus revitalizing the political struggle and giving it the momentum it had lacked. He was elected head of the MCP virtually with absolute powers and by 1961 the MCP was the most viable and militant party in all of Africa, with a membership standing at 250,000. 'Unity, Loyalty, Obedience and Discipline' became the official tenets of Malawi, with derision, intimidation and violence against opponents suddenly becoming a nasty characteristic of public life from this point onwards. Ultimately, the Devlin Report on the State of Emergency imposed by the colonial administration in Nyasaland (during which Banda and 1,500 others were imprisoned) vindicated Banda's claim that most Africans opposed federation, and set the country's course towards independence in a more united and mobilized way than most African colonies. Banda's victory over Britain stood at the core of his legitimacy then and has done so ever since: a quarter of a century after the event, up until the multiparty elections in the 1990s that were to see his final demise, this personal triumph figured centrally in his public speeches. The MCP swept the polls in August 1961 gaining 99 per cent of the vote in a 95 per cent turnout. Many opposition candidates did not even get *one* vote, fearing to appear at the polls to cast their own ballot. The MCP repeated its sweep in the 1964 elections preceding independence, with opposition groups intimidated from nominating their candidates.

Despite its image of unity *vis-à-vis* Britain, the MCP leadership was deeply divided on a host of programmatic and ideological issues as well as on leadership style. An impossible situation had been created by the elevation to absolute power of an arch-conservative, domineering older individual, by a young radical clique that saw itself as the country's pace-setters and the power behind the throne. To Banda this age gap was further ground for unquestioning obedience and deference to his views, a fact leading to a major 1964 cabinet crisis that saw the defeat, and escape to Zambia and Tanzania, of those who had brought Banda to power. From their exile, several tried to raise armed opposition against the regime, but without success.

The 1964 crisis was the only time (until the 1990s) that Banda was ever challenged. His victory led to purges that consolidated his idiosyncratic personal rule, setting the pattern for the remainder of his lengthy reign. Though jockeying for political advantage took place on the part of his lieutenants, Banda's supremacy was never challenged. Firmly consolidating a highly conservative, pro-Western personal rule, Banda treated cabinet ministers as errand-boys, dominated all decision-making, and personally supervised every facet of government activity, domestic and foreign policy.

Banda's 'special relationship' with South Africa – in the course of which diplomatic relations were established in 1967, Prime Minister Vorster paid a State Visit in 1970 and massive assistance was granted for the construction of Malawi's new capital of Lilongwe – greatly soured relations with other African states, and especially Tanzania and Mozambique. This was compounded by personal antipathy between Nyerere and Banda, a sentiment going back to the 1960s when Banda had tried to secure a territorial corridor to the coast at Tanzania's expense, and worsened by Tanzania's granting of sanctuary to Banda's 1964 foes, and Banda's allowing Pretoria to mount Renamo's offensive against Maputo in the 1980s. Relations with Zambia have also been thorny, in part due to Banda's claim on northeast Zambia, part of his early vision of a 'Greater Malawi', and the fact that refugees from Banda's rule sought sanctuary in Zambia, with Malawi's Secret Service mounting operations against them. Very early on, Banda wrote off the OAU as irrelevant (noting that it was a tragedy that 'too many ignorant people are in a position of power and responsibility' in Africa[1] making Malawi a virtual pariah in its own continent). At the same time, Malawi's opposition to the seating of China and East Germany at the United Nations, her refusal to initiate diplomatic relations with the Arab world (conditioned by Banda's anti-Arab prejudices stemming from memories of the slave era) have set off the country from most others.

Harsh security measures were entrenched throughout Malawi, including provisions for public executions. When modern (expatriate-staffed) courts disagreed with Banda's concepts of justice, the powers and jurisdiction of traditional courts, headed by pliable chiefs, were expanded, so that 'Malawian' justice would prevail. It was to these courts that Banda's political foes were later brought for trial, many to be sentenced to death. Banda's strict personal moral code and demand for orthodoxy saw the imposition of a dress code (barring such things as beards and miniskirts) and a literary censorship that saw bans on periodicals, newspapers, movies and books (not just Karl Marx and *Penthouse*, but also *The Godfather*). Nor are expatriates immune from Banda's wrath: in September 1969 Peace Corps activities were

---

[1] *Hansard*, Zomba, 17 May 1966, p. 564.

terminated because of alleged complaints about their 'slovenliness', and in 1971 an American instructor at the University who protested about harassment of Jehovah Witnesses was expelled from the country. So was a British woman who publicly called a Banda speech 'rubbish'. Others were hauled to court for wearing 'indecent' apparel, and 250 Goans were expelled in 1976 for 'disrespect' to the President attested by their switching off a radio broadcast of Banda's speech during a wedding reception.

Political freedoms were likewise curtailed and a one-party system was entrenched under Life-President Banda, all as part of the quest for unity. The latter was even justified on quasi-theological grounds: 'there is no opposition in Heaven. God himself does not want opposition – that is why he chased Satan away. Why should Kamuzu have opposition?'[2] Yet though there was no freedom of speech or competitive politics in Malawi, and Banda thoroughly dominated decision-making in the country, the regime defied categorization as a simple dictatorship. Firstly, despite polemical diatribes against its economic policies ('growth without development', and criticism of the bias in favour of estate agriculture and against smallholders), the regime was developmentally inclined, and certainly not a self-seeking tyranny. Moreover, by African standards Malawi's political system was institutionalized. The party was not a mere shell, and some relatively free speech was possible during local party branch meetings, though mostly on local issues. There, popular views often paralleled Banda's own opinions – as was visible in the 1993 elections which, though ushering in the end of the Banda era, underlined the fact that he still retained not inconsiderable support in Chewa rural areas even after a reign of thirty years.

Malawi's evolution likewise reflected Banda's personal predispositions in the socio-economic sphere. Although with time changes did take place, the emphasis of Banda era was on: developing the country's infrastructure (paved roads, railways); restraint in budget allocations for social services (such as education, health) not seen as directly economically productive; a clamp on wage-levels (rural and urban) that saw the development of only minimal rural–urban wage disparities in order to prevent a rural–urban exodus, but at the expense of acute poverty in rural areas; and a strong bias in favour of large-scale commercial agriculture that boosted State exports and revenues, thus transforming Malawi to what some viewed as Africa's economic Cinderella.

Great dangers existed for Malawians near the pinnacle of power, as

[2] *Malawi News*, 20 December 1964.

attested by the constant expulsions of party members, district chairmen and Secretaries General. Most were ousted on the amorphous grounds of 'gross breach of party discipline' – meaning anything annoying Banda. Every year between 1970 and 1990 an average of seven constituencies remained unrepresented in Parliament due to such expulsions; and of the 150 members expelled during 1964-81, forty eventually ended in prison and only two of ten who voluntarily resigned from Parliament during this period remained at liberty. One specific feature of the Banda reign was the fall from grace of every potential successor. The position of Secretary General of the MCP has *not* been the gateway to power, as most incumbents were to discover.

The mid-1970s were particularly tumultous years in Malawi as an internal power struggle (camouflaged as a conspiracy) erupted, bringing in its wake a repression that engulfed the entire country. There were some 2,000 arrests, including many Northerners, mostly Tongan, and amongst them all sixteen staff of the National Statistical Office and two Ministerial statisticians. In February 1976 the only prominent Northerner was purged as Attorney General and Minister of Justice. The University, seen by Banda as a hotbed of radicals had its Principal, Registrar, and many lecturers and students arrested. (A department of Political Science had never been authorized in Malawi!)

The crisis abated with the arrest of the MCP Secretary General and the senior police officer in charge of the Special Branch, who were tried (by a traditional court) for sedition and hanged in September 1977. Both became scapegoats for the repression of 1975-76, and though most detainees were released, few were rehabilitated. In 1980 another power struggle saw the three most influential people after Banda lose their posts, if only because being in line for the succession of the now ageing Banda was in itself enough to ensure their downfall. During 1980-83 other MCP influentials died or fell from grace, reports of their murders being fully revealed only in 1994 after Banda's eclipse. Indeed, between 1976 and 1983 all four MCP Secretaries General were either executed, killed or purged from their posts, with similar eclipses of secondary leaders.

One leader who perennially revolved around the summit of power, seemingly immune from any purge, was John Tembo. An ambitious opportunist and extremely rich to boot, Tembo was part of the 'Kadzamira–Tembo' clique, that included his niece, Cecilia Kadzamira, for decades Banda's 'Official Hostess' and in control of the portals of the Presidential Office; his brother, David, head of the ADMARC marketing giant; and Cecilia's brothers, David, Vice

Introduction

Chancellor of the University of Malawi, and John, Postmaster General. A Ngoni from Dedza with powerful allies in the Police, Malawi's first Finance Minister, and between 1971 and 1984 Governor of the Reserve Bank (dropped under foreign pressure as he was viewed incompetent), Tembo was much disliked in the country and without a power base in the MCP. However, as Banda's health deteriorated, Tembo took up his position at the centre of the stage (as Banda's Chichewa interpreter, Treasurer-General of the MCP and possible heir apparent). Only the relatively peaceful transition in 1993-94 averted a widely expected intramural tug-of-war and possible Tembo victory. In the transition, the aged (according to some, senile) President was forced to concede a multiparty election by domestic and international pressures, in which the MCP received only a minority of the vote. Although there were some who clamoured for Banda's arrest, he was allowed to remain in the seclusion of one of his State residences as Chihuaba assumed presidential power.

The Bibliography

A surprisingly large body of literature exists on Malawi – objectively a fairly small and insignificant country – and this literature is being strongly augmented on an annual basis. Although the selection that follows is fairly comprehensive, it is only a small cross-section of the most important material. In this brief bibliographical note there is space only to alert the reader to three problems. First, the literature on some themes or topics has not been significantly augmented from that obtaining when the first edition of this book was published nearly two decades ago.

Secondly, there is a dearth of books or articles on the political evolution during the Banda era. This is understandable in light of the difficulties of undertaking serious research during this period, but is striking in comparison to the steady stream of outstanding works published in other fields, notably history and religion. And finally, it should be noted that although Malawian scholars have not yet had a great impact on the discipline with either books or articles in the overseas press, their contributions are vital and should not be bypassed. Their work is best seen in the university's various academic publishing series and the country's several scholarly journals.

Dissertations

Frank Alexander. 'Missions in Malawi', MA thesis, Fuller Theological Seminary, 1969.

Edward Alter Alpers. 'The role of the Yao in the development of trade in East-Central Africa', PhD thesis, University of London, 1966.

Eta Elizabeth Banda. 'A study of family life education experiences among the Chewa grandmothers, mothers and daughters in Malawi', PhD thesis, University of Maryland, 1991.

Timothy Kiel Barnekov. 'An inquiry into the development of native administration in Nyasaland, 1888-1939', MA thesis, San Jose State College, California.

Howard Bernard Bickers. 'A missionary strategy for evangelism in Central Africa: an examination of people-movement strategy in the historical cultural context of Malawi', PhD thesis, Southwestern Baptist Theological Seminary, 1977.

Jaspine Dabson Chimpanga Bilima. 'James Malinki of Malawi: Church leader in cross-cultural ministry', PhD thesis, St. Andrews University, 1993.

Keith Bloomfield. 'The petrology of the basement complex in part of southern Nyasaland with particular reference to infracrustal rocks', PhD thesis, Leeds University, 1963.

Robert Benson Boeder. 'Malawians abroad: a history of labor emigration from Malawi to its neighbours, 1890 to the present', PhD dissertation, Michigan State University, 1974.

Bruce P. Browne. 'A politico-geographical analysis of Malawi's borderlands', MA thesis, Michigan State University, 1972.

C. H. W. Bullough. 'Traditional birth attendance in Malawi', MD thesis, University of Glasgow, 1980.

Lorna Michael Butler. 'Bases of women's influence in the rural Malawian domestic group', PhD thesis, Washington State University, 1976.

Dissertations

J. C. Chakanza. 'A general survey of independent Churches in Malawi, 1900-1978', MLitt thesis, University of Aberdeen, 1979.

Martin Leon Chanock. 'British policy in Central Africa, 1908-1926', PhD thesis, University of Cambridge, 1968.

Aleck Humphrey Che-Mponda. 'The Malawi–Tanzania border and territorial dispute, 1968: a case study of boundary and territorial imperatives in the new Africa', PhD dissertation, Howard University, 1972.

Prainy Lucian Chikhula. 'The implementation of basic human needs as a tool of economic development: some evidence from Malawi's sectoral growth', PhD thesis, SUNY/Buffalo, 1983.

Charles D. Chilimampunga. 'Rural–urban migration and economic development in Malawi', PhD thesis, University of Waterloo (Canada), 1992.

Moira Primula Frances Chimombo. 'Overgeneralization in negation: a comparison of first and second language acquisition', EdD thesis, Columbia University Teachers College, 1981.

Steve Bernard Miles Chimombo. 'Contemporary Malawian novels', EdD thesis, Columbia University Teachers College, 1980.

B. M. Chimwaza. 'Food and nutrition in Malawi', PhD thesis, University of London, 1982.

Dennis Danny Chimwenje. 'Curriculum planning and decision-making process in secondary schools in Malawi', EdD thesis, University of Massachusetts, 1990.

G. H. R. Chipande. 'Smallholder agriculture as a rural development strategy: the case of Malawi', PhD thesis, University of Glasgow, 1983.

Chinyamata Chipeta. 'Family farm organization and commercialization of agriculture', PhD thesis, Washington University, 1976.

Obyrne Japhet Mapopa Chipeta. 'The early history of the Tumbuka c. 1400-1700: from economic and political enlargement of scale to economic decline and political fragmentation', MA thesis, Dalhousie University, 1982.

Wiseman Chijere Chirwa. '*Theba* is power: rural labor, migrancy and fishing in Malawi, 1980-1988', PhD thesis, Queens University (Canada), 1992.

Michael Wayne Conner. 'The art of the Jere and Maseko of Malawi 1818-1964', PhD dissertation, Indiana University, 1991.

Diana Catherine Crader. 'Hunters along farmers: faunal remains from Chenchere II rockshelter, Malawi', PhD thesis, University of California/Berkeley, 1981.

Cynthia Ann Crosby. 'A history of the Nyasaland Railway, 1895-1935: a study in colonial economic development', PhD thesis, Syracuse University, 1974.

Cyril Vernon Cutting. 'Chemical aspects of some Nyasaland soils with reference to the production of tung oil and tea', PhD thesis, University of London, 1956.

Zan-dong Ding. 'Shallow crustal structure in northern Lake Malawi from two-ship expanded spread profile', PhD thesis, Duke University, 1991.

Karen Elise Fields. 'Revival and rebellion in colonial central Africa: social and political consequences of missionary enterprise', PhD thesis, Brandeis University, 1977.

Steven Michael Friedson. 'The dancing prophets of Malawi: Music and healing among the Tumbuka', PhD dissertation, University of Washington, 1991.

Derrick Kanyerere Gondwe. 'The incidence and economic effects of indirect taxation in Malawi', PhD thesis, University of Manitoba, 1978.

Loveness Gondwe. 'Factors in the design of an English language syllabus for engineering students at the Malawi polytechnic', PhD thesis, University of East Anglia, 1988.

Ronald E. Gregson. 'Work, exchange and leadership: the mobilization of agricultural labor among the Tumbuka of the Henga Valley', PhD thesis, Columbia University, 1969.

Bernard Anderton Harawa. 'The Teachers' Union of Malawi: its emergence, development and activities from 1943 to 1973', EdD thesis, Columbia University, 1974.

Deborah Ann Harding. 'The phonology and morphology of Chinyanja', PhD thesis, University of California/Los Angeles, 1966.

Trevor Hill. 'The phonetics of a Nyanja speaker', MA thesis, University of London, 1948.

Jacob Ogbonnaya Ibik. 'Law of marriage in Nyasaland', PhD thesis, University of London, 1966.

Leslie Austin Lionel James. 'Education in the Rhodesias and Nyasaland, 1890-1963', PhD thesis, New York University, 1965.

C. T. Jenkins. 'Management and management education in a less well-developed economy: the case of Malawi', PhD thesis, Aston University, 1986.

Power Joey. 'Individual enterprise and enterprising individuals: African entrepreneurship in Blantyre and Limbe, 1907-1953', PhD thesis, Dalhousie University (Canada), 1990.

Selby Hickey Joffe. 'Political culture and communication in Malawi: the hortatory regime of Kamuzu Banda', PhD thesis, Boston University, 1973.

Yusuf Medadlly Juwayeyi. 'The later prehistory of southern Malawi: a contribution to the study of technology and economy during the later Stone Age and Iron Age periods', PhD thesis, University of California/Berkeley, 1981.

Zemani David Kadzamira. 'Local politics and the administration of development in Malawi', PhD thesis, University of Manchester, 1974.

Patrick Augustine Kalilombe. 'From "outstation" to "small Christian communities": a comparison between two pastoral methods', PhD thesis, Graduate Theological Union, 1983.

Owen J. Kalinga. 'The Ngonde kingdom of northern Malawi, 1600-1895', PhD thesis, University of London, 1974.

Ezekiel Kalipeni. 'Internal migration and development in Malawi: A geographic perspective', PhD thesis, University of North Carolina at Chapel Hill, 1986.

I. A. K. Kandawire. 'Local leadership and socio-economic changes in Chingale area of Zomba district in Malawi', PhD thesis, University of Edinburgh, 1972.

Jonni Miika Kanerva. 'Focus and phrasing in Chichewa phonology', PhD thesis, Stanford University, 1990.

Martin Cecil Kanyuka. 'Moral regulation of young offenders in Malawi: a study of the Chilwa Approved School', PhD thesis, University of Toronto, 1989.

Thomas Peter Kapito. 'Yao resistance to Christian marriage? possibilities of a local theology of marriage', PhD thesis, University of Ottawa, 1989.

Jonathan B. M. Kaunda. 'Malawi: development policy and the centralized state – a study of Liwonde Agricultural Development Division', PhD thesis, University of East Anglia, 1988.

David John Killick. 'Technology in its social setting: bloomery iron smelting at Kasungu, Malawi 1860-1940', PhD thesis, Yale University, 1990.

Paul A. Kishindo. 'Agricultural development at the grass-roots: a study of smallholders in Malawi', PhD thesis, University of Hull, 1983.

Irving Leslie Kornfield. 'Evolutionary genetics of endemic Cichlid fishes (Pisces: Cichlidae) in Lake Malawi, Africa', PhD thesis, SUNY/Stony Brook, 1974.

B. S. Krishnamurthy. 'Land and labour in Nyasaland, 1891-1914', PhD thesis, University of London, 1964.

Isaac C. Lamba. 'The history of post-war education in colonial Malawi 1945-1961', PhD thesis, University of Edinburgh, 1984.

Harold Marius Lange. 'The development of higher education in an emergent country: Malawi, Africa, 1960-1967', EdD thesis, University of Southern California, 1973.

Harry Wells Langworthy. 'A history of Undi's kingdom to 1890; aspects of Chewa history in East Central Africa', PhD thesis, Boston University, 1969.

C. J. Lawless. 'An investigation into the use of programmed learning materials in Malawi secondary schools', PhD thesis, University of Reading, 1973.

D. H. Laycock. 'Experiments in the growing and harvesting of tea in Nyasaland', MSc thesis, University of Leeds, 1955.

U. Lindskog. 'Child health and household water supply. An intervention study from Malawi', Linköping University, 1987.

Thomas Franklin Lowry. 'An integration of American guidance principles with the education and culture of Malawi', PhD thesis, University of North Dakota, 1977.

Roderick J. Macdonald. 'A history of African education in Nyasaland, 1875-1945', PhD thesis, University of Edinburgh, 1969.

William Eugene Mackie. 'Radio broadcasting in Malawi: a search for identity and service', PhD thesis, University of Missouri, 1971.

William Emmet McFarren. 'History in the land of flames: the Maravi states of pre-colonial Malawi', PhD thesis, University of California, Berkeley, 1986.

Murlene McKinnon. 'Commerce, Christianity and the gunboat: an historical study of Malawi lake and river transport, 1850-1914', PhD thesis, Michigan State University, 1977.

Hugh W. Macmillan. 'The origins and development of the African Lakes Company: 1878-1908', PhD thesis, University of Edinburgh, 1970.

Emily Nyamazao Maliwa. 'The history of nationalism and intellectual movements in Nyasaland', MA thesis, University of Chicago, 1961.

Emily Nyamazao Maliwa. 'Customary law and administration of justice, 1890-1933', MPhil thesis, University of London, 1967.

A. C. Mapanje. 'The use of traditional literary forms in modern Malawian writing in English', MPhil thesis, University of London, 1975.

Geoffrey Lusekelo Du Mhango. 'The economics and success of "people's participation" in the production and management of low-income urban housing in developing countries', PhD thesis, University of California, 1990.

Dissertations

D. Milazi. 'Malawian migration in relation to the South African farming and mining economy', PhD thesis, Free University of West Berlin, 1975.
R. Mulomboji Mkandawire. 'A study of extention work under two agricultural settings in Malawi', PhD thesis, University of East Anglia, 1984.
Selina Chimika Mhango Mkandawira. 'An investigation of protein-energy malnutrition in Malawi with special reference to children in the age-group infancy to five years', EdD thesis, Columbia University Teachers College, 1991.
Joest Jacob Mnemba. 'The battle for the African church: developing a conception and praxis for the ecumenical church in Malawi', PhD thesis, Lutheran School of Theology at Chicago, 1986.
C. M. Moyo. 'Local participation in rural development projects: the case of Malawi', PhD thesis, University of Edinburgh, 1984.
Kenneth W. Mufuka. 'The role of a missionary in the colonization of Malawi, 1875-1927: an assessment of the career of Dr. Robert Laws', MA thesis, University of St. Andrews, 1971.
Steve S. Mwiyeriwa. 'Vernacular literature of Malawi, 1854-1975, an annotated bibliography', MLA thesis, University of Malawi, 1978.
C. R. Namponya. 'Agriculture in Malawi: an annotated bibliography, 1930-1974', MA thesis, University of Malawi, 1976.
Clement H. Ng'ong'ola. 'Land law and economic development in Malawi', PhD thesis, University of London, 1983.
D. Nkhwazi. 'Presidential leadership in Malawi', PhD thesis, University of Hamburg, 1971.
G. T. Nurse. 'The physical characters of the Maravi', PhD thesis, University of Witwatersrand (South Africa), 1975.
Gregory John Orr. 'Aspects of the second language acquisition of Chichewa noun class morphology', PhD thesis, University of California/Los Angeles, 1987.
Melvin E. Page. 'Malawians in the Great War and after, 1914-1925', PhD thesis, Michigan State University, 1977.
Kings M. Phiri. 'Chewa history in central Malawi and the use of oral tradition', PhD thesis, University of Wisconsin, 1975.
S. H. Phiri. 'Some aspects of spatial interaction and reaction to governmental policies in a border area: a study in the historical and political geography of rural development in the Zambia/Malawi and Zambia/Mozambique frontier zone, 1870-1979', PhD thesis, University of Liverpool, 1981.
Ann Maureen Matekwe Phoya. 'An exploration of the factors that influence early prenatal care enrollment and compliance behaviour among rural Malawian pregnant women', DNSc thesis, Catholic University of America, 1993.

Simon Arthur Roberts. 'The growth of an integrated legal system in
    Malawi: a study in racial distinctions in the law', PhD thesis,
    University of London, 1967.
Andrew C. Ross. 'Origins and development of the Church of Scotland
    Mission, Blantyre, Nyasaland, 1875-1926', PhD thesis, University
    of Edinburgh, 1968.
F. E. Sanderson. 'Nyasaland migrant labour in British Central Africa,
    1890-1939', MA thesis, Manchester University, 1960.
Matthew Schoffeleers. 'Symbolic and social aspects of spirit worship
    among the Mang'anja', DPhil thesis, Oxford University, 1968.
Matthew Schoffeleers. 'Symbolic and spirit workshop among the
    Mang'anja', DPhil thesis, Oxford University, 1968.
H. Simukonda. 'Rural transformation and smallholder agriculture in
    Malawi: a case-study of the Karonga rural development project',
    PhD thesis, University College of Swansea, 1983.
Harvey Jefferey Sindima. 'Malawian churches and the struggle for
    life and personhood: crisis and rupture of Malawian thought and
    society', PhD thesis, Princeton Theological Seminary, 1987.
Richard G. Stuart. 'Christianity and the Chewa: the Anglican case,
    1885-1950', PhD thesis, University of London, 1974.
Roger Tangri. 'The development of modern African politics and
    emergence of a nationalist movement in colonial Malawi', PhD
    thesis, University of Edinburgh, 1970.
Leroy Vail. 'Aspects of the Tumbuka verb', PhD thesis, University
    Wisconsin, 1975.
Betty Wilbert. 'Education in Malawi', MA thesis, Howard University,
    1965.
Arnold Paul Wendroff. 'Trouble-shooters and trouble-makers:
    witchfinding and traditional Malawian medicine', PhD thesis, City
    University of New York, 1985.
David Wilson. 'The improvement of basic data used in educational
    planning: a case study – Malawi', PhD thesis, Syracuse University,
    1969.
Eric R. de Winter. 'Health services of a district hospital in Malawi',
    PhD thesis, University of Amsterdam, 1972.

The Country and Its People

1 Malawi.
Martha S. B. Lane. Chicago, Illinois: Children's Press, 1990. 126p.
This is a book aimed at young readers. It consists of an introduction to the geography, history, government and economy of Malawi, and describes the lifestyles of its people. It contains colour illustrations throughout. Somewhat similar, though aimed at a different age-group, is Renfield Sanders, *Malawi* (New York: Chelsea House Publishers, 1990. 103p.).

2 Malawi.
In: *Africa Today.* London: Africa Books, 1991, p. 1209-33.
This is a compact overview of Malawi's history, economy, politics and social framework, followed by seven pages of statistical data (some from 1983). It includes lists of the government of Malawi, its diplomatic representatives abroad, and foreign representatives in Lilongwe.

3 Malawi.
In: *Africa*, edited by Sean Moroney. New York: Facts on File, 1989, vol. 1, p. 313-26.
A compact overview of all aspects of Malawi: its geography, history, population, and recent social, economic and political evolution.

4 Malawi in pictures.
Thomas O'Toole. Minneapolis, Minnesota: Lerner Publications, 1988. 64p.
This book is a revised edition of Bernardine Bailey, *Malawi* (New York: Sterling Publishing, 1973). The work describes the topography, history, society, economy and government of Malawi, and is illustrated with photographs. See also Vera Garland and Frank Johnston, *Malawi, lake of stars* (Blantyre: Central Africana, 1993. 160p.).

1

5 **The Shire Highland.**
John Buchanan. Blantyre: Blantyre Publishing, 1982. [n.p.]. bibliog.
This is a reprint of the classic description of the country and its agricultural resources
originally published in 1885. John Buchanan first went to Malawi as a missionary,
and after his dismissal consequent to the Blantyre Mission scandal, became a
prosperous businessman.

6 **Twenty-five years of independence in Malawi, 1964-1989.**
B. F. Kandoole, K. M. Phiri. Blantyre: Dzuka Publishing, 1989. 116p.
bibliog.
A laudatory review, accompanied by many colour illustrations, of Malawi's record of
progress in all spheres since independence. There exists another more glossy book,
including 100 pages of photographs, issued to commemorate Malawi's 10th
anniversary of independence: *Smiling Malawi* (Zomba: Government Printer, 1976.
143p.).

Malawi in maps.
See item no. 20.

Area handbook for Malawi.
See item no. 470.

Historical dictionary of Malawi.
See item no. 481.

Know Africa.
See item no. 483.

Travel and Tourism

7 **Guide to the Mulanje massif.**
   F. Easwood. Johannesburg: Lorton Publications, 1979. 74p. maps.

A guide to the mountain trails and attractions of the massif dominating the skyline in southern Malawi. For a recent guide to the entire southern region of the country, see Vera Garland's *Blantyre and the southern region of Malawi: an official guide* (Blantyre: Central Africana, 1991. 163p.).

8 **The land of the lake: a guide to Malawi.**
   David Tattersall. Blantyre: Blantyre Periodicals, 1982. 116p. maps.

Until the more recent spate of guides this was the standard tourist manual on Malawi. It contains full details about the country's hotels, restaurants, sports facilities, national parks and different tourist circuits. Its drawbacks are that the book is full of distracting advertisements, and information on more esoteric attractions is scarce. See also the older *Malawi: holiday guide* (Blantyre: Department of Tourism, 1972. 63p.). For wildlife (of which there is progressively less) see the brief section on Malawi in *African wildlife safaris* (New York: Facts on File, 1989). For a rare illustrated guide of northern Malawi, a region that is much more scenic in a wild way, see Margaret Roseveare and Lee Myers, *Mzuzu and the northern region of Malawi: an official guide* (Blantyre: Central Africana, 1991. 93p.).

9 **Lilongwe and the central region of Malawi.**
   Alison Matthews (et al.). Blantyre: Central Africana, 1991. maps.

Since the construction of Malawi's new capital and international airport at Lilongwe most international visitors now land there (rather than, as before, at Blantyre) and stay on the Lake. This manual, therefore, concentrates on providing tourist information on these areas.

10 **Malawi.**
A. Hulsbomer.   Chalfont St. Peter, England: Bradt Publications, 1991.
139p. maps.
This recent book is a concise summary of the country's history, society and culture. It
includes tourist information interspersed with maps and plates.

11 **Malawi.**
Geoff Crowther.   In: *Africa on a shoestring.*   Hawthorne, Australia;
Berkeley, California: Lonely Planet Publications, 1989, p. 321-40.
Periodically updated, this is one of the better tourist manuals to budget travel in
Africa. It is, however, less detailed than the several books exclusively on Malawi
tourism. Nevertheless, the chapter contains useful information on budget options both
in urban centres and in the countryside.

12 **Malawi.**
Alan Rake.   In: *Traveller's Guide to Central and Southern Africa.*
London: IC Publications, 1990, 7th ed., p. 100-15.
A brief description of the country, its tourist sites and the available accommodation.
For similar information, see 'Malawi' in the periodically updated UTA Airlines
publication (for example: 1989, p. 194-207). UTA used to fly twice weekly on the
rather unusual Paris–Libreville–Lilongwe route.

13 **Malawi: wildlife, parks and reserves.**
Judy Carter.   London: Macmillan, 1987. 176p. maps.
This is a guidebook to Malawi's national parks and reserves. Several such tourist
publications have been issued. One good example is *Malawi – the warm heart of
Africa* (Blantyre: Mastward, 1978. 160p.).

14 **The Malawi cookbook.**
Annabel Shaxson, Pat Dickson, June Walker.   Zomba: Government
Printer, 1985. 3rd. ed. 164p.
This is a very popular cookbook in Malawi (as attested by the fact that a fourth
edition is scheduled). Aimed at expatriates in Malawi and tourists from abroad, it
contains a surprisingly comprehensive array of unusual and not so unusual recipes,
some of which would require access to ingredients not normally available overseas
(e.g. grasshoppers, red locusts, and other insects). For another more recent
publication, published by the Malawi Congress Party's women's branch, see
Malawi's traditional and modern cooking (Lilongwe: CCAM, 1992. 261p.).

15 **Visitor's guide to Malawi.**
Martine Maurel.   Edison, New Jersey: Hunter Publishing, 1990. 203p.
maps.
This book is a very detailed and comprehensive tourist guide to Malawi, and includes
many regional maps, description of routes and potential hazards, as well as prices of
accommodation throughout the country.

16 **Zomba mountains: a walkers' guide.**
H. M. Cundy, K. E. Cundy. Blantyre: Malawi Correspondence
College, 1975. 33p.
An illustrated guide to walks possible on the much-frequented Zomba mountain near
Chancellor College. One of Malawi's most delightful hotels is perched on top of the
mountain. The booklet includes references to edible plants found in the area.

Malawi in maps.
See item no. 20.

The amphibians of Malawi.
See item no. 37.

The birds of Malawi.
See item no. 39.

Malawi's national parks and game reserves.
See item no. 50.

Mammals of Malawi.
See item no. 51.

Ten (or so) primates of Malawi.
See item no. 57.

Blantyre historical guide.
See item no. 435.

Blantyre's early buildings.
See item no. 436.

Historical buildings of Malawi.
See item no. 437.

Geography and Geology

17 **Dambos and environmental change in Malawi.**
J. R. Whitlow. In: *Small channelless valleys in the tropics: characteristics, formation, utilization*, edited by Michael F. Thomas, Andrew S. Goudie. Berlin: Borntraeger, 1985, p. 147-69.
This description of the geomorphology and sedimentology of the dambos in the Lilongwe plains and those in the Nyika plateau shows how they differ from each other.

18 **Geomorphology and the Mlanje mountain.**
Colin A. Baker. *Society of Malawi Journal*, vol. 19, pt. 1 (Jan. 1966), p. 21-31.
An examination of the Precambrian Mlanje mountain dominating the skyline of southern Malawi. For three other surveys, see K. Bloomfield and Anthony Young, 'The geology and geomorphology of Zomba Mountain', *Nyasaland Journal*, vol. 14, pt. 2 (July 1961), p. 54-80; E. C. Thatcher and K. E. Wilderspin, *The geology of the Mchinje–Upper Bua area* (Zomba: Government Printer, 1968. 72p.); W. G. G. Cooper and K. Bloomfield, *The geology of the Tambani–Salambidwe area* (Zomba: Ministry of Lands and Surveys Bulletin, no. 13 (1961). 61p.).

19 **Malawi: a geographical study.**
John G. Pike, G. T. Rimmington. London: Oxford University Press, 1965. 229p. maps.
Though dated, this work remains the standard book on Malawi's physical and social geography.

20 **Malawi in maps.**
Swanzie Agnew, Michael Stubbs.   London: University of London
Press, 1972. 143p. maps. bibliog.
A comprehensive geography of Malawi presented through a series of maps. These are
accompanied by commentary by experts on the country's agriculture, climate, soil
erosion, vegetation, demography and cattle distribution.

21 **Malawi meteorites, 1899-1981.**
M. J. Crow.   *Society of Malawi Geographers* (Blantyre), vol. 36, no. 1
(1983), p. 16-32. maps.
Malawi, with its high-altitude ranges, is well suited for meteorite falls, and several of
those that have come down in the past are described. These include the Kota Kota fall
(discovered in 1905), and the meteorite falls at Zomba (1899), Mtola (1944), Dowa
(1966) and Machinga (1981).

22 **Malawi: official standard names approved by the U. S. Board on
Geographic Names.**
United States, Geographic Names Division.   Washington, DC: Board
on Geographic Names, 1970, 161p. map.
This is the official US gazetteer that contains some 10,200 alphabetically arranged
entries for villages, towns and topographical features of Malawi, and their precise
geographical coordinates. The publication is somewhat dated since it does not contain
some of the official place-name changes of the 1970s.

23 **The Malawi Rift.**
R. Crossley, M. J. Crow.   In: *Geodynamic evolution of the Afro-Arabian
Rift system.*   Rome: Accademia Nazionale dei Lincei, 1980, p. 78-88.
maps. bibliog.
This is a geographical and geological study of the Malawi Rift Valley, within which is
found Lake Malawi. The area is still seismologically active. For more material on the
Rift Valley, see R. Crossley, 'Controls of sedimentation in the Malawi Rift Valley',
Sedimentary Geology (Amsterdam), vol. 40 (1948), p. 33-50. See also D. P. Piper (et
al.), 'A stratigraphic and structural reappraisal of central Malawi: results of a
geotraverse', *Journal of African Earth Sciences* (Oxford), vol. 8, no. 1 (1989), p. 79-90.

24 **Maps and surveys of Malawi: a history of cartography and the land
survey profession.**
Colin G. C. Martin.   Cape Town: A. A. Balkema, 1980. 270p. maps.
bibliog.
Martin has produced a remarkably comprehensive study of the history of cartography
and land surveys in Malawi from the 15th century to 1980.

25 **Mineral exploration in Malawi.**
J. C. Chatupa. *Malawi Geographer* (Zomba), no. 19 (1979), p. 40-57. map. bibliog.

An overview of Malawi's known mineral resources, and all the geochemical and geophysical prospecting taking place in 1978. See also D. Ottley, 'Mineral resources potential of Malawi', *Mining Magazine* (San Francisco), (Feb. 1989), p. 128-30; S. W. Morel, 'Malawi glimmerites', *Journal of African Earth Sciences* (Oxford), vol. 7, no. 7/8 (1988), p. 987-98; and S. W. Morel, 'Petrology and geothermometry of the Little Michiru complex, Malawi', *Mineralogical Magazine*, vol. 53, no. 3 (1989), p. 285-91.

26 **The national atlas of Malawi.**
Lilongwe: National Atlas Coordinating Committee, 1983. 79p. maps.

This atlas includes a comprehensive collection of maps of Malawi's natural environment, land resources, agriculture and industry. It includes a gazetteer (p. 71-9) with a list of place-names.

27 **Notes on the climate of Malawi.**
I. W. Lakoni. *Malawi Geographer* (Zomba), vol. 18 (1978), p. 14-23. maps.

A brief explanation of Malawi's climatology, supplemented by maps, charts and a diagram. The author is a member of the Malawi Meteorological Services. See also *Monthly and annual rainfall in Malawi during the 30 years, 1941 to 1970* (Chileka: Malawi Meteorological Service, 1981. 198p.); and I. N. Lancaster, 'Relationship between altitude and temperature in Malawi', *South African Geographical Journal* (Braamfontein), vol. 62, no. 1 (April 1980), p. 89-97. For a comprehensive compendium of climatological tables see *Climatological tables for Malawi* (Chileka: Meteorological Services, 1982. 70p.).

28 **A short history and annotated bibliography on soil and water conservation in Malawi.**
E. J. Mwendera. Maseru, Lesotho: SADDC, 1989. 160p.

This book comprises five pages of text and 145 fully annotated entries on soil conditions and water resources in Malawi. See also T. F. Shaxson, 'A map of distribution of major biotic communities in Malawi', *Society of Malawi Journal*, vol. 30, pt. 1 (Jan. 1977), p. 35-48.

29 **Variations in the level of Lake Malawi.**
R. Crossley. *Malawi Geographer* (Zomba), no. 19 (1979), p. 5-18.

This article, illustrated with diagrams, explains the causes for Lake Malawi's not inconsiderable periodical changes of level. See also R. S. Drayton (et al.), *A regional analysis of river floods and low flows in Malawi* (Lilongwe: Water Resources Branch, 1980. 79p.); R. S. Drayton, *A preliminary survey of water resources of Malawi* (Lilongwe: Water Resources Branch, 1980. 37p.); John G. Pike, 'The hydrology of Lake Malawi', *Society of Malawi Geographers* (Zomba), vol. 21, no. 2 (July 1968), p. 20-47; H. Neuland, 'Abnormal high water levels of Lake Malawi? An attempt to assess the future behaviour of the lake water levels', *GeoJournal*, vol. 9, no. 4 (1984),

p. 323-34; and John G. Pike, 'The sunspot/lake level relationship and the control of Lake Malawi', *Society of Malawi Journal*, vol. 21, pt. 2 (July 1968), p. 48-59.

Draft environmental profile of Malawi.
See item no. 32.

Livingstone's African journal, 1853-1856.
See item no. 94.

Area handbook for Malawi.
See item no. 470.

Ecology and
Environment

30 **Colonialism, capitalism and ecological crisis in Malawi:
a re-assessment.**
John McCracken.   In: *Conservation in Africa*, edited by D. Anderson,
R. Grove.   Cambridge: Cambridge University Press, 1987, p. 63-77.
map. bibliog.

McCracken investigates the spread of tsetse fly belts in colonial Malawi in order to
evaluate the validity of the contention that contemporary ecological catastrophes are
directly traceable to degradations of a viable precolonial ecology by the spread of
capitalism and colonialism. He suggests such conclusions are oversimplifications at
least with respect to the spread or contraction of tsetse fly belts.

31 **Confronting an unsolvable problem: deforestation in Malawi.**
David French.   *World Development*, vol. 14, no. 4 (1986), p. 531-40.

French argues that the low price of firewood from customary lands, and the low
financial returns from tree planting for firewood purposes, make the process of
deforestation in Malawi simply irreversible. This reality imposes on the government
quite different tree-planting strategies than would be the case if the process were
reversible. He enumerates some of those strategies. See also the various contributions
in M. Ngulube (et al.), *Proceedings of the national forestry research symposium*
(Zomba: Forestry Research Institute, 1990. 262p.).

32 **Draft environmental profile of Malawi.**
Robert G. Varady.   Washington, DC: Department of State,
US National Committee for Man and the Biosphere, 1982. 196p.

Prepared under contract by the Office of Arid Lands Studies at the University of
Arizona, this book is a voluminous inventory of all information available in the
United States on the environment and natural resources of Malawi. It is one in a series
of such studies for countries receiving US bilateral assistance. The work covers
Malawi's geology, mineral, water and energy resources, climate, land use, flora and

fauna, wildlife, prevalent diseases and much more. The appendices include a wide array of tables, from those listing wild flowers (as of 1975), grasses (1938) and edible fungi, to sources of private and public foreign aid.

33 Malawi.
Richard Scobey. In: *Energy and development in Southern Africa*, edited by Phil O'Keefe, Barry Munslow. Stockholm: Royal Swedish Academy of Sciences; Uppsala: Scandinavian Institute of African Studies, 1984, vol. 1, p. 171-86.

A detailed analysis of the energy consumption and commercial and non-commercial energy supplies in Malawi, one of nine country studies in this two-volume work. Projections indicate that by the year 1995 the limits of the population capable of being sustained on existing arable land in Malawi will have been reached, a conclusion also reached by other scholars. In like manner the population's annual fuel needs will rapidly begin to exceed existing (and irreversibly depleted) fuel supplies, a fact leading to periodical shortages of firewood. Since prospects of economic growth are quite limited, the study paints overall a bleak picture for the future of Malawi.

34 Population growth and environmental degradation in Malawi.
Ezekiel Kalipeni. *Africa Insight* (Pretoria), vol. 22, no. 4 (1992), p. 273-82. map.

This is a very recent survey of the serious environmental degradation going on in Malawi, with the author arguing that much of the damage is linked directly to population growth and the pressure this puts on the limited land resources.

35 A note on the underground water resources of the Protectorate.
D. N. Holt. *Nyasaland Journal*, vol. 12, pt. 2 (July 1959), p. 60-82.

Though dated, this is an important and comprehensive survey of the underground water resources of Malawi. For an update see Swanzie Agnew, *The waters of Malawi: developments since independence* (Zomba: Chancellor College Geography and Earth Sciences Department, 1976. 49p.). See also A. D. C. Kombe, 'The role of protected areas in catchment conservation in Malawi', in *National Parks conservation and development*, edited by J. A. McNeely, K. R. Miller (Washington, DC: Smithsonian Institution Press, 1984, p. 115-17).

Malawi in maps.
See item no. 20.

National atlas of Malawi.
See item no. 26.

Short history and annotated bibliography on soil and water conservation in Malawi.
See item no. 28.

Lake Malawi National Park: a case study of conservation planning.
See item no. 47.

Drought, migration and chronology in the Lake Malawi littoral.
See item no. 78.

Famine analysis and family relations: 1949 in Nyasaland.
See item no. 82.

The Lower Shire Valley: its ecology, population distribution, ethnic divisions and systems of marriage.
See item no. 176.

Rapid population growth and poverty generation in Malawi.
See item no. 225.

Flora and Fauna

36 **African cichlids of Lakes Malawi and Tanganyika.**
Herbert R. Axelrod, Warren E. Burgess. Neptune City, New Jersey:
T. F. H. Publications, 1986. 11th ed. 413p.

This eleventh edition of a classic, is a massive, very comprehensive study, supported
by many illustrations, some in colour, of the prevalence and types of cichlids – a
small tropical fish – that are found in large numbers in the waters of Lakes Malawi
and Tanganyika. A few years later the definitive work, exclusively focused on Lake
Malawi fishlife was published: Ad Koning, *Koning's book of cichlids and all the
other fishes of Lake Malawi* (Neptune City, New Jersey: T. F. H. Publications, 1990.
495p.). See also an illustrated work by Mary Ellen Sweeney. *The proper care of
Malawi cichlids* (Neptune City, New Jersey: T. F. H. Publications, 1993. 256p.).

37 **The amphibians of Malawi.**
Margaret M. Stewart. Albany: State University of New York, 1967.
163p.

This study is an illustrated inventory of Malawi's sixty species of amphibians.

38 **The biogeography of montane small mammals in Malawi.**
D. C. D. Happold, M. Happold. *Journal of Biogeography* (Oxford),
vol. 16, no. 4 (1989), p. 353-67. map. bibliog.

A study of the biogeography of Malawi mammals revealing a 'continuous presence of
a forest–grassland mosaic which must have shown altitudinal change in response to
changing climates in the past' (p. 353). See also C. O. Dudley, 'The history of the
decline of the larger mammals of the Lake Chilwa Basin', *Society of Malawi Journal*,
vol. 32, no. 2 (July 1979), p. 27-41; and R. Charles Long, 'A list with notes of the
mammals of the Nsanje-Port Herald District', *Society of Malawi Journal*, vol. 26,
no. 1 (Jan. 1973) p. 60-78.

Flora and Fauna

39   **The birds of Malawi.**
Constantine Walter Benson, F. M. Benson.   Limbe, Malawi: Montfort
Press, 1977. 263p. maps. bibliog.

This revised edition of the original 1953 book, is a comprehensive inventory of
Malawi's birds, a gazetteer of the precise localities where they are to be found, and
their scientific and more common English names. A comparable, but more recent
book, is Kenneth B. Newman, Nigel G. B. Johnston-Stewart and Bob Medland, *Birds
of Malawi* (Johannesburg: Southern Book Publishers, 1992. 110p.). A great deal of
literature has been published on Malawi birds. For some of the more important
contributions, see Nigel G. B. Johnston-Stewart, 'Evergreen forest birds in the
southern third of Malawi', *Nyala*, vol. 10, no. 2 (1984), p. 99-120; R. J. Dowsett,
'Site-fidelity and survival rates of some montane forest birds in Malawi', *Biotropica*
(Washington, DC), vol. 17, no. 2 (1985), p. 145-54; G. G. M. Schulten, G. B.
Harrison 'An annotated list of birds recorded at Lake Chirwa', *Society of Malawi
Journal*, vol. 28, no. 2 (July 1975), p. 6-30; Françoise Dowsett-Lemaire, 'Breeding
productivity and the non-breeding element in some montane forest birds in Malawi',
Biotropica (Washington, DC), vol. 17, no. 2 (1985), p. 137-44; R. J. Dowsett, 'The
past and present distribution of montane birds in Malawi', *Nyala* vol. 7, no. 1 (1981),
p. 25-46; D. Stead, 'The birds of montane evergreen forests of southern Malawi',
Nyala, vol. 4, no. 1 (July 1978), p. 24-34; and 'Aquatic birds of Blantyre', *Nyasaland
Journal*, vol. 13, no. 1 (Jan. 1960), p. 7-17.

40   **Causes of mortality of nyala in Lengwe National Park.**
F. X. Mkanda, Simon M. Munthali.   *African Journal of Ecology*
(Oxford), vol. 29, no. 1 (March 1991), p. 28-36. bibliog.

This article explores the reasons for the high mortality rates of the nyala in one of
Malawi's national parks. The author analyses the nutritional and reproductive state of
the nyala herds at Lengwe National Park, and reveals that a high percentage of the
animals were in poor condition irrespective of the amount of dry-season rainfall. This
was seen as indicating that nyala mortality 'may not have been caused by starvation
alone' (p. 29).

41   **Dictionary of plant names in Malawi.**
Blodwen Lloyd Binns.   Zomba: Government Printer, 1972. 184p.

An inventory of the scientific and vernacular names of most plant species found in
Malawi, and especially those of agricultural significance. See also the same author's
'Ethnobotany of plant names in Malawi', *Society of Malawi Journal*, vol. 29, no. 1
(Jan. 1976), p. 46-57; and *A First checklist of the herbaceous flora of Malawi*
(Zomba: Government Printer, 1968. 113p.).

42   **Distribution and abundance of the common ungulates of Nyika
National Park, Malawi.**
Simon M. Munthali, Hector M. Banda.   *African Journal of Ecology*
(Oxford), vol. 30, no. 3 (Sept. 1992), p. 203-12. bibliog.

Based upon a ground and air sample-count, the authors determine that the populations
of almost all the ungulates at Nyika National Park in northern Malawi have increased
over the past fourteen years. The only exception were the zebras, whose numbers
have remained stagnant.

43   **Eucalypts in Malawi.**
John A. Whitelock. *Society of Malawi Journal*, vol. 38, no. 2 (1985),
p. 29-36.

This article is a brief description of the origins and prevalence of eucalyptus trees, a species which is non-indigenous to Malawi but which has adapted very well with some stands over 120 feet tall. For another species logged and used in Malawi for house and furniture construction, see 'Some notes on the taxonomy, distribution, ecology and economic importance of *Widdringtonia*, with particular reference to *W. whytei*', *Nyasaland Journal*, vol. 13, no. 1 (Jan. 1960), p. 65-86.

44   **The evergreen forests of Malawi.**
John Doneric Chapman, F. White.   Oxford: Commonwealth Forestry
Institute, 1970. 190p. map. bibliog.

During his fifteen years with the Forestry Department Chapman visited all of Malawi's forests and undertook much original research. One outcome is this study of the environment and plant geography of the country's evergreen forests. It is followed by individual analyses of ten forest ranges.

45   **A first check list of the herbaceous flora of Malawi.**
Blodwen Binns.   Zomba: Government Printer, 1972. 184p.

This comprehensive compendium of Malawi's flora is by a Professor of Botany who in 1972 was at the University of Malawi. See also the standard, though dated, three-volume study of the flora of the entire region from Botswana to Mozambique: A. W. Excell (et al.), *Flora Zambesiaca* (London: Crown Agents, 1961-70).

46   **The grasslands of Malawi.**
George Jackson.   *Society of Malawi Journal*, vol. 22, no. 1 (Jan.
1969), p. 7-17; vol. 22, no. 2 (July 1969) p. 73-81.

This two-part article is a botanical inventory of Malawi's grasslands. See also the author's 'The vegetation of Malawi', *Society of Malawi Journal*, vol. 21, no. 2 (July 1968), p. 11-19. For an earlier comprehensive inventory see George Jackson and P. O. Wiehe, *An annotated check list of Nyasaland grasses, indigenous and cultivated* (Zomba: Government Printer, 1958).

47   **Lake Malawi National Park: a case study of conservation planning.**
A. Trevor Croft.   *Parks* (Washington, DC), vol. 6, no. 3 (1981),
p. 7-11.

An overview of the planning and implementation of the Lake Malawi Park project that was approved in principle in 1976. For other studies on the country's other various parks, see R. H. V. [sic] 'An outline of a management plan for Kusungu National Park, Malawi', in *Problems in management of locally abundant wild animals*, edited by P. A. Jewell (et al.) (London: Academic Press, 1981); D. Stead and C. O. Dudley 'Liwonde National Park – the mammals', *Nyala* (Zomba), vol. 3, no. 2 (Dec. 1977), p. 29-38; D. E. Stead, 'Liwonde National Park – the birds', *Nyala* (Zomba), vol. 5, no. 1 (June 1979), p. 12-27; and J. E. Clarke, *Protected Areas Master Plan* (Lilongwe: Department of National Parks and Wildlife, 1983. 3 vols).

Flora and Fauna

48   The living jewels of Lake Malawi.
Peter Reinthal. *National Geographic*, vol. 177, no. 5 (May 1990), p. 42-51.
One little-known fact is that, for various reasons, Lake Malawi boasts more fish species than any other lake in the world. This colourful popular article by ichthyologist Reinthal documents the unusual lifestyles of some of these species, including the cichlids of which between 500 and 1,000 varieties may exist, and which are widely harvested for the aquariums of the world. See also D. Twaddle and N. G. Willoughby, 'Annotated checklist of the fish-fauna of the River Shire south of Kapachira Falls', *Nyala* (Zomba), vol. 5, no. 2 (Dec. 1979), p. 74-92; and R. G. Kirk, 'The fishes of Lake Chilwa', *Society of Malawi Journal*, vol. 20, no. 1 (Jan. 1967), p. 35-48.

49   The loranths of Malawi.
John Feehan. *Nyala*, vol. 10, no. 1 (1984), p. 99-120.
A comprehensive study of tropical mistletoes and, in particular, the varieties found in Malawi.

50   Malawi's national parks and game reserves.
John L. Hough.   Blantyre: Wildlife Society of Malawi, 1989. 229p. maps. bibliog.
Hough's book is a definitive, comprehensive and detailed guide to Malawi's wildlife, and includes details on hiking trails and information on Malawi's five parks and four game reserves. For an earlier work that also includes illustrations of paw-prints for the purpose of identifying wildlife, see G. D. Hayes, *A guide to Malawi's national parks and game reserves* (Limbe: Montfort Press, 1979.166p. maps).

51   Mammals of Malawi: an annotated checklist and atlas.
W. F. Ansell, R. J. Dowsett.   St. Ives, England: Trendrine Press, 1988. 170p. maps. bibliog.
A major revision of Sweeney's dated manual (R. C. H. Sweeney, *A preliminary annotated checklist of the mammals of Nyasaland* (Blantyre: Nyasaland Society, 1959). After an introduction on the geography of mammal habitats, the main text follows, interspersed with 88 black-and-white plates. There is a systematic and detailed list, by class and order of mammals, followed by an annotated gazetteer with place-names, a lengthy bibliography and extended indexes. For a briefer graphic presentation see the authors' 'An atlas of the mammals of Malawi', *Nyala*, vol. 6, no. 1 (1980), p. 47-50.

52   Mythical and real snakes of Chitipa District.
Bruce J. Hargreaves.   *Society of Malawi Journal*, vol. 35, no. 1 (Jan. 1984), p. 40-52. maps. bibliog.
Hargreaves gives an account of the more commonly found snakes of Malawi, as well as of mythical snakes and serpents that are widely believed by the population to exist. Among the latter 'species' is an eight-headed snake allegedly found wherever there are mineral deposits, a flying snake, and a twenty-yard-long snake that is in awe of human twins. For the early definitive study of Malawi's forty-eight species of snakes, see R. C. H. Sweeney, *Snakes of Malawi* (Zomba: Government Printer, 1961. 200p.). For a more recent compendium of the country's snakes see John Royle,

An introduction to the common snakes of Malawi (Blantyre: Wildlife Society of Malawi, 1989. 47p.). For works on other species found in Malawi, see D. C. D. Happold and M. Happold, 'The natural history of bats in Malawi', *Nyala*, vol. 11, no. 2 (1987), p. 57-62; P. Hanney, 'The harsh-furred rat in Nyasaland', *Mammalogy* (Baltimore), vol. 45 (1964), p. 345-58; and W. Noel Gray, 'Some unusual snails of Lake Malawi', *Nyala*, vol. 6, no. 1 (June 1980) p. 19-28.

53 Orchids of Bvumbe.
I. F. LaCroix, T. M. LaCroix. *Society of Malawi Journal*, vol. 36, no. 2 (1983) p. 12-18.

A botanical study of the orchids in the Thyolo district of Malawi's Southern Region, a densely populated and heavily cultivated area, where fifty-six species of orchids were surprisingly recorded in 1979, all growing within a radius of one mile. See also Brian Morris, 'The orchids of Malawi', *Society of Malawi Journal*, vol. 35, no. 1 (1982), p. 7-23; and Brian Morris, 'Epiphytic orchids of the Limbuli stream, Mtanje', *Society of Malawi Journal*, vol. 18, no. 2 (July 1965), p. 59-70. For other flower species see Brian Morris, 'Spring flowers of *Brachystegia* woodland: Arums and gingers', *Society of Malawi Journal*, vol. 40, no. 2 (1987), p. 39-48; and Audrey Moriarty, *Wild flowers of Malawi* (Johannesburg: Purnell, 1975. 166p.).

54 Preliminary annotated list of Malawi forest insects.
R. F. Lee. Zomba: Government Printer, 1971. 111p.

This is a classified and annotated inventory of Malawi's forest insects, following research conducted by the Forest Research Institute.

55 Preliminary list of some edible fungi.
Jessie Williamson. *Society of Malawi Journal*, vol. 26, no. 1 (Jan. 1973), p. 15-27.

This article is a study and inventory of Malawi's edible fungi by a nutritionist long-resident in Malawi. See also the same author's 'Some edible fungi of Malawi', *Society of Malawi Journal*, vol. 27, no. 2 (July 1974), p. 47-74.

56 Succulents of Malawi.
Bruce J. Hargreaves. *Society of Malawi Journal*, vol. 32, no. 1 (Jan. 1979), p. 31-44.

A description and inventory of Malawi's succulents – plants whose cells have adapted for water storage. For an earlier article see the author's 'Succulents of Chitipa – the muddy place', *Society of Malawi Journal*, vol. 30, no. 1 (Jan. 1977), p. 28-35.

57 The ten (or so) primates of Malawi.
Bruce J. Hargreaves. *Society of Malawi Journal*, vol. 37, no. 2 (1984), p. 24-38. bibliog.

An illustrated description of ten lower, and higher, primates (monkeys) found in Malawi. See also R. J. Dowsett and N. D. Hunter, 'Birds and mammals of Mangochi mountain', *Nyala*, vol. 6, no. 1 (1980), p. 5-18; and D. C. D. Happold and M. Happold, 'Small mammals of Zomba Plateau', *African Journal of Ecology* (Oxford), vol. 24 (1986), p. 77-87.

58 **Trees of Malawi, with some shrubs and climbers.**
John S. Pullinger, Alison M. Kitchen.   Blantyre: Blantyre Printers and Publishers, 1982. 229p. map. bibliog.

This definitive study is a detailed inventory of Malawi's trees, shrubs and climbers, presented in a very useful manner with side-by-side text and colour sketches, and with a botanical and Chichewa glossary of terms. There is also an index and a brief bibliography.

59 **The useful plants of Malawi.**
Jessie Williamson.   Limbe, Malawi: Montfort Press, 1974. 2nd ed. 337p. map. bibliog.

A comprehensive botanical compendium and description of Malawi's plants classified according to their use and including their nutritional value. The work has an index of English and Malawi names, and a section discussing fungi that are edible.

60 **The vegetation of the Mlanje mountains, Nyasaland.**
John Doneric Chapman.   Zomba: Government Printer, 1962. 78p. map.

Chapman's work is an ecological botany of Mulanje, a massif rising in southern Malawi.

African wildlife safaris.
See item no. 8 [annot.].

Malawi wildlife, parks and reserves.
See item no. 13.

Zomba mountains: a walkers' guide.
See item no. 16.

Archaeology

61 **Archaeology in Malawi.**
J. Desmond Clark. *Society of Malawi Journal*, vol. 19, no. 2
(July 1966), p. 15-25.
Clark provides details on excavations conducted in northern Malawi where evidence
was unearthed of continuous habitation since 60,000 BC. The author was very active
in numerous digs in the 1950s and 1960s when he served as Curator of North
Rhodesia's (now Zambia's) Rhodes–Livingstone Museum; he was later to become
Professor of Archaeology at the University of California. See also G. Y. Mgomezulu,
'Malawi archaeology revisited', *Society of Malawi Journal*, vol. 32, no. 2 (1979),
p. 7-24.

62 **The first stone artifacts to be found *in situ* within the Plio-Pleistocene
Chiwondo beds in northern Malawi.**
Zefe M. Kaufulu, Nicola Stern. *Journal of Human Evolution*
(London), vol. 16, no. 7/8 (Nov.-Dec. 1987), p. 729-40. maps. bibliog.
This is an analysis of the attributes and sedimentary context of stone artifacts
recovered from northern Malawi, that provide the earliest evidence of the presence of
hominids in Malawi, and, indeed, in all of south-central Africa.

63 **Hunters in Iron Age Malawi: the zooarchaeology of Chencherere
rockshelter.**
Diana Catherine Crader. Lilongwe: Malawi Ministry of Education
and Culture, 1984. 239p. bibliog. (Department of Antiquities,
Publication no. 21).
A detailed and valuable analysis of the faunal remains from the Lower Stone Age site
of the Chencherere II rock shelter. The past ecology of the site is reconstructed in
relation to the present environmental setting, as is the manner in which animals were
captured and butchered, and the relations between the hunter-gatherer, and food-
producers living nearby. Other evidence on this area is reported on in J. Desmond

Archaeology

Clark, 'Archaeological investigations of a painted rock shelter in Central Malawi', *Society of Malawi Journal*, vol. 26, no. 1 (Jan. 1973), p. 28-46. See also J. Desmond Clark and C. V. Haynes, 'An elephant butchery site at Mwanganda's village, Karonga, Malawi, and its relevance for Paleolithic archaeology', *World Archaeology* (London), vol. 1 (1969), p. 390-411.

64 **Iron Age of northern Malawi: an archaeological reconnaissance.**
K. R. Robinson. Lilongwe: Ministry of Education and Culture, 1982. 126p. bibliog. (Department of Antiquities, Publication no. 20).

This is a report on excavations in an Iron Age site in the northernmost Karonga district during 1965-66, and on similar work on sites in the Upper Kasitu valley (Mzimba district) undertaken in 1979. Robinson has published extensively on her work at other excavations: see, in particular, *The Iron Age of the southern Lake area of Malawi* (Zomba: Government Press, 1970. 131p. (Department of Antiquities, Publication no. 8)); *The Iron Age of the Upper and Lower Shire, Malawi* (Zomba: Government Press, 1973. 167p. (Department of Antiquities, Publication no. 13)); *The Nkotakota Lake shore and marginal areas, Malawi: an archaeological reconnaissance* (Blantyre: Government Press, 1979. 57p. (Department of Antiquities, Publication no. 19)); and 'A preliminary report on the archaeology of Ngonde, northern Malawi', *Journal of African History*, vol. 7, no. 2 (1966), p. 169-88; the latter reported on excavations in the ancient capital of the Ngonde in Karonga district.

65 **Iron-smelting in the upper North Rukuru basin of northern Malawi.**
S. Davidson, P. N. Moseley. *Azania* (Nairobi), vol. 23 (1988), p. 57-99. maps.

This long article is a locational record, and inventory, of iron implements found in some thirty Iron Age sites of iron-smelting in the upper North Rukuru basin in north Malawi, between Livingstonia and Karonga. See also D. B. Wenner and J. van der Merwe, 'Mining for the lowest grade ore: traditional iron production in northern Malawi', *Geoarchaeology* (New York), vol. 2, no. 3 (1987), p. 199-216; and Augustine W. C. Msiska, 'A note on iron working and early trade among the Phoka of Rumphi, Malawi', *Society of Malawi Journal*, vol. 34, no. 1 (1981) p. 36-44.

66 **Late Quaternary vegetation history of the Nyika Plateau, Malawi.**
M. E. Meadows. *Journal of Biogeography* (Oxford), vol. 11, no. 3 (1984), p. 209-22. maps. bibliog.

A reconstruction of the history of vegetation in the Nyika Plateau over the past 5,000 years. Radiocarbon dating and other evidence suggests that the existing patches of forest were present as far back as 12,000 years ago, a very surprising element of environmental stability that contradicts previous assertions of heavier vegetation in the past. See also K. Yemane (et al.), 'Lacustrine environment during Lower Beaufort (Upper Permian) Karoo deposition in northern Malawi', *Palaeogeography, Palaeoclimatology, Palaeoecology*, vol. 70, no. 1-3 (1989), p. 165-78.

67   The origins and development of agriculture in Southern Africa: the
      place of Malawi.
      Gadi G. Y. Mgomezulu.   *Journal of Social Science*, vol. 8 (1980/81),
      p. 1-27. map.
An evaluation of the contributions of archaeological research to the understanding of
the origins and development of agriculture in Malawi.

68   Preliminary report on some fossils found from the Chinondo bed in
      Karonga District.
      S. C. Coryndon.   *American Anthropologist* (Menasha, Wisconsin),
      vol. 68 (1966), p. 59-66.
Coryndon reports on the results of excavations in Malawi's northern Karonga district.
See also J. E. Mawby, 'Fossil vertebrates from Northern Malawi', *Quarternaria*
(Rome), vol. 13 (1970), p. 319-23; and N. E. Lindgren and J. M. Schoffeleers, *Rock
art and Nyau symbolism in Malawi* (Zomba: Malawi Ministry of Education and
Culture, 1978 (Department of Antiquities, Publication no. 18)).

History

69   **Adventures in Nyasaland: a two-year struggle with Arab slave-dealers in Central Africa.**
L. Monteith Fotheringham.   London: Sampson Low, 1891. 304p.
The classic account of the travails of the northern Ngonde people *vis-à-vis* Arab slave raids in the area, written by an African Lakes Company agent in Karonga.

70   **British Central Africa.**
Sir Harry Hamilton Johnston.   New York: Edward Arnold, 1897.
544p. Reprinted, New York: Negro Universities Press, 1960.
This book is written by Johnston, Commissioner and consul-general of British Central Africa, and administrator of the British South Africa territory north of the Zambezi river – a vain, authoritarian and highly prejudiced individual – who, by virtue of his talent for writing and drawing, and his interests in linguistics, botany and ethnology, left a rare comprehensive record of Nyasaland's early decades, with over 200 sketches and plates. Johnston also wrote his autobiography, *The story of my life* (London: Chatto & Windus, 1923. 536p.), which, together with his brother's book on him, highlights his dictatorial mannerisms *vis-à-vis* natives and aides alike. For the latter book see Alex Johnston, *The life and letters of Sir Harry Johnston* (New York: Jonathan Cape & Harrison Smith, 1929. 350p.). One eminent historian argues that Johnston's personal failings notwithstanding, his talent for prompt (and aggressive) action brought slavery to a rapid conclusion and ushered in peace in the region. See Roland A. Oliver, *Sir Harry Johnston and the scramble for Africa* (London: Chatto & Windus, 1957. 368p.). For a biography of one of Nyasaland's governors see Robert B. Boeder, *Alfred Sharpe of Nyasaland. Builder of Empire* (Blantyre: Society of Malawi, 1982. 152p.).

71 **Capitaos and chiefs: oral tradition and colonial society in Malawi.**
   Tony Woods.   *International Journal of African Historical Studies*
   (New York), vol. 23, no. 2 (1990), p. 259-68.
This article is an exploration of Malawian historiography, illustrating the kinds of
pitfalls that can be encountered by scholars utilizing oral tradition, expert informants,
or for that matter the Malawi archives that became more open to researchers in the
1980s. The author focuses on several concrete historical issues that at the time were
deeply resented by the native populations – the hammocks on which early Europeans
used to be transported around the country; the mannerisms of the European planter
class; and the origins of Malawi's chiefs, who, according to some sources, did not
exist prior to 1913.

72 **Central African emergency.**
   Clyde Sanger.   London: Heinemann, 1960. 342p. bibliog.
One of the best of several accounts of Britain's efforts to force Nyasaland to join the
Central African Federation. Nysaland's vehement resistance to the federation, which
was dominated by what was then South Rhodesia and had a racial policy worse than
South Africa's, led to the Central African Emergency and catapulted Kamuzu Banda
to power.

73 **Central Malawi in the 19th century.**
   Harry W. Langworthy.   In: *From Nyasaland to Malawi: studies in
   colonial history*, edited by R. J. Macdonald.   Nairobi: East African
   Publishing House, 1976, p. 1-43.
A study of early Chewa society in three regions in Central Malawi, illustrating the
author's thesis that external influences together with the changed basis of wealth in
the region resulted in political conflicts and growing disunity and splinterization. For
Langworthy's study of the Chewa kingdom of Undi (spanning an area currently in
contemporary Mozambique) see 'Conflict among rulers in the history of Undi's
Chewa kingdom', *Transafrican Journal of History*, vol. 1, pt. 1 (Jan. 1971), p. 1-23.

74 **The Chinde concession, 1891-1923.**
   Colin Baker.   *Society of Malawi Journal*, vol. 33, no. 1 (Jan. 1980),
   p. 6-18.
This is an analysis of the creation, physical layout and activities of the Chinde
concession at the mouth of the Zambezi River during the three decades of its
existence. The concession served as a point of transshipment of goods and personnel
for Nyasaland, and was abandoned with the construction of the railroad linking the
colony with the port of Beira in Mozambique, a route that provided much speedier
weekly passenger and freight service.

75 **The Chiwaya war. Malawians in World War I.**
   Melvin E. Page.   Boulder, Colorado: Westview Press, 1992. 256p.
Based on extensive use of oral resources, this is is an important study of how most of
the adult male population of Malawi was dragged into involvement in the war effort,
either actively as *askaris* (soldiers) or as *tenga-tenga* (military labourers).

76 Coercion and control in Nyasaland: aspects of the history of a
    colonial police force.
    John McCracken. *Journal of African History* (Cambridge), vol. 27,
    no. 1 (1986), p. 127-47.

In this article, McCracken examines the evolution and changing function of the
Nyasaland police force from its inception in the 1890s to self-government in 1952. It
was initially composed of small groups of untrained former soldiers, but the return to
Nyasaland of 'dangerous' migrant labourers from South Africa led, in 1920, to the
creation of a centralized, trained force that was primarily meant to protect urban
dwellers and their property. Recruits, initially disproportionately drawn from the Yao
ethnic group, were attracted to the force much less by the force's rates of pay (which
were low) than by the status, privileges, and uniforms they obtained.

77 Cullen Young, Yesaya Chibambo, and the Ngoni.
    Peter G. Forster. *Society of Malawi Journal*, vol. 44, no. 1 (1991),
    p. 34-61. bibliog.

Forster's article is an exploration of an old historical dispute: the alleged falsification
of oral history in Reverend Young's strong anti-Ngoni (and pro-Tumbuka) early
studies (1923 and 1932) of northern Malawi, in contrast to the more balanced 1942
work of Reverend Chibambo. Forster concludes that while bias is certainly visible in
Young's work, there is no evidence of conscious falsification of oral history.

78 David Livingstone: a catalogue of documents.
    G. W. Clendennen, I. C. Cunningham. Edinburgh: National Library of
    Scotland, 1979. 348p.

The definitive, and extremely comprehensive, listing of all the manuscript writings of
the famous explorer, missionary, scientist and humanitarian. The material is found in
sixty-six private and public collections. For additional material located subsequent to
the publication of the above work, see I. C. Cunningham, *David Livingstone: a
catalogue of documents. A supplement* (Edinburgh: National Library of Scotland,
1985. 85p.). For a third important compendium of 140 of Livingstone's letters and
documents, some twenty of which do not appear in Clendennen's work (and which
are stored in the Livingstone Museum in Livingstone, Zambia), see Timothy Holmes,
David Livingstone: letters and documents, 1841-1872 (London: James Currey, 1990.
202p.).

79 Drought, migration and chronology in the Lake Malawi littoral.
    J. B. Webster. *Transafrican Journal of History* (Nairobi), vol. 9, no. 1
    (1980), p. 70-90.

This is an interesting attempt to assess the reasons for the patterns of migration of
several peoples, notably the ancient Chewa (Maravi) from their original habitat (in
contemporary Zaïre and allegedly circa 1300, but according to other scholars much
later) to the Lake Malawi region and Mozambique. The author reconstructs the
drought cycles in antiquity, and suggests those were the main factors behind the
migrations.

80   Economics and ethnicity: the Italian community in Malawi.
      John McCracken. *Journal of African History* (Cambridge), vol. 32,
      no. 2 (1991), p. 313-32.
A rare study of the Italian community, one of the smallest to establish itself in
colonial Nyasaland (seventy people in the 1920s). It played an economic role out of
all proportion to its small size. By the 1940s over thirty estates were in Italian hands,
and one member, Ignacio Conforzi, was the colony's leading entrepreneur.

81   The establishment and expansion of the Lambya kingdom
      c1600-1750.
      Owen J. M. Kalinga.   *African Studies Review* (Waltham,
      Massachusetts), vol. 21, no. 2 (Sept. 1978), p. 55-66. bibliog.
A study, replete with detailed king-lists, of the small Lambya kingdom in the northern
Chitipa district of Malawi, about which there are few other written sources. For the
history of other small states, see the same author's 'The Balowoka and the
establishment of states west of Lake Malawi', in *State formation in eastern Africa*,
edited by A. I. Salim (Nairobi: Heinemann, 1984, p. 36-52); and Harry W.
Langworthy, 'Mkanda's Kingdom to the mid-nineteenth century: a history of the
Malawi–Zambia watershed of Mchinji and Chipata districts', *Journal of Social
Science*, vol. 12 (1985), p. 1-20. See also Owen Kalinga, 'Colonial rule, missionaries
and ethnicity in the North Nyasa District, 1891-1938', *African Studies Review*,
vol. 28, no. 1 (1985), p. 57-72, as well as the same author's 'European settlers,
African apprehensions, and colonial economic policy: the North Nyasa Native
Reserves Commission of 1929', *International Journal of African Historical Studies*,
vol. 17, no. 4 (1984), p. 641-56.

82   Expedition in east-central Africa, 1888-1891.
      Carl Wiese.   Norman, Oklahoma: University of Oklahoma Press,
      1983. 383p. bibliog. (Translated from the 1889 Portuguese edition,
      edited by Harry Langworthy).
Born in 1860 in Germany, Wiese left for Mozambique in 1883 to travel through
Zambia and Malawi, hunting elephants. This book, reporting on his experiences, has a
strong anti-British and pro-Portuguese bias, and it is linguistically awkward because
of his imperfect command of the language. Serialized in Lisbon in 1891-92, his
accounts of encounters with the Ngoni and Chewa are of interest to scholars of
Malawi.

83   Famine analysis and family relations: 1949 in Nyasaland.
      Megan Vaughan.   *Past and Present* (Oxford), no. 108 (1985),
      p. 177-205.
An analysis of the serious famine of 1949 in Blantyre district. The author plays down
the role of background natural and/or ecological conditions, and underlines instead
the negative role played by the British administration in the colony, and local
markets, in contrast to the positive response of long-distance kinship ties. The author,
one of the foremost historians of Malawi, concludes that 'if we are going to
understand the impact of famine, we must see it in the context of the whole web of
economic and social relations, from the level of the household to that of the state'
(p. 205). This article was the precursor for the author's wider study *The story of an*

African famine: gender and famine in twentieth century Malawi (Cambridge: Cambridge University Press, 1987. 191p. bibliog.).

84 From interest groups to party formation in colonial Malawi.
Denis Venter. *Journal of Contemporary African Studies* (Pretoria), vol. 14, no. 1/2 (Oct. 1984-April 1985), p. 241-60.

Venter examines the African interest groups of the early 20th twentieth century, comprising Nyasaland's embryonic middle class – clerks, teachers, petty businessmen – which, influenced by 'non-conformist religious organizations' (i.e. the Scottish missionary societies), organized to protect, promote and express African interests in the colony, in due course giving rise to the Malawi Congress Party. See also J. Van Velsen, 'Some early pressure groups in Malawi', in *The Zambezian past: studies in Central African History*, edited by E. Stokes and R. Brown (Manchester: Manchester University Press, 1966. 407p.). The European community in the country, fully backed by the local administration, strenuously opposed African nationalist strivings as documented *inter alia* in Robin H. Palmer's 'European resistance to African majority rule in Nyasaland: the Settlers' and Residents' Association of Nyasaland', *African Affairs*, no. 271 (1973), p. 256-72.

85 From Nguni to Ngoni: a history of the Ngoni exodus from Zululand and Swaziland to Malawi, Tanzania, and Zambia.
Desmond Dudwa Phiri. Lilongwe: Likuni Publishing House, 1982. 187p. bibliog.

One of several accounts of the history of the 19th-century northward exodus of a branch of the South African Zulu, some elements of which subjugated Chewa and other groups they found in central and northern Malawi, and settled among them. (Other elements are currently found in neighbouring countries.) In due course the Zulu (Nguni) became known in Malawi as the Ngoni. By the early decades of the 20th century they had, because of their small numbers, partly absorbed the culture of their former vassals, the Chewa.

86 From porters to labor extractors: the Chikunda and Kololo in the Lake Malawi and Tchiri River area.
Allen Isaacman, Elias Mandala. In: *The workers of African trade*, edited by C. Coquery-Vidrovitch, Paul E. Lovejoy. Beverly Hills, California: Sage, 1985, p. 209-42. map. bibliog.

This is a study of the history of forced labour in Central Africa, and the transformation of Chikunda and Kololo porters, canoemen and mercenaries from slaves to free labourers, and eventually as suppliers of forced labour.

87 The Great War and Chewa society in Malawi.
Melvin E. Page. *Journal of Southern African Studies* (Oxford), vol. 6, no. 2 (April 1980), p. 171-82.

A study of the resilience of Chewa society in Nyasaland. They succeeded, aided by their Nyau secret society rites, in facing a multiplicity of challenges inclining it to disintegration during the First World War.

88 **The history of the Chewa.**
Samuel Josiah Ntara, Harry W. Langworthy.   Wiesbaden, Germany:
Franz Steiner Verlag, 1973. 3rd ed. 172p.
This book is composed of a collection of historical personal narratives collected by
Ntara among various Chewa chiefs in Central Malawi. They are commented on by
Langworthy, who sets them within a wider historical perspective based on his own
fieldwork in the region.

89 **A history of the Malawi police force.**
C. Marlow.   Zomba: Government Printer, 1971. 42p.
This brief outline of the history of the police force in Nyasaland recounts that the first
unit, in the absence of serious crime until then, was set up only in 1921. For material
on the origins of the Malawi armed forces, see the extremely detailed book by
H. Moyse-Bartlett: *The King's African Rifles: a study of the military history of East
and Central Africa, 1890-1945* (Aldershot, England: Gale and Polden, 1956. 727p.);
and 'Nyasaland' in Anthony Clayton and David Killingray, *Khaki and Blue: military and
police in British colonial Africa* (Athens, Ohio: Ohio University Center for
International Studies, 1989, p. 67-77).

90 **A history of the Ngonde kingdom of Malawi.**
Owen J. M. Kalinga.   New York: Mouton, 1985. 176p. bibliog.
Kalinga's book is a major pioneering study, based on oral history and traditions, of
the small Karonga kingdom at the northern tip of Lake Malawi. The author, who is
from that region, has become one of Malawi's prime historians, especially of the
Ngonde people. He offers a new interpretation of the kingdom's emergence (circa
1600) when the Kyungu dynasty settled in the Lake Malawi region after migrating
from the inter-lacustral area of Central Africa. The area they settled in already had a
pre-Kyungu political system, elements of which were integrated into the new
kingship they established, based on divine rule (a trait of the inter-lacustral peoples).
Their seclusion was first shattered by the intrusion of Swahili military prowess in the
19th century, and then, later, by British overlordship. For further material on the
Ngonde see the author's 'Trade, the Kyungus, and the emergence of the Ngonde of
Malawi', *International Journal of African Historical Studies* (Boston), vol. 12, no. 1
(1979), p. 17-39; 'The Koronga war: commercial rivalries and politics of survival',
Journal of African History (London), vol. 21 (1981), p. 209-18; 'The British and the
Kyungus: a study of the changing status of the Ngonde rulers during the period 1891-
1933', *African Studies* (Johannesburg), vol. 38, no. 2 (1979), p. 167-81; and 'Towards
better understanding of socio-economic change in 18th and 19th century Ungonde',
Cahiers d'Etudes Africaines, vol. 24, no. 1 (1984), p. 87-100. See also the earlier P. J.
Howson, *A short history of Karonga* (Zomba: Government Printer, 1972. 54p.).

91 **Independent African: John Chilembwe and the origins, setting and
significance of the Nyasaland native uprising of 1915.**
George Shepperson, Thomas Price.   Edinburgh: Edinburgh University
Press, 1987. 574p. bibliog.
This book is the classic, much cited, and pioneering study into the motives that
triggered the uprising of 1915 in Nyasaland, the event which is widely regarded as the
first stirrings of Malawian proto-nationalism. The revolt, led by Chilembwe – a
Western-trained and ordained minister, and head of an independent Church – was a

reaction to the acute discrimination and demeaning attitude of settlers and the settler-biased colonial administration to the native population. The authors describe the personality and formative experiences of both Chilembwe and Joseph Booth, his radical, egalitarian missionary mentor, prior to outlining in a very detailed manner the revolt itself. Only three Europeans died (and two were wounded) in the skirmishes: as the authors note, 'For a rebellion against foreign rule, it had been, on the face of it, singularly ineffective. But . . . it was the quality, rather than the quantity, of Chilembwe's movement which gave it significance' (p. 267). For additional insights on this much-studied revolt see also George Simeon Mwase and Robert I. Rotberg, *Strike a blow and die: a narrative of race relations in colonial Africa* (Cambridge, Massachusetts: Harvard University Press, 1967. 135p.); Robert I. Rotberg, 'Psychological stress and the question of identity: Chilembwe's revolt reconsidered', in *Protest and power in Africa*, edited by Robert I. Rotberg and Ali A. Mazrui (New York: Oxford University Press, 1970, p. 337-73); Desmond Dudwa Phiri, *John Chilembwe* (Lilongwe: Longman, 1975. 106p.); Landeg White ' "Tribes" and the aftermath of the Chilembwe rising', *African Affairs*, vol. 83, no. 333 (Oct. 1984), p. 511-41; and Ian Linden and Jane Linden, 'John Chilembwe and the new Jerusalem', *Journal of African History*, vol. 12, no. 4 (1971), p. 629-51.

92   **The *Jumbe* of Kota Kota and some aspects of the history of Islam in Malawi.**
      George Shepperson.   In: *Islam in tropical Africa*, edited by I. M.
      Lewis.   London: Hutchinson, 1969, p. 253-65.
A brief overview of the Swahili Kota Kota slave centre on Lake Malawi (*Jumbe* was the title of their rulers), and the mercantile Yao community arriving from Mozambique, the main proponents of Islam in the region. The faith did not put down deep roots in Malawi because of its association with the slave-raiding activities of the Jumbe sultanate and the Yao, and the destruction of Arab and Yao military power by the British stemmed its possible future growth. See also Harry W. Langworthy, 'Swahili influence in the area between Lake Malawi and the Luangwa River', *African Historical Studies*, vol. 4, pt. 3 (1971), p. 575-602.

93   **Kaluluma Chilembwe Phiri, 1859-1959.**
      Kelvin N. Banda.   *Society of Malawi Journal*, vol. 42, no. 2 (1989),
      p. 11-33.
Banda has written a fascinating biography of the Chewa chief who lived among the invading Ngoni as a slave, and later as a notable chief. His life spanned the era of the slave trade, ethnic wars, the British Protectorate and the first stirrings of independence.

94   **Land and politics in Malawi 1875-1975.**
      B. Pachai.   Kingston, Ontario: Limestone Press, 1978. 245p. bibliog.
A valuable and masterful study of the history of Malawi from pre-colonial days, intertwining colonial land and labour policy with the role played by missionaries in the territory.

95 **Livingstone's African journal, 1853-1856.**
David Livingstone, edited by I. Schapera.   London: Chatto and
Windus, 1963. 2 vols.

This is the journal of the great missionary's travels in central Africa. They are
outlined in great detail, and have been referred to by J. W. Gregory as 'the greatest
single contribution to African geography which has ever been made'. For a collection
of essays on Livingstone's achievements by some of the top scholars of Malawi
(Shepperson, McCracken, Page, and others), see *Livingstone: man of Africa;
memorial essays 1873-1973* (London: Longman, 1973. 245p.). For two revisionist
accounts, that give greater stress to Livingstone's multiple personal and professional
failures, and argue that much of the credit heaped upon him was really due to the
contributions of others, see Judith Listowel, *The other Livingstone* (London: Julien
Friedmann, 1974. 312p.) and Tim Jeal, *Livingstone* (New York: Putnam, 1973.
427p.). For the account of the search for the explorer after reports reached London
about his death see Edward D. Young (the naval officer commissioned to undertake
it), *The search after Livingstone* (London, 1868. 262p.).

96 **Magomero: portrait of a village.**
Landeg White.   New York: Cambridge University Press, 1987. 288p.
bibliog.

This is a beautifully written, sensitively treated, and universally acclaimed micro-
study 'from inside' of Magomero, a small village of several hundred people at the
bend of the Namadzi river in the Shire Highlands, the site of the first (disastrous)
settlement of the Universities' Mission to Central Africa, and, later, the centre of the
1915 Chilembwe uprising. The book recounts with extraordinary compassion the
history of the region from 1859 to the present day, and in the process establishes itself
as a prime source on the slave trade, Christian missions, land alienation, and the
emergence of nationalism.

97 **The making of an imperial slum: Nyasaland and its railways,
1895-1935.**
Leroy Vail.   *Journal of African History*, vol. 16, pt. 1 (1975),
p. 89-112.

A biting critique of Britain's decision to build the railroad to the Indian Ocean
without (as elsewhere) any colonial subsidies, leading to the pauperization of
Nyasaland by its construction costs. Much the same theme is to be found in Vail's
'Railway development and colonial underdevelopment: the Nyasaland case', in *The
roots of rural poverty in Central and Southern Africa*, edited by Robin Palmer and
Neil Parsons (London: Heinemann, 1977, p. 369-95).

98 **The making of the 'Dead North': a study of the Ngoni rule in
northern Malawi c. 1855-1907.**
Leroy Vail.   In: *Before and after Shaka: Papers in Nguni history.*
edited by J. B. Peires.   Grahamstown (South Africa): Institute of
Social and Economic Research, 1981, p. 230-67.

Vail takes a critical look at the Nguni conquests in northern Malawi, the political
system they established over populations they conquered there, and their subsequent
military decline at the turn of the century due to their rejection of modern weaponry

technology (rifles). See also the two articles by Jack Thompson: 'The origins, migration and settlement of the Northern Ngoni', *Society of Malawi Journal*, vol. 34, no. 1 (1981), p. 6-35; and 'The Ziehl case: an early example of the interaction between the British colonial administration and the Ngoni of Northern Malawi', *Society of Malawi Journal*, vol. 35, no. 1 (1982), p. 41-51. The latter relates the reasons for the voluntary acquiescence to British rule of the Ngoni in northern Malawi.

99 **Malawi: a political and economic history.**
John G. Pike. London: Pall Mall, 1968. 248p.

This is one of the first post-independence books on Malawi's historical evolution written by an hydrologist-turned-historian. The book ignores much of the region's economic history and the proto-nationalism of the pre-Second World War period. Together with some authors Pike dates the arrival of the Maravi (from whom the Chewa descended) at the Lake to the 15th century, though other historians put their arrival much later. See for example M. D. D. Newitt, 'The early history of the Maravi', *Journal of African History*, vol. 23, no. 1 (1982), p. 145-62, which argues for a mid-17th-century date. For an earlier but still useful study that is more comprehensive than its title suggests, see Michael Gelfand, *Lakeside pioneers: socio-medical study of Nyasaland, 1875-1920* (Oxford: Blackwell, 1964. 330p.). For earlier histories of the region see the two books by A. J. Hanna: *The beginnings of Nyasaland and north-eastern Rhodesia 1859-95* (Oxford: Oxford University Press, 1956. 281p.) and *The story of the Rhodesias and Nyasaland* (London: Faber, 1960. 288p.). All earlier works, however, must be supplemented by revisionist historiography (and its more searching and scathing analysis of colonial policy and settler policies) that started emerging in the 1970s.

100 **Malawians to remember: John Chilembwe.**
Desmond Dudwa Phiri. Lilongwe: Longman, 1976. 106p.

A biography of the leader of the 1915 uprising, part of a monograph series on historic Malawian figures. Also in the series are books on Inkosi Gomani II (1973), James Frederick Sangala (1974) and Charles Chidongo Chinula (1975).

101 **'Marginal men': the colonial experience in Malawi.**
John McCracken. *Journal of Southern African Studies*, vol. 15, no. 4 (Oct. 1989), p. 537-64.

Utilizing Shepperson's biographical approach to understand Malawi's colonial evolution, McCracken focuses on three culturally 'marginal men' – Tom Boquito, Donald Malota and Frederic Njilima – all products of the 'Christianity and commerce' or 'Bible and plough' values inculcated by early missionaries in Nyasaland. The three were also influenced by sojourns abroad, by the Chilembwe uprising, and by other personal experiences. Boquito, for example, was rescued from slavery by David Livingstone, while Njilima's father, a Chilembwe associate, was executed by the British.

102 **Masokwa Elliot Kenan Kamwana Chirwa: his religious and political activities, and impact in Nkhata Bay 1908-1956.**
Wiseman Chijere Chirwa. *Journal of Social Science*, vol. 12 (1985), p. 21-43. map.
This article is an historical overview of Watchtower doctrine, and of Kamwana and his teachings in Nkhata Bay prior to his relocation to South Africa.

103 *Mwali* **and the Luba origins of the Chewa: some tentative suggestions.**
Ian Linden, Jane Linden. Berkeley: University of California Press, 1974. 223p.
Oral tradition has it that the Chewa descended from the Maravi who migrated to the vicinity of Lake Malawi from what is today Zaïre. The Lindens suggest this point of origin is proved by the fact that the title of the wife of the head of the Maravi empire (*Mwali*) as well the Shona term *Mwari* are variations of *Mwadi* among the Luba around Lake Kisale in Zaïre. For data on the original inhabitants (the Akafula) of the land the Maravi were to inhabit, see G. T. Nurse's 'The name "Akafula"', *Society of Malawi Journal*, vol. 20, pt. 2 (July 1967), p. 17-22. For an intriguing speculation about the historical implications of the differing average heights of Malawians see the same author's *Height and history in Malawi* (Zomba: Government Printer, 1969. 39p.).

104 **The myth of the capitalist class: unofficial sources and political economy in colonial Malawi 1895-1924.**
Tony Woods. *History in Africa* (Atlanta), vol. 16 (1989), p. 363-73.
Basing his analysis on expatriate newspapers of the period, Woods concludes that – contrary to recent radical revisionist historiography – the colony's early 'capitalists were a badly fragmented class, antagonistic to the colonial administration . . . paralyzed . . . allowing the state to enact legislation which was often antithetical to capitalists' ambitions and prerequisites' (p. 363).

105 **Narrative of an expedition to the Zambezi and its tributaries.**
David Livingstone, Charles Livingstone. London: J. Murray, 1865. 608p. (Reprinted in 1971 by Johnson Reprint, New York).
The narrative of six visits to the Shire river and Lake Malawi by Livingstone and his brother between 1859 and 1864. Of all of Livingstone's writings this work is possibly the most germane to Malawi, and includes an encyclopaedic array of data, ranging from the decorations of native calabashes to the nature of crocodile eggs. See also David Livingstone, *Missionary travels and researches in South Africa* (Freeport, New York: Books for Libraries Press, 1972. 732p. Reprint of the 1857 edition); *The Zambezi journal and letters of Dr. John Kirk 1858-1863*, edited by Reginald Foskett (Edinburgh: Oliver & Boyd, 1965. 2 vols). The latter are the notes and diaries (and to a much lesser extent the scientific journal) of the medical officer and botanist who accompanied Livingstone on his Zambezi expedition.

History

106   The nature and substance of Mang'anja and Kololo traditions:
      a preliminary survey.
      E. C. Mandala.   *Society of Malawi Journal*, vol. 31, no. 1
      (Jan. 1978), p. 6-22.

Mandala explores the conscious manipulation of oral traditions for purposes of 'caste-climbing' among the southernmost Mang'anja who claim identification with the ancient Phiri. For similar problems of dealing with oral traditions and legends, in this case with respect to the Mbona cult, see Matthew Schoffeleers' 'Oral history and the retrieval of the distant past: on the use of legendary chronicles as sources of historical information' in *Theoretical explorations in African religion*, edited by W. van Bings-bergen, M. Schoffeleers (London: Kegan Paul, 1985, p. 164-88); and J. Matthew Schoffeleers, 'Ideological confrontation and the manipulation of oral history: a Zambesian case', *History in Africa* (Los Angeles), vol. 14 (1987), p. 257-73.

107   The Nguru penetration into Nyasaland 1892-1914.
      Thomas Galligan.   In: *From Nyasaland to Malawi: studies in
      colonial history*, edited by R. J. Macdonald.   Nairobi: East African
      Publishing House, 1976, p. 108-23.

The Nguru, currently better known as the Lomwe, arrived in Malawi in several waves, the most recent as refugees from the turmoil and civil strife in Mozambique in the 1970s. They now constitute, according to several estimates, 20 per cent of Malawi's population. The author describes the first major wave (1892-1914), when they fled the atrocities of the brutal Portuguese administration and private concessions in Mozambique and the resulting famines. Most settled in the Shire Highlands and worked for low wages on the European estates that most Chewa shunned in favour of work in Zambia and South Africa.

108   Notes on the history of the lakeside Tonga of Nyasaland.
      Jaap Van Velsen.   *African Studies*, vol. 18, pt. 3 (1959), p. 105-17.

This article is a reconstruction of the pre-1870 history of the Tonga people, and an indication of the manner in which oral legends have been manipulated and changed by various factions to suit their needs.

109   Notes on the history of the Tumbuka-Kamanga peoples in the
      northern province of Nyasaland.
      T. Cullen Young.   London: Cass, 1970. 192p. (Reprint of the 1932
      edition).

A study of Tumbuka history from their oral legends by a Livingstonia missionary. See also Leroy Vail, 'Suggestions towards a reinterpreted Tumbuka history' in *Malawi: the history of a nation*, edited by Bridglal Pachai (London: Longman, 1973, p. 148-67). For the intrusion of systematic slavery among the Tumbuka, see C. J. W. Fleming, 'The peculiar institution among the early Tumbuka', *Society of Malawi Journal*, vol. 25, pt. 1 (Jan. 1972), p. 5-10. For the role of armed lake-steamers in ending the slave trade in the region, see Lewis Gann's 'The end of the slave trade in British Central Africa', *Rhodes-Livingstone Journal*, no. 16 (1954), p. 25-51.

110   **The Ntumbe.**
      G. T. Nurse.   *Society of Malawi Journal*, vol. 30, pt. 2 (July 1977),
      p. 11-17. bibliog.
A brief outline of the origins of the Ntumbe subdivision of the Chewa ethnic group in
Central Malawi. The Ntumbe are descendants of Chewa who were captured and
acculturated by the Ngoni in the Ntcheu district. They have been virtually ignored by
most scholars since they straddle the border with Mozambique.

111   **Nyasaland mails and stamps.**
      C. D. Twynam.   *Nyasaland Journal*, vol. 1, pt. 1 (Jan. 1948) p. 11-25.
Twynam has written a fascinating study of the history of postal mail and of postage
stamps in Malawi. At the time the article was written there were only 48 post offices
in the entire country. See also Colin Baker, 'British Central Africa's first Postmaster
General – Ernest Edward Harrhy', *Society of Malawi Journal*, vol. 44, no. 1 (1991),
p. 62-5. For philatelists, another early work that includes 150 illustrations out of some
1,335 stamp cancellations is a gold-mine: H. C. Dann, *The cancellations of the
Rhodesias and Nyasaland* (London: Robson Lowe, 1950. 85p.), as is *A guide to the
postage stamps of the Rhodesias and Nyasaland* (Salisbury: Mashonaland Philatelic
Study Group, 1974. 63p.). In the United States, the standard reference work on
Nyasaland's and Malawi's stamps is *Scott standard postage stamp catalogue* (Sidney,
Ohio: Scott Publishing. annual. 4 vols).

112   **Nyassa, a journal of adventures.**
      Edward Daniel Young.   Blantyre: Rotary Club of Blantyre, 1984.
      239p. (Reprint of a 1877 edition limited to 250 copies and published in
      London by John Murray).
Early account of travel and exploration in the Lake Malawi region.

113   **Peasants, planters and the colonial state: the case of Malawi, 1905-
      1940.**
      John McCracken.   *Journal of Eastern African Research and
      Development*, vol. 12 (1982), p. 21-35.
An important attempt to modify the picture of Malawi as no more than a labour
reserve for the mines of Southern Africa. McCracken underlines this was true only for
the underdeveloped northern part of Malawi; in the south a European settler-
dominated economy developed, while in the central region African peasants were
predominant. See also the author's 'Underdevelopment in Malawi: the missionary
contribution', *African Affairs*, vol. 76, no. 303 (April 1977), p. 195-209, where he
explores in greater depth the negative repercussions of the missionary role in northern
Malawi. For a somewhat romanticized account of the early years in Nyasaland,
written by an official in Alfred Sharpe's administration, see H. L. Duff, *Nyasaland
under the Foreign Office* (London: George Bell & Sons, 1906. 422p. Reprinted in
New York: Negro Universities Press, 1960).

114   **Political change and the Chewa and Yao of the Lake Malawi region, c. 1750-1900.**
      Kings M. Phiri.   In: *State formation in eastern Africa*, edited by A. I.
      Salim.   Nairobi: Heinemann Educational Books, 1984, p. 53-69.
This study examines the turbulent late 18th and 19th centuries that saw a decline in Chewa power and the rise of Yao and Ngoni hegemony in southern Malawi. A similar contribution to the historiography of this period is contained in the author's 'Traditions of power and politics in early Malawi: a case study of Kasungu district from about 1750 to 1933', *Society of Malawi Journal*, vol. 35, no. 1 (1982), p. 24-40; 'The pre-colonial history of Southern Malawi: an interpretive essay', *Journal of Social Science* (Zomba), vol. 8 (1980/81), p. 28-46; and 'Pre-colonial states of Central Malawi: towards a reconstruction of their history', *Society of Malawi Journal*, vol. 41, pt. 1 (1988), p. 1-29.

115   **Politics and Christianity in Malawi, 1875-1940: the impact of the Livingstonia Mission in the Northern Province.**
      John McCracken.   London: Cambridge University Press, 1977. 324p.
This is a seminal and eminently readable study of the immense and lasting impact of the teachings of the Livingstonia Mission in northern Malawi. Not only did the Mission's activities train a valuable and much sought-after stratum of artisans, but the critical and independent thinking that was encouraged produced the first group of nationalists in the colony. Paradoxically, as McCracken shows in an article published in the same year as this book, this very success of the Livingstonia Mission was for long to negatively affect the northern region, as Mission trainees spurned its economic backwardness for jobs elsewhere. See John McCracken, 'Underdevelopment in Malawi: the missionary contribution', *African Affairs*, vol. 76, no. 303 (April 1977), p. 195-209.

116   **A pre-colonial history of Malawi.**
      John G. Pike.   *Nyasaland Journal*, vol. 18, pt. 1 (Jan. 1965), p. 22-54.
Pike divides the pre-colonial history of the region into six periods, placing the arrival of the Maravi at Lake Maravi in the 15th century, and that of the Tumbuka chiefdom in the 18th century.

117   **The race to discover Lake Malawi.**
      Karl Wand.   *Society of Malawi Journal*, vol. 35, no. 1 (Jan. 1984),
      p. 10-39. maps.
A detailed account of the explorations and death of the German Dr Albrecht Roscher during 1859-60, as outlined by the German Ambassador to Malawi, 1979-82. Though Livingstone 'discovered' the lake, Roscher arrived at the site only two months later, and became its first victim.

118 **The river-god and the historians: myth in the Shire Valley and elsewhere.**
Christopher Wrigley. *Journal of African History*, vol. 29, no. 3 (1988), p. 367-83.

Raising the issue of myth and reality, and offering other comparative evidence, Wrigley powerfully disputes aspects of distant Maravi history, and specifically the alleged early rise of a centralized Lundu kingdom as early as the year 1600; its military assistance by Zimba refugee-warriors; and historical interpellations from mythical oral history of the origin of the Mbona secret cult in the region, and especially its progenitor – all themes directly associated with the life-long work in Malawi of Matthew Schoffeleers. Concerning the Mbona cult, Wrigley suggests, for example, that 'the entire tradition of Mbona consists of ancient myth, modified by the convulsions of the late nineteenth century' (p. 363). For Schoffeleers' rejoinder to Wrigley's critique, see his 'Myth and history: a reply to Christopher Wrigley', *Journal of African History*, vol. 29, no. 3 (1988), p. 385-90.

119 **The rise of nationalism in Central Africa: the making of Malawi and Zambia.**
Robert I. Rotberg. Cambridge, Massachusetts: Harvard University Press, 1965. 362p. bibliog.

Though much new material and analysis has since emerged, as well as revisionist historiography, this is the only book-length and still seminal study of the emergence of nationalism in Malawi. Rotberg has traced its progress from the traumatic but ill-fated Chilembwe rebellion through the rise of civic groups, religious organizations and proto-parties.

120 **Seeds of trouble: government policy and land rights in Nyasaland, 1946-1964.**
Colin Baker. London: British Academic Press, 1993. 215p. bibliog.

Written by one of Malawi's prime historians, this book is the history of land policy in colonial Malawi, the emergence of large agricultural estates, and of the infamous *thangata* system of African tenancy rights in exchange for labour. Baker's treatment of these issues is more detailed than that found in earlier works (these tend to focus mostly on the exploitative *thangata* system). It is also more systematic, and more holistic in that he approaches the issue in a comprehensive manner. He details colonial and settler thinking and problems with respect to land and labour, the workings of the various Colonial Committees after the Second World War (the 1946 Abrams Committee, and the 1947 Land Planning Committee); Sir Geoffrey Colby's reactions to these; the 1953 African disturbances; and the eventual abolition of *thangata*. He concludes by bringing the picture up to independence, with the land acquisition and resettlement efforts of 1955-64.

121 **Silent majority: a history of the Lomwe in Malawi.**
Robert Boeder. Pretoria: Africa Institute of South Africa, 1984. 84p. maps.

A concise and valuable study of the impetus behind the migration from Mozambique to Malawi of the Lomwe, today second in number to the Chewa. Already described as 'One of the greatest population movements of southern Africa' (p. 1), the Lomwe have since been further augmented by additional migrants seeking to escape the turmoil in Mozambique. Over the decades the Lomwe have succeeded in raising themselves from estate labourers on low-paying plantations, to positions of social and economic importance.

122 **The story of Malawi's capitals: old and new, 1891-1969.**
Bridglal Pachai. *Society of Malawi Journal*, vol. 24, pt. 1 (Jan. 1971), p. 35-56.

An historical study of Malawi's three capitals – Blantyre, Zomba and Lilongwe. See also Paul A. Cole-King, *Lilongwe: a historical study* (Zomba: Government Press, 1971. 53p.).

123 **Strike a blow and die: a narrative of race relations in colonial Africa.**
Gideon Simeon Mwase, edited by Robert I. Rotberg. Cambridge, Massachusetts: Harvard University Press, 1967. 135p.

This book includes, *inter alia*, an account of the Chilembwe uprising of 1915, given to Mwase by a follower of Chilembwe when he and Mwase were inmates at Zomba prison.

124 **Swahili influence in the area between Lake Malawi and the Luangwa River.**
Harry W. Langworthy. *African Historical Studies*, vol. 4, pt. 3 (1971), p. 575-602. map.

An assessment of the impact of the intrusion of Swahili Arabs in Malawi and Zambia, and especially the Jumbe of Nkhota Khota. Unlike other scholars, the author focuses on their non-slave-raiding commercial activities. See also Marcia Wright and Peter Lary, 'Swahili settlements in northern Zambia and Malawi', *African Historical Studies*, vol. 4, pt. 3 (1971), p. 547-73, an article which focuses on the Swahili commercial and slave-raiding activities and networks, and the British reaction to them in the era before the imposition of colonial rule. For a study of the latter see I. C. Lamba, 'The scramble for Malawi: a case study in humanitarian imperialism', *Journal of Social Science*, vol. 6 (1977), p. 96-108.

125 *Thangata* **– forced labour or reciprocal assistance?**
J. A. Kamchitete Kandawire. Zomba: University of Malawi, 1979. 161p.

Originally the author's Edinburgh University PhD thesis, this work is the first in-depth analysis of the infamous *thangata* 'land-for-labour' exploitative system in which forced labour held native farmers captive in European estates and farms during the colonial era. The work is also a comprehensive study of land policy in Nyasaland, with all of its limitations and negative repercussions. Another study assesses the exploitation of Malawians as soldiers and labourers during the First World War, an experience from which the first nationalist strivings emerged: Melvin E. Page, 'The war of *thangata*: Nyasaland and the East African campaign, 1914-18', *Journal of African History*, vol. 19, pt. 1 (1978), p. 87-100.

---

126   *Ubureetwa* and *thangata*: the catalysts to peasant political
      consciousness in Rwanda and Malawi.
      Catharine Newbury.   *Canadian Journal of African Studies*, vol. 14,
      no. 1 (1980), p. 97-111.

Newbury compares Malawi's *thangata* system of land-for-labour used by settlers to
obtain much-needed indigenous manpower for their estates during the colonial era,
and the somewhat similar *ubureetwa* system in Rwanda, utilized by chiefs to exploit
their subjects. The end result of the exploitative way in which these two practices
were used during the modern era was the same: growing collective awareness of the
injustice of the non-reciprocal system, erosion of its legitimacy, its rejection as unfair,
and periodical peasant unrest or violent manifestations.

127   'War came from the Boma': military and police disturbances in
      Blantyre, 1902.
      Sean Morrow.   *Society of Malawi Journal*, vol. 41, no. 2 (1988),
      p. 16-29.

This article analyses the Blantyre disturbances of October 1902 by units of the King's
African Rifles *en route* to assist in quelling a revolt in Somalia. Morrow illustrates
that the local settlers' outrage at the incident at the time was more over their loss of
local manpower, than over its treatment.

128   White farmers in Malawi: before and after the depression.
      Robin Palmer.   *African Affairs*, vol. 84, no. 335 (1985), p. 211-45.

Palmer examines the reasons why the European estate sector that developed in
Malawi was completely different from the similar one that was erected in the
neighbouring Rhodesias, and why it was a failure to boot. By 1938 only thirty-five tea
estates, employing eighty Europeans remained in Malawi, with a progressive shift in
economic power to African sharecroppers.

129   Work and control in a peasant economy: a history of the lower
      Tchiri valley in Malawi, 1859-1960.
      Elias Coutinho Mandala.   Madison, Wisconsin: University of
      Wisconsin Press, 1990. 402p. bibliog.

Based on archival and oral history sources tapped (during 1973-80) for a PhD
dissertation, this excellent book is one of the most thorough, meticulous and well-
documented works on Malawi. The study focuses on the evolving role of peasants in
the country and is a wide-ranging and masterful analysis of the indigenous rural
economy, farmers' responses to the new colonial order and the demands it made upon
them as productive agents as well as a pool of human labour.

130   Working conditions and worker responses on Nyasaland tea
      estates, 1930-1953.
      Robin Palmer.   *Journal of African History*, vol. 27, no. 1 (1986),
      p. 105-26.

An analysis of the notoriously poor wages and working conditions, including
thangata labour, prevailing on the European tea estates prior to independence. Much
of the 20-30,000 labour force was made up of Lomwe, escaping even worse

History

conditions in neighbouring Mozambique. By the 1950s, however, severe labour shortages on the estates resulted in millions of pounds of tea being unpicked, and greater labour militancy erupted in the Thyolo riots of 1953. The latter in turn led to the colonial government's purchase of half of the million acres of freehold estate land expropriated from local chiefs at the onset of the colonial era. See also the author's 'The Nyasaland tea industry in the era of international tea restrictions, 1933-1950', *Journal of African History*, vol. 26, no. 2/3 (1985), p. 215-39. In another article Palmer utilizes the archives of the International Tea Committee to throw light on the international politics of tea, and the regional perspective as Malawi, Kenya, Tanzania and Uganda each established their own tea industries. See 'The politics of tea in Eastern Africa 1933-1948', *Journal of Social Science*, vol. 13 (1986), p. 69-90.

131 **The Yao in the Shire Highlands 1861-1915: political dominance and reaction to colonialism.**
Violet Lucy Jhala. *Journal of Social Science*, vol. 9 (1982), p. 1-21. map.

Jhala attempts to fill some gaps in Yao historiography, hitherto focused on the Yao's migration from Mozambique, strong resistance to colonialism and modernization, and their social organization at the time of the imposition of British rule. She concentrates on the Yao's prominence in trade with the east coast, marginalization under colonial rule, and their later upward mobility via careers in the army/police. See also Edward A. Alpers, 'Trade, state and society among the Yao in the 19th century', *Journal of African History*, vol. 10, pt. 3 (1969) p. 405-20; and Kings M. Phiri, 'Yao intrusion into southern Malawi, Nyanja resistance and colonial conquest', *Transafrican Journal of History* (Nairobi), vol. 13 (1984), p. 157-66.

132 **The Zimba and the Lundu State in the late sixteenth and early seventeenth centuries.**
Matthew Schoffeleers. *Journal of African History*, vol. 28 (1987), p. 337-55.

This article is a specific rejoinder to Newitt's 1982 contention that the Maravi state system in the region emerged in the first half of the 17th century. According to Schoffeleers, the Lundu state alone (which he describes) was already in existence as early as 1590.

133 **The Zwangendaba succession.**
C. J. W. Fleming. *Society of Malawi Journal*, vol. 25, pt. 2 (July 1972), p. 38-48.

Fleming gives an account of the Ngoni migration (under their chief, Zwangendaba) from Zululand in South Africa into Zambia and Malawi and on to Lake Tanganyika. After Zwangendaba's death Ngoni unity collapsed and the various groups dispersed, some to settle in Malawi. See also Thomas T. Spear, *Zwangendaba's Ngoni 1821-1890: a political and social history of a migration* (Madison, Wisconsin: University of Wisconsin African Studies Program, Occasional Paper no. 4, 1972). For the unsettled conditions in Zululand that brought about the great migration northward (the *Mfecane*), see J. D. Omer-Cooper, *The Zulu aftermath* (London: Longman, 1966. 208p.).

The Shire Highland.
See item no. 5.

Twenty-five years of independence in Malawi, 1964-1989.
See item no. 6.

Colonialism, capitalism and ecological crisis in Malawi.
See item no. 30.

Anglican missionaries and a Chewa *dini*.
See item no. 134.

The Bimbi shrine in the Upper Shire and its relationship with Yao chiefs, 1830-1925.
See item no. 136.

The Cape Dutch Reformed Church in Malawi.
See item no. 137.

Catholics, peasants, and Chewa resistance in Nyasaland.
See item no. 138.

The history and political role of the Mbona cult among the Mang'anja.
See item no. 141.

The history of the Universities' Mission to Central Africa, 1859-1865.
See item no. 142.

The interaction of the M'Bona cult and Christianity.
See item no. 144.

Islam in Malawi.
See item no. 145.

The legacy of the Scottish missionaries in Malawi.
See item no. 147.

Mainstream Christianity to 1980 in Malawi, Zambia and Zimbabwe.
See item no. 149.

A martyr cult as a reflection of changes in production.
See item no. 150.

Memoir of Bishop Mackenzie.
See item no. 151.

Metamorphoses of the Yao Muslims.
See item no. 152.

Missions and politics in Malawi.
See item no. 153.

My African reminiscences 1876-1895.
See item no. 154.

Religious independency in Nyasaland.
See item no. 161.

The resistance of Nyau societies to the Roman Catholic missions in colonial Malawi.
See item no. 163.

Reverend Hanock Msokera Phiri and the establishment in Nyasaland of the African Methodist Episcopal Church.
See item no. 164.

River of blood: the genesis of a martyr cult.
See item no. 165.

The romance of Blantyre.
See item no. 166.

Science and magic in African technology.
See item no. 167.

The story of the Universities' Mission to Central Africa.
See item no. 168.

Witnesses and Watchtower in the Rhodesias and Nyasaland.
See item no. 170.

Bread with freedom and peace.
See item no. 180.

Capitalism, kinship and gender in the Lower Tchire (Shire) valley of Malawi.
See item no. 192.

Kamazu Banda of Malawi.
See item no. 258.

Malawi: the politics of despair.
See item no. 261.

Civil response to war: the Nyasaland civil service, 1914-1918.
See item no. 272.

The evolution of local government in Malawi.
See item no. 273.

Religion

134 **Anglican missionaries and a Chewa *dini* conversion and rejection in Central Malawi.**
Richard Stuart. *Journal of Religion in Africa* (Leiden), vol. 10, no. 1 (1979), p. 46-69.
This is an account of the Chewa people's original resistance to Christianity and mission-based bush-schools in Central Malawi, as manifested through a resurgence of Nyau initiation ceremonies and *dini*, a religion based on Nyau.

135 **An annotated list of independent churches in Malawi, 1900-1981.**
J. Chaphadzika Chakanza. Zomba: University of Malawi Department of Religious Studies, 1983. 71p.
This publication is a revised second edition of the 1980 publication of the same name. It adds over thirty churches to the original 143 independent ones identified as having emerged in Malawi since the turn of the century. Some of these churches were fundamentalist, going back to the Scriptures; others adopted what, from a Christian point of view, were heresies; while still others combined in essence traditional African practices (polygamy, initiation rites) with Christian dogma and practice. See also John Parratt, 'African independent Churches in Malawi', *Journal of Social Science* (Zomba), vol. 10 (1983), p. 111-19.

136 **The Bimbi shrine in the Upper Shire and its relationships with Yao chiefs, 1830-1925.**
James Amanze. *Journal of Social Science*, vol. 9 (1982), p. 37-50.
A contribution to a study of the history and political role of traditional religious cults, and specifically the lesser-studied Bimbi shrine in Malawi. Basing his work on oral legends, the author pieces together several mythical origins of the shrine, and suggests that with the collapse of the Maravi state system the Bimbi shrine became an important culturally unifying centre. The fact that the subsequent Yao military

intrusions granted autonomy to the shrine encouraged a stable pattern of Nyanja–Yao relations to be established.

137 **The Cape Dutch Reformed Church Mission in Malawi: a preliminary historical examination of its educational philosophy and application, 1899-1931.**
Isaac C. Lamba. *Transafrican Journal of History* (Nairobi), vol. 12 (1983) p. 51-74.
This is an important overview of the little-studied Cape Dutch Reformed Church Mission (DRCM) in Malawi. The author unequivocally concludes that the DRCM, by trying to reach as many people as possible with a policy of providing 'bare literacy for a people classified as children', produced 'semi-literacy under thousands of semi-qualified teachers . . . contributing to underdevelopment' (p. 67) even as its political philosophy nurtured political quietism. See also the earlier, more laudatory self-image of the Church in J. L. Pretorius, 'The story of the Dutch Reformed Church Mission in Nyasaland,' *Nyasaland Journal*, vol. 10, no. 1 (Jan. 1957), p. 11-22.

138 **Catholics, peasants, and Chewa resistance in Nyasaland, 1889-1939.**
Ian Linden, Jane Linden. Berkeley: University of California Press, 1974. 223p. bibliog.
Prefacing his work by the hope that 'this book will not be grist to the mill of anyone wishing to denigrate the Catholic Church in Malawi', Linden proceeds to provide an important history (often revisionist) of the relatively understudied Catholic missionary activity in Malawi, and African's resistance to it. 'Populist' in contradistinction to the 'elitism' of the Protestant thrust in Malawi, the Church made inroads among conservative Chewa peasants (of whom nearly a million are currently Catholic) but produced few modernizers, or proto-nationalists, these being largely the product of the Scottish Church.

139 **Chewa visions and revisions of power: transformation of the Nyau dance in Central Malawi.**
Deborah Kaspin. In: *Modernity and its discontents*, edited by Jean and John Comaroff. Chicago, Illinois: University of Chicago Press, 1993, p. 34-57. bibliog.
A detailed and fascinating description and analysis of Nyau, the 'focal institution of community life' (p. 34) in Chewa villages of central Malawi. Nyau was a legacy of royal rituals, that survived after royalty disappeared. According to Kaspin, 'Nyau is implicated in the consolidation of the rural community, the creation of boundaries between familiar and unfamiliar domains, the metamorphization of experience, and the representation of political and productive power...[becoming] a synonym for a larger cultural order, for the signs and symbols that define the substructure of rural Chewa consciousness' (p. 57). For another fascinating description of the Nyau secret rites and the masks used (with nine pages of plates), see Gerhard Kubik and Moya Aliya Malamusi (an Austrian musicologist and his Malawian collaborator), *Nyau: Maskenbunde im südlichen Malawi* (Nyau: Mask societies in southern Malawi) (Vienna: Verlag der Österreichischen Akademie der Wissenschaften, 1987. 62p.).

140   **Chisumphi theology and religion in Central Malawi.**
Ian Linden.   In: *Guardians of the land: essays on Central African territorial cults*, edited by J. Matthew Schoffeleers.   Gwelo, Zimbabwe: Mambo Press, 1978, p. 187-208.
This study of the oral traditions, beliefs and rites associated with Malawi's three major indigenous religious institutions – territorial rain-shrines, Nyau secret societies, and spirit possession cults – offers insights into the theology of the Chewa supreme god, Chisumphi. See also Temwa Luhanga (et al.), *Papers on regional cults* (Zomba: University of Malawi Department of Religious Studies, 1983), which includes three essays on different cults. For some of the earlier published material, see the three articles by W. H. J. Rangeley: 'Nyasaland rain shrines', *Nyasaland Journal*, vol. 5, no. 2 (July 1952), p. 31-50; 'M'Bona – the rain maker', *Nyasaland Journal*, vol. 6, no. 1 (Jan. 1953), p. 8-27; and 'Territorial cults in the history of Central Africa', *Journal of African History*, vol. 14, no. 4 (1973), p. 581-97.

141   **The history and political role of the Mbona cult among the Mang'anja.**
Matthew Schoffeleers.   In: *The historical study of African religions*, edited by T. O. Ranger, I. N. Kimambo.   Berkeley: University of California Press, 1972, p. 73-94.
A detailed examination of the Mbona cult and the shrine at Khulubi on the Upper Shire river. One of Malawi's most ancient, its influence at one time extended right to the Indian Ocean. Schoffeleers notes that the cult integrated the Mang'anja in every sphere of life from the 14th century onwards, 'being an embodiment of Mang'anja identity, society and aspirations for over six centuries' (p. 92). For a comparison of shrines among the northern and southern Chewa see the same author's 'The Chisumphi and Mbona cults in Malawi', in *Guardians of the land: essays on Central African territorial cults*, edited by Matthew Schoffeleers (Gwelo, Zimbabwe: Mambo Press, 1978, p. 147-86). See also Matthew Schoffeleers' 'Cult idioms and the dialectics of a region', in *Regional cults*, edited by R. P. Werbner (New York: Academic Press, 1977, p. 219-39).

142   **The history of the Universities' Mission to Central Africa, 1859-1965.**
A. E. M. Anderson-Morshead, A. G. Blood.   London: Universities' Mission to Central Africa, 1955-62. 3 vols. + suppl.
This is the official record of the activities of the Universities' Mission to Central Africa (UMCA). For the UMCA's unique floating steamer missions see the collection of essays in *What we do in Nyasaland*, edited by Dora Yarnton Mills (London: Universities' Mission to Central Africa, 1911. 266p.). See also R. Laws, *Reminiscences of Livingstonia* (Edinburgh: Oliver & Boyd, 1934. 242p.); Godfrey Dale, *Darkness or light* (London: Universities' Missions to Central Africa, 1925. 280p.); and W. P. Livingstone, *Laws of Livingstonia* (London: Hodder & Stoughton, 1921. 385p.).

Religion

143 **The influence of the Livingstonia Mission upon the formation of welfare associations in Zambia, 1912-31.**
David J. Cook. In: *Themes in the Christian history of Central Africa,* edited by T. Ranger, J. Weller. London: Heinemann, 1975, p. 98-134.

The Livingstonia Mission had an influence well beyond the boundaries of colonial Nyasaland, as Africans educated there moved to neighbouring territories, utilizing their new skills or knowledge. This chapter recounts the Mission's impact and activities in Zambia (North Rhodesia) where, *inter alia*, former President Kaunda's father, educated at Livingstonia, was active in setting up schools, a church and a mission.

144 **The interaction of the M'Bona cult and Christianity.**
Matthew Schoffeleers. In: *Themes in the Christian history of Central Africa,* edited by T. Ranger, J. Weller. London: Heinemann, 1975. p. 14-29.

This article is a sympathetic overview of the history of the interaction between Christian missionaries, who were vehemently opposed to the Mbona cult, and followers of the cult in southern Malawi. These last even saw parallels between the lives of Mbona and Christ.

145 **Islam in Malawi.**
David S. Bone. *Journal of Religion in Africa* (Leiden), vol. 13, no. 2 (1982), p. 126-38.

A brief survey of the origins of Islam in Malawi, and the specific beliefs and practices of the 10 per cent of the population who profess it. Most of these are the Yao, who freely converted, some prior to their arrival in Malawi in the 19th century; also Muslim are some 20,000 Chewa in the Nkotakota region who were forced to convert under the influence of the Arab *Jumbe* dynasty there in the 1840s. For the Yao, see A. Thorold's 'Yao conversion to Islam', *Cambridge Anthropology* (Cambridge), vol. 12, no. 2 (1987), p. 18-28. The Christian missionary reaction is to be found in David S. Bone's twin articles: 'The Christian missionary response to the development of Islam in Malawi, 1875-1986', *Bulletin on Islam and Christian–Muslim relations in Africa* (Birmingham), vol. 2, no. 3 (1984), p. 1-23, and vol. 5, no. 4 (1987), p. 7-24. For the Muslim society's initial suspicion of, and rejection of, Western education see David S. Bone, 'The Muslim minority in Malawi and Western education', *Journal of the Institute of Muslim Minority* (London), vol. 6, no. 2 (1985), p. 412-19. In general the colonial administration remained neutral about the spread of Islam in so far as it primarily involved what were regarded as industrious and loyal Yao; see Robert Greenstein, 'The Nyasaland government's policy towards African Muslims', in *From Nyasaland to Malawi: studies in colonial history,* edited by R. J. Macdonald (Nairobi: East African Publishing House, 1976, p. 144-68). For a bibliography on this topic see 'Islam in Malawi: an annotated bibliography' (Zomba: University of Malawi Department of Religious Studies, 1983).

146   **Jordan Msumba, Ben Ngemela and the Last Church of God and His Christ, 1924-1935.**
Owen J. M. Kalinga.   *Journal of Religion in Africa* (Leiden), vol. 13, no. 3 (1982), p. 207-18. bibliog.
This is a study of one of the most successful breakaway churches, founded in northern Malawi in 1924, which despite its great popularity among peasants, has hardly attracted the attention of scholars. Kalinga, who has written extensively on the northern Ngonde kingdom, offers a reconstruction of the origins of the church, and focuses on two of its founders.

147   **The legacy of the Scottish missionaries in Malawi.**
Harvey J. Sindima.   Lewiston, New York: Edwin Mellen Press, 1992. 152p. bibliog.
Sindima's succinct overview of the Scottish evangelization policy and strategy in Malawi underlines the degree to which Malawi history was intermeshed with the activities of Scottish missionaries. He argues that they did not have a policy of stressing the training and ordaining of Africans; when they actually did so it was more out of budgetary motives, manpower deficiencies, and the fear of losing qualified catechists either to other churches or their setting up their own independent churches.

148   **Letters of Charles Domingo.**
Charles Domingo, edited by Harry W. Langworthy.   Zomba: University of Malawi Department of Religious Studies, 1983. 72p.
This monograph contains the collected papers of Charles Domingo written between 1910 and 1912. They are addressed mostly to Joseph Booth in Cape Town, to be forwarded to the Seventh Day Baptist officials in Plainfield, New Jersey. For in-depth interpretation of the Seventh Day Baptist movement see Kenneth P. Lohrentz, 'Joseph Booth, Charles Domingo, and the Seventh Day Baptists in Northern Nyasaland, 1910-12', *Journal of African History*, vol. 12, no. 3 (1971), p. 461-80; and Harry W. Langworthy, 'Charles Domingo, Seventh Day Baptists and independency', *Journal of Religion in Africa* (Leiden), vol. 2 (1985), p. 96-121.

149   **Mainstream Christianity to 1980 in Malawi, Zambia and Zimbabwe.**
John C. Weller (et al.).   Gwelo, Zimbabwe: Mambo Press, 1984. 224p. bibliog.
The authors outline the history of mainstream Christianity in the three countries.

150   **A martyr cult as a reflection of changes in production: the case of the Lower Shire valley, 1590-1622 A.D.**
Matthew Schoffeleers.   *African Perspectives* (Leiden), no. 2 (1978), p. 19-33. bibliog.
A detailed discussion of the Mbona cult, its origins, organization and development. The centre of the cult was near contemporary Nsanje in the former Maravi state of Lundu. Differences between cult worship here and elsewhere in Chewa regions, and the relative absence of Nyau secret societies (of pre-Chewa days) lead Schoffeleers to

Religion

postulate that Lundu expelled the existing autochtonous population at the end of the
16th century with the aid of a mercenary Zima army. See also the same author's
'Trade warfare and social inequalities in the Lower Shire valley 1590-1622', *Society
of Malawi Journal*, vol. 33, no. 2 (1980), p. 6-24.

151 **Memoir of Bishop Mackenzie.**
Harvey Goodwin. Cambridge: Deighton, Bell, 1864. 438p.
Based on Mackenzie's private letters (he died early in 1862), this is the story of the
ill-fated first Christian mission set up at Magomero.

152 **Metamorphoses of the Yao Muslims.**
Alan Thorold. In: *Muslim identity and social change in subsaharan
Africa*, edited by Louis Brenner. Bloomington: Indiana University
Press, 1993, p. 78-90.
A brief but comprehensive study of Islam among the Yao. The latter came into
contact with Muslim influences via their trade with coastal communities in the 17th
and 18th centuries. The author identifies the the major sects and their influences on
the different segments of the Yao population found around the southern tip of Lake
Malawi.

153 **Missions and politics in Malawi.**
Nyamayaro K. Mufuka. Kingston, Ontario: Limestone Press, 1977.
279p. maps. bibliog.
This book is a thorough, fundamental and very useful overview of both the positive
and the negative repercussions of the intense missionary proselytizing in Nyasaland,
intertwined with an analysis of the socio-economic evolution of the colony. As the
author stresses, of the various orders that came to spread the gospel in Africa 'only
one group stands out...who practiced what they preached' (p. iii) – the Scottish
missionaries who, both locally and in Great Britain, consistently sided with African
interests and aspirations. See also Peter G. Forster, 'Missionaries and anthropology:
the case of the Scots of Northern Malawi', *Journal of Religion in Africa* (Leiden),
vol. 16, no. 2 (1986), p. 101-20; Peter G. Forster, *T. Cullen Young: missionary and
anthropologist* (Hull, England: Hull University Press, 1989. 251p.); Jack Thompson,
'True love and roots: a centenary re-assessment of the work of William Koyi among
the Ngoni', *Society of Malawi Journal*, vol. 39, no. 2 (1986), p. 15-25.

154 **My African reminiscences 1876-1895.**
William Percival Johnson. London: Universities' Mission to Central
Africa, 1926. Reprinted New York: Negro Universities Press, 1966. 236p.
Johnson gives an overly modest account of the mission station on the eastern shore of
Lake Malawi that for several years was solely staffed by him. See also D. Y. Mills,
*A hero man: the life and adventures of William Percival Johnson, Archdeacon of
Nyasa* (London: Universities' Mission to Central Africa, 1931. 278p.).

155 **Nyau in Kotakota District.**
W. H. Rangeley. *Nyasaland Journal*, vol. 2, pt. 2 (July 1949),
p. 35-49; vol. 3, pt. 2 (July 1950), p. 19-33.
This early analysis of the Nyau secret society in Chewa society pays special attention
to the masks used and is written in a fascinating style. Rangeley was a European born
in Nyasaland who in due course became commissioner of the Southern Province.

156 **Pentecolism and neo-traditionalism: the religious polarization of a
rural district in southern Malawi.**
Matthew Schoffeleers. Amsterdam: Free University Press, 1985.
51p. bibliog.
This illustrated monograph is a religious history of Nsanje and the spread of
pentecolism in that area of Malawi. Schoffeleers identifies the demographic
characteristics, gender and age groups of those participating in both the indigenous
Mboni cult and in the Church, and suggests a strong affinity between the emergence
of a lower middle class among the traditional peasant population and the spread of
pentecolism. In particular the slow crumbling of possession cults enabled 'several
thousands of women to become available for recruitment into more centrally
organized religious movements' (p. 37).

157 **Plant-induced 'spirit possession' in Malawi.**
Bruce J. Hargreaves. *Society of Malawi Journal*, vol. 39, no. 1
(1986), p. 26-35.
A detailed description of a possession dance performed regularly in the Lower Shire
river valley, and four of the specific plants used to induce trances during it. See also
J. M. Schoffeleers, *Evil spirits and the rites of exorcism in the Lower Shire valley of
Malawi* (Limbe: Montfort Press, 1967); and J. M. Schoffeleers, 'Social functional
aspects of spirit possession in the Lower Shire valley of Malawi', in *Religious Studies
Papers* (1969), p. 51-63.

158 **Provisional annotated chronological list of witch-finding
movements in Malawi, 1850-1980.**
J. Chaphadzika Chakanza. *Journal of Religion in Africa* (Leiden),
vol. 15, no. 3 (1985), p. 227-43.
A listing of twenty-one anti-witch movements – banned in 1911 – that describes their
activities. These included forcing suspects to drink a toxic *mwabri*, which if vomited
proved innocence. The author includes references to original source material.

159 **Religion in Malawi.**
David S. Bone. Zomba: University of Malawi Department of
Religious Studies, 1983. 26p.
A directory of scholars, in Malawi and abroad, involved in research on religion in
Malawi. The list includes sixty-five individuals, their academic affiliations, specific
interests and some of their publications.

160 **Religion, language and tribal myth: the Tumbuka and Chewa of Malawi.**
H. L. Vail. In: *Guardians of the land: essays on Central African territorial cults*, edited by J. Matthew Schoffeleers. Gwelo, Zimbabwe: Mambo Press, 1978, p. 209-34.

A comparison of several Tumbuka beliefs and customs with those of the Chewa to the south, illustrating how southern Tumbuka beliefs remarkably overlap those of the Chewa, while those of the northern Tumbuka do not. The author notes that the Tumbuka and Chewa had a common religious base in the distant past, but that this was altered in the north over the years. See also T. Cullen Young, 'The idea of God in Northern Nyasaland', in *African idea of God*, edited by Edwin W. Smith (Edinburgh: Edinburgh University Press, 1950, p. 36-58).

161 **Religious independency in Nyasaland: a typology of origins.**
John Parratt. *African Studies* (Johannesburg), vol. 38, no. 2 (1979), p. 183-200.

An overview of the differing origins of the independent religious movements and churches that sprang up in colonial Nyasaland. In the south these were largely due to the indefatigable work of. Joseph Booth; elsewhere the return home of migrant labourers, discrimination against African ministers and personality clashes within existing churches triggered religious independency. Much the same material, and conclusions, but in greater depth, is found in an earlier book by R. L. Wishlade: *Sectarianism in southern Nyasaland* (London: Oxford University Press, 1965. 162p.). See also Roderick J. MacDonald, 'Religious independency as a means of social advance in Northern Nyasaland in the 1930's', *Journal of Religion in Africa* (Leiden), vol. 3, no. 2 (1970), p. 106-29.

162 **Religious revitalization in Malawi: the African ancestors' religion.**
J. Chaphadzika Chakanza. *Journal of Humanities* (Zomba), no. 3 (Dec. 1989), p. 43-54.

An overview of the emergence in the 1970s of the Makolo ancestors' sect in Blantyre, Thyolo, Mulanje and Chiradzula. Preachers attracted crowds at bus stops and markets, and intermittent flurries of leaflets won over large numbers of converts. Without any particular cogent theological or social message, and appealing especially to those unaffected by modernization in urban slums and rural backwaters, the sects decried Malawians' abandonment of their ancestral faiths for the 'European' God, and stressed the falsification of many of Christ's teachings by the Christian churches.

163 **The resistance of Nyau societies to the Roman Catholic missions in colonial Malawi.**
Matthew Schoffeleers, Ian Linden. In: *The historical study of African religions*, edited by T. O. Ranger, I. Kimambo. Berkeley: University of California Press, 1972, p. 252-76. bibliog.

Authored by two of the towering scholars of traditional Malawian religions, this study surveys the secret Nyau societies that resisted the proselytizing efforts of Catholic missions and remain prevalent in Chewa society to this day. Nyau refers not only to the sect, but to their masks, apparel, dances and rites, and to an all-embracing claim of ethnic identity transmitted through participation. Participation in the cult was directly and indirectly forbidden by both the colonial administration and the Church in Malawi, but when independence was achieved President Banda began using the practices as a means of nation-building. See also the author's 'The Nyau societies: our present understanding', *Society of Malawi Journal*, vol. 29, no. 1 (Jan. 1976), p. 59-68; and *Catholics, peasants and Chewa resistance in Nyasaland* (London: Heinemann, 1974. 223p.).

164 **Reverend Hanock Msokera Phiri and the establishment in Nyasaland of the African Methodist Episcopal Church.**
Roderick J. MacDonald. *African Historical Studies*, vol. 3, no. 1 (1970), p. 75-87.
A biography of Phiri and his role in furthering the Methodist Church in Southern Africa. Phiri, President Banda's uncle and the one instrumental in getting him to the United States, joined the African Methodist Episcopal Church in South Africa in 1923, and became a major force in setting up schools and missions in Malawi, Tanganyika, Northern Rhodesia and Zaïre.

165 **River of blood: the genesis of a martyr cult in southern Malawi, c. A.D. 1600.**
J. Matthew Schoffeleers. Madison, Wisconsin: University of Wisconsin Press, 1992. 325p. bibliog.
This book is a veritable *tour de force* by the Dutch Catholic priest and religious anthropologist, long-time missionary in Malawi, and currently Professor Emeritus at the Free University of Amsterdam. It is an exceedingly readable account not only of the Mbona cult from its origins to the present day, but also a reconstruction of the early history of southern Malawi, its ethnic groups, their evolution and coalescence around the cult. Schoffeleers describes in detail the three-part ritual cycle of the communal rain-prayers, provides texts of seven cult myths from different historical periods (in English and Chimang'anja), and underlines how oral tradition about the cults constitutes a rich repository of historical data. He concludes his study with a 13-page bibliography.

166 **The romance of Blantyre: how Livingstone's dream came true.**
Alexander Hetherwick. Blantyre: Blantyre Synod Bookshop, 1962. 260p.
The history of the Blantyre Mission, cathedral, school and press, by one of the country's prime missionaries and the one in charge of the Blantyre Synod between 1883 and 1928. For one 'popular' outline of the author's work in Nyasaland see the highly laudatory W. P. Livingstone, *A prince of missionaries* (London: James Clarke, 1931. 206p.).

167 **Science and magic in African technology: traditional iron smelting in Malawi.**
Nikolaas J. Van der Merwe, Donald H. Avery. *Africa* (London), vol. 57, no. 2 (1987), p. 143-72.
A reconstruction of the role that magic and other factors played in iron-smelting at two historic sites in Malawi. These were Chulu and Phoka in central and northern Malawi, respectively.

Religion

168 **The story of the Universities' Mission to Central Africa.**
Henry Rowley. New York: Negro Universities Press, 1969. 424p.
(Reprint of 1867 edition by Saunders, Ittley & Co., London).

The story of the travails of the Universities' Mission to East Central Africa from its commencement under Bishop Mackenzie in Magomero to its withdrawal. The work contains vivid descriptions of the many difficulties encountered during the trip to Nyasaland (via the Zambezi) and during the Mission's stay in the Highlands, Magomero and Chibisa.

169 **Transition and change: a study of the psychological impact of Gule.**
Joseph Kuthemba Mwale. *Journal of Social Science* (Zomba), vol. 8 (1980-81), p. 126-47.

The study is based on interviews of 520 Chewa initiated youths and examines the psychological and socialization effects on them of Wamkulu initiation rites. The results supported several hypotheses, including the increase in self-esteem of those partaking in them. See also Ian Linden, 'Chewa initiation rites in Nyau Gule Wamkulu societies', in *Themes in the Christian history of Central Africa*, edited by T. O. Ranger, J. Weller (London: Heinemann, 1975, p. 30-44).

170 **Witnesses and Watchtower in the Rhodesias and Nyasaland.**
James R. Hooker. *Journal of African History*, vol. 6, no. 1 (1965), p. 91-106.

A review of the history of the two sects in central Africa. Believing as they do that evil spreads through involvement in political and commercial structures, the members of Watchtower and Jehovah's Witnesses eschew any involvement with formal structures of government. During the colonial era they were warily kept under surveillance, but after independence their refusal to accept the authority of the state led to their persecution, and even the expulsion of their members from Malawi. See also 'Jehovah's Witnesses in Malawi', *Africa Report*, vol. 21, no. 1 (Jan.-Feb. 1976), p. 37-9, where the persecution of the cult is documented.

171 **Y. Z. Mwasi and the origins of the Blackman's Church.**
John Parratt. *Journal of Religion in Africa* (Leiden), vol. 9, no. 3 (1978), p. 193-206.

The Blackman's Church was one of the most important secessions from the Livingstonia Synod. It expressed the frustrations felt by African ministers in colonial Africa. This article traces, through the writings of Mwasi, the roots and reasons for Mwasi's split from Livingstone.

Independent African: John Chilembwe and the origins, setting and sigificance of the Nyasaland native uprising of 1915.
See item no. 91.

The *Jumbe* of Kota Kota and some aspects of the history of Islam in Malawi.
See item no. 92.

Land and politics in Malawi 1875-1975.
See item no. 94.

Magomero: portrait of a village.
See item no. 96.

'Marginal men': the colonial experience in Malawi.
See item no. 101.

Masokwa Elliott Kenan Kamwana Chirwa.
See item no. 102.

Politics and Christianity in Malawi, 1875-1940.
See item no. 115.

The river-god and the historians: myth in the Shire Valley and elsewhere.
See item no. 118.

Strike a blow and die.
See item no. 123.

Evil spirits and rites of exorcism in the Lower Shire Valley.
See item no. 176 [annot.].

The Yao village.
See item no. 179.

Catholic directory of Malawi.
See item no. 476.

Demography

172 **Demographic data resources for colonial Malawi.**
Justice R. Ngoleka Mlia. In: *Demography from scanty evidence:
central Africa in the colonial era*, edited by Bruce Fetter. Boulder,
Colorado: L. Rienner, 1990, p. 81-100. maps. bibliog.
This is a history of censuses conducted in Malawi, the methodologies employed and
the range of demographic data available at the time. The author underlines the
limitations of the data collected in the past by census takers, and hence its
unreliability, and outlines the socio-economic characteristics of the populations then
and now. Other analyses of early censuses include Gilroy Coleman, 'The African
population of Malawi: census 1901-1966', *Society of Malawi Journal*, vol. 27, pt. 1
(Jan. 1974), p. 27-41 and pt. 2 (July 1974), p. 36-46. These make much the same
points about the unreliability of early censuses.

173 **Malawi population census, 1977.**
National Statistics Office. Zomba: Government Printer, 1984. 2 vols.
The 1977 census was the second since Malawi's independence, and was conducted
with the aid of the UNDP and with fiscal assistance from the British government. The
two volumes include one subtitled 'Analytical report' that outlines administrative and
methodological details regarding the 1977 census, and a second subtitled 'Analytical
report' that is primarily composed of statistics on a variety of variables. The tables
include data on all aspects of the population, including domestic and foreign
migration, sex and age composition, education and literacy. The population of
Malawi was put at just over 5.5 million as against 4 million in 1966, indicating a high
growth rate of 2.9 per cent, a figure which was to increase by 1987. For Malawi's
1966 census see *Malawi: population census 1966: final report* (Zomba: Government
Printer, 1971. 49p.).

174 **Population and housing census 1987: preliminary report.**
National Statistics Office. Zomba: Government Printer, 1987. 28p.
    maps.

This report, mostly in the form of tables from Malawi's most recent census, includes data on housing, the first time this kind of information was collected in conjunction with a census. The census was also the first conducted in its entirety by local staff. The data reveal that Malawi's population remained overwhelmingly rural (89 per cent as against 92 per cent in 1977, and 95 per cent in 1966), and had grown at an accelerated 3 per cent per annum to roughly 8 million. Fully half the population resided in the southern region, which comprises 34 per cent of the land mass, as compared with 39 per cent in the central (38 per cent of the land) and 11 per cent in the northern region (28 per cent of the country's surface). The statistics are roughly comparable with data collected in previous censuses. As was visible for some time even without the census, the country's high rate of population growth was sharply increasing the country's already very high population density, with consequent pressures on the country's limited available arable land and forests (tapped for firewood) and extremely grave repercussions for the near future. Other information collected revealed that there were more women than men in Malawi, and that 50 per cent of the population had never attained formal education except those living in Blantyre, Kasungu, Chitipa, Karongo, Nkhata Bay and Mzimba. A huge three-volume final report of the 1987 census appeared six years later, but is not widely available abroad yet: see National Statistics Office, *Malawi population and housing census 1987* (Zomba: Government Printer, 1993. 3 vols).

Population growth and environmental degradation in Malawi.
See item no. 34.

Drought, migration and chronology in the Lake Malawi littoral.
See item no. 79.

Projections of internal migration in Malawi.
See item no. 186.

Malawi family formation survey, 1984.
See item no. 223.

Area handbook for Malawi.
See item no. 470.

The People

175 **Children of their fathers: growing up among the Ngoni of Nyasaland.**
Margaret Read.   London: Methuen, 1959. 176p.

This is a dated (but still very useful) detailed anthropological study of socialization in traditional Ngoni society in colonial Nyasaland. For a broader study by the same author, based on empirical work in the 1930s, see *The Ngoni of Nyasaland* (London: Oxford University Press, 1956. 212p. Reprinted in 1970 by Cass (London)).

176 **The Lower Shire Valley: its ecology, population distribution, ethnic divisions and systems of marriage.**
Matthew Schoffeleers.   Limbe, Malawi: Montfort Press, 1968. 86p. bibliog.

Written by the Dutch priest-scholar whose contributions to the understanding of Malawi history, culture and traditional religion have been monumental, this slim book is an outline of the complex matrix of peoples and their cultures found in the Lower Shire Valley. The book is ideally complemented by his earlier volume stressing traditional rites in the region: *Evil spirits and rites of exorcism in the Lower Shire Valley of Malawi* (Limbe, Malawi: Montfort Press, 1967).

177 **Peoples of the Lake Nyasa region.**
Mary Tew.   London: Oxford University Press, 1950. 131p. bibliog.

Part of the Ethnographic Survey of Africa series, this is the definitive anthropological classification study of the Chewa, Tumbuka, Yao, Ngonde, Tonga, Ngoni and other groups in Malawi. For a more comprehensive study of the Tonga see Jaap Van Velsen, *The politics of kinship: a study in social manipulation among the lakeside Tonga of Nyasaland* (Manchester: Manchester University Press, 1972. 338p.).

178 **Some changes in the matrilineal family system among the Chewa of Malawi since the nineteenth century.**

Kings M. Phiri.   *Journal of African History* (Cambridge), vol. 24, no. 2 (1983), p. 275-74. map. bibliog.

An account of the important changes that have taken place over time in the basic patterns of Chewa matrilineal society. These were occasioned by the slave trade, the Nguni invasions and their patrilineal system, and the effect of early colonialism and missionary teachings on traditional Chewa life. The changes involve marriage contracts, family residential patterns, exercise of domestic authority and control of children, all which have seen the powerful growth of patriliny inconsistent with the Chewa's original matrilineal social organization. For the specific effect of the Swahili slave-sultanate in Nkhota-Kota on Chewa culture and society see Sol Liwewe, *Swahili-Arab impact on Chewa society in Central Nkota-Kota c. 1840-1920* (Zomba: History Seminar paper no. 9, 1982). See also Paul Kishindo, 'The emergence of a virilocal pattern of residence among the matrilineal people of Central Malawi and its implications for smallholder agriculture', *Eastern Anthropologist* (Lucknow), vol. 41, no. 2 (1988), p. 157-63; and D. N. Kaphagawani (et al.), 'Chewa cultural ideals and system of thought as determined from proverbs', *Journal of Social Science*, vol. 10 (1983), p. 100-10.

179 **The Yao village: a study in the social structure of a Malawian tribe.**

J. Clyde Mitchell.   Manchester: Manchester University Press, 1956. 236p. bibliog. maps.

This is still the classic study of the Yao ethnic group, a largely Muslim trading group (in ivory and slaves) that reached the lower Lake region from Mozambique and imposed their sovereignty over the villages they came upon. The book is based on fieldwork research in two Yao villages in the mid to late 1940s, and focuses on the origins and cultural influences on the Yao of Islam (from the coast), and the evolution of their social structures and lineages in Malawi. See also an earlier classic, originally published as far back as 1919 by the Nyasaland government, that includes text and oral testimonials in both English and Yao: Yohanna B. Abdallah, *The Yaos* (London: Cass, 1973. 136p.). Still useful is W. H. J. Rangeley, 'The AmaCinga Yao', *Nyasaland Journal*, vol. 15, pt. 2 (1962), p. 40-70.

Adventures in Nyasaland.
See item no. 69.

Cullen Young, Yesayu Chibambo, and the Ngoni.
See item no. 77.

From Nguni to Ngoni.
See item no. 85.

The history of the Chewa.
See item no. 88.

History of the Ngonde kingdom of Malawi.
See item no. 90.

The People

The *Jumbe* of Kota Kota and some aspects of the history of Islam in Malawi.
See item no. 92.

Magomero: portrait of a village.
See item no. 96.

The making of the 'Dead North': a study of Ngoni rule in northern Malawi c. 1855-1907.
See item no. 98.

Mwali and the Luba origin of the Chewa.
See item no. 103.

The Nguru penetration into Nyasaland 1892-1914.
See item no. 107.

Notes on the history of the Lakeside Tonga.
See item no. 108.

Notes on the history of the Tumbuka-Kamanga peoples in the northern province of Nyasaland.
See item no. 109.

The Ntumbe.
See item no. 110.

Political change and the Chewa and Yao of the Lake Malawi region.
See item no. 114.

Politics and Christianity in Malawi 1875-1940.
See item no. 115.

Silent majority: a history of the Lomwe in Malawi.
See item no. 121.

Swahili influence in the area between Lake Malawi and the Luangwa river.
See item no. 124.

The Yao in the Shire Highlands 1861-1915.
See item no. 131.

The Zwangendaba succession.
See item no. 133.

Catholics, peasants and Chewa resistence in Nyasaland, 1889-1939.
See item no. 138.

The history and political role of the Mbona cult among the Mang'anja.
See item no. 141.

A martyr cult as a reflection of changes in production.
See item no. 150.

Metamorphoses of Yao Muslims.
See item no. 152.

Religion, language and tribal myth: the Tumbuka and Chewa of Malawi.
See item no. 160.

The resistance of Nyau societies to the Roman Catholic missions in colonial Malawi.
See item no. 163.

River of blood: the genesis of a martyr cult in southern Malawi.
See item no. 165.

The Indian minority of Zambia, Rhodesia and Zimbabwe.
See item no. 221.

Area handbook for Malawi.
See item no. 470.

Labour and Migration

180 **Bread with freedom and peace: rail workers in Malawi, 1954-1975.**
Tony Woods. *Journal of Southern African Studies* (Oxford), vol. 18, no. 4 (Dec. 1992), p. 727-38.
A study of the relationship between labour militancy and the struggle for independence through the analysis of the country's railroad workers' trade union. The Malawi Congress Party heightened workers' expectations, a fact which, the author suggests, was behind the labour unrest of the 1990s.

181 **Dimensions of conflict: emigrant labor from colonial Malawi and Zambia, 1900-1945.**
Joel W. Gregory, Elias Mandala. In: *African population and capitalism*, edited by Dennis D. Cordell, Joel W. Gregory. Boulder, Colorado: Westview Press, 1987, p. 221-40.
Basing their work on demographic data, the authors reinterpret the relationship between agriculture, migration and the capitalist drive. They reconstruct patterns of migration from colonial Malawi and Zambia during the period 1900-45, that were partly abetted by the colonial regime's coercive measures to spur labour away from the subsistence sector to plantations or mining. The resultant decline in agrarian productivity in the late 1930s 'made it more difficult for elders to rely upon agriculture as a source of accumulation. Like the Ngoni before them, elders in the valley began to look to migration as a more reliable tool for accumulation' (p. 239). See also E. P. Makombe, 'The impact of the 1907 agreement on Malawi labour migration to the Zimbabwean colonial market', *Scandinavian Journal of Development Alternatives*, vol. 11, no. 2 (June 1992), p. 95-123; F. E. Sanderson, 'The development of labour migration from Nyasaland', *Journal of African History*, vol. 2 (1961), p. 259-71; and G. Coleman, 'Some implications of international labour migration from Malawi', *East African Geographical Review*, vol. 12 (April 1974), p. 87-101.

182 **From socialization to personal enterprise: a history of the Nomi labor societies in the Nsanje district of Malawi, 1891-1972.**
Matthew Schoffeleers. *Rural Africana*, no. 20 (Spring 1973), p. 11-25.
A description of the communal work societies in Nsanje that pool their income for purposes of a joint festivity at the end of the planting season.

183 **Labour in Nyasaland: an assessment of the 1960 railroad workers' strike.**
John McCracken. *Journal of Southern African Studies* (Oxford), vol. 14, no. 2 (Jan. 1988), p. 279-90.
As McCracken notes, despite the drive for 'obsessive detail' of research into Malawi's immediate pre-independence era, 'one significant area remains untouched' (p. 279) – the history of labour relations in the country. This article is a pioneering study of labour militancy in the Blantyre-Limbe area from the late 1940s through to the 1960 strike of the railway workers on which 'not even one sentence' (p. 279) had been written hitherto. Following independence, the Banda regime succeeded in 'eliminating all but the most trivial examples of independent worker action' (p. 280).

184 **Land and labor in rural Malawi.**
Rural Africana (East Lansing), edited by Melvin Eugene Page. Special issue no. 20 (1973).
A collection of articles including the editor's 'Land and labor in Malawi' (p. 3-10); M. Schoffeleers' 'From socialization to personal enterprise' (p. 11-26); Martin Chanock's 'Notes for an agricultural history of Malawi' (p. 27-36); and others.

185 **The pattern of internal migration in response to structural change in the economy of Malawi, 1966-1977.**
Robert Christiansen. *Development and Change* (London), vol. 15, no. 1 1984), p. 125-51. maps. bibliog.
Important survey of the patterns of internal demographic shifts as reflected by the censuses in Malawi. Originally there was a net migration from the economically depressed and underdeveloped north to the southern region, but after the construction of the new capital in Lilongwe there was also an influx to the central region. The migrations are economically inspired, gravitating to regions where employment opportunities exist. However, the migration patterns are somewhat unusual because the majority of migration is not from rural to urban areas, but an intra-rural (rural–rural) flow of people.

186 **Projections of internal migration in Malawi: implications for development.**
Edwin S. Segal. *Journal of Modern African Studies*, vol. 23, no. 2 (June 1985), p. 315-29.
This article focuses in greater depth on district-level population movements as reflected by the 1977 census, projecting them into long-term estimates of population distributions and policy implications. One of the key aspects of both internal migration and urbanization in Malawi has been the slow growth of small towns rather

than the development of massive urban sprawls, and this has been partly an outgrowth of conscious policy, stressing decentralization of economic and social services and curtailing the growth of the civil service and urban opportunities, as well as de-emphasizing a too large spread between rural and urban wages.

187 **The return of Malawian labour from South Africa and Zimbabwe.**
Robert E. Christiansen, Jonathan E. Kydd. *Journal of Modern African Studies*, vol. 21, no. 2 (June 1983), p. 311-26.

This is a penetrating analysis explaining how Malawi, for long a net exporter of hundreds of thousands of migrant workers to neighbouring countries, including to the mines of South Africa, was able to withdraw over half of its labour force overseas a decade after independence and integrate it into its domestic economy. See also F. E. Sanderson, 'The development of labour migration from Nyasaland', *Journal of African History*, vol. 2 (1961), p. 259-71.

188 **The role of the Ngoni and Lomwe in the growth of the plantation economy in the Shire Highlands, 1890-1912.**
H. H. K. Bhila. *Journal of Social Science*, vol. 5 (1976), p. 28-43.

An examination of the recruitment of Ngoni and (especially) Lomwe arriving in large numbers in Nyasaland, escaping the hardships in Mozambique, to work on the European plantations in south Malawi. Such groups had to be recruited in large numbers in the absence of Chewa interest in this hard and low-paid work.

189 **The role of trade unions and employers' associations in economic development and employment creation in Malawi.**
C. Chipeta. Geneva: International Institute for Labour Studies, 1976. 24p.

A brief (and overly optimistic) assessment of the potential role of Malawi's employee and employers' associations in the developmental and job-creation processes.

190 **We won't die for fourpence: Malawian labor and the Kariba dam.**
Robert B. Boeder. *Journal of Modern African Studies*, vol. 15, no. 2 (1977), p. 310-15.

This is a description of the strike of Malawian labourers during the construction of the Kariba dam in Zambia in 1959.

Land and politics in Malawi 1875-1975.
See item no. 94.

Peasants, planters and the colonial state.
See item no. 113.

Seeds of trouble: government policy and land rights in Nyasaland, 1946-1964.
See item no. 120.

Thangata – forced labor or reciprocal assistance?
See item no. 125.

Ubereetwa and *thangata*: the catalysts to peasant political consciousness.
See item no. 126.

Working conditions and worker responses on Nysaland tea estates.
See item no. 130.

Malawi labor migration and life in southern Africa.
See item no. 301.

Land and labor in rural Malawi.
See item no. 316.

Gender Issues

191 **Bureaucracy and rural women: illustrations from Malawi.**
David Hirschmann. *Rural Africana*, no. 21 (Winter 1985), p. 51-63.
Hirschmann has studied the attitudes towards rural women of policy-makers in
Malawi. Despite some movement away from gender stereotypes, 'patriarchy, private
insecurity, bureaucratic caution about change, notably in gender roles, and an
unhelpful view to peasant farmers in general' still affect the way a woman's role in
the economy is perceived. The role they play, however, is major and vital, especially
in light of the fact that so many males have migrated in search of work outside the
country. For a similar thrust see also Jonathan Mayuyuka Kaunda, 'Agricultural credit
policy, bureaucratic decision-making and the subordination of rural women in the
development process: some observations on the Kawinga project, Malawi', *Journal of
Southern African Studies* (Oxford), vol. 16, no. 3 (Sept. 1990), p. 413-30.

192 **Capitalism, kinship and gender in the lower Tchire (Shire) valley
of Malawi 1860-1960: an alternative theoretical framework.**
Elias C. Mandala. *African Economic History* (Madison, Wisconsin),
vol. 13 (1984), p. 137-69. map. bibliog.
Mandala surveys the changing role of gender in the process of class formation as a
consequence of the capitalist mode of production in the Shire valley. The author
covers much the same ground in his 'Peasant cotton agriculture, gender and
intergenerational relationships: the lower Tchire (Shire) valley of Malawi, 1906-
1940', *African Studies Review*, vol. 25, no. 2/3 (June-Sept. 1982), p. 27-44.

193 **Changing relations of production in southern Malawi's
households: implications for involving women in development.**
Jean Davidson. *Journal of Contemporary African Studies*, vol. 11,
no. 1 (1992), p. 72-83.
This article explores why the emphasis of key donor agents on cooperative
development as a method of uplifting women's incomes has not been particularly

successful in Malawi, in contrast to the record in other countries. According to the author the failure is 'attributed to a lack of sensitivity to existing relations of production' (p. 72).

194 **Chewa women's songs: a verbal strategy of manipulating social tensions.**
Enoch Timpunza Mvula. *Women's Studies International Forum* (Oxford), vol. 9, no. 3 (1986), p. 265-72. bibliog.

The author argues in this article that Chewa work songs are not just expressive behaviour aimed at entertaining hard workers, but also firm expressions of gender roles. The hand-pounding songs are 'one of the most powerful modes of verbal expression' for a Chewa woman who wishes to communicate her concerns. The pounding is a verbal strategy that a woman employs 'to negotiate with and manipulate others within her environment' (p. 265). The author has written a similar article on the Tumbuka entitled 'Tumbuka pounding songs in the management of familial conflict', in *Cross Rhythms*, edited by Daniel Avorgbedor and Kwesi Yankah (Bloomington, Indiana: Trickster Press, 1987, p. 93-113). See also Enoch T. Mvula, 'The pounding song as a vehicle of social consciousness', *Outlook*, vol. 1 (July 1982), p. 31-55.

195 **A comparison of rural women's time-use and nutritional consequences in two villages in Malawi.**
Lila Engberg (et al.). In: *Gender issues in farming systems research and extension*, edited by Susan V. Poats (et al.). Boulder, Colorado: Westview Press, 1988, p. 99-110.

This study, supported by four tables of statistical data, measures the use of time in functioning rural households in two Malawi villages. It also establishes correlations between women's cash-crop agrarian activities and (negative) consequences on family nutrition. For an earlier quantification of rural work undertaken by women in five villages see Barbara A. Clark, 'The work done by rural women in Malawi', *Eastern Africa Journal of Rural Development*, vol. 8, no. 1/2 (1975), p. 80-91.

196 **Food production and income generation in a matrilineal society: rural women in Zomba, Malawi.**
David Hirschmann, Megan Vaughan. *Journal of Southern African Studies*, vol. 10, no. 1 (1983), p. 86-99.

A description of various food-producing and income-generating activities that are common in rural households in the district of Zomba and that are undertaken by women.

197 **Household units and historical process in southern Malawi.**
Megan Vaughan. *Review of African Political Economy* (London), no. 34 (Dec. 1985), p. 35-45.

A general study of gender relations and the status of women in Malawi as they are affected by changing commodity production patterns. The effect is not uniform; the author indicates how in one instance (involving the development of a cash-crop industry) the economic and political status of women was enhanced, while in another (in the tobacco industry) their position was definitely marginalized.

198 **Income-generating activities and rural women in Malawi: a search for a viable strategy.**
G. H. R. Chipande, M. M. Mkwezalamba. *Journal of Social Science*, vol. 13 (1986), p. 91-103.

The two authors, members of the University of Malawi's Economics Department, outline several possible occupational options aimed at increasing the income of rural women, since they have limited access to non-farm sources of employment, bear heavy domestic burdens, and do not fully participate in agricultural development projects aimed at uplifting smallholders. For one effort to better harness the labour of women (the Women in Agricultural Development Project funded by USAID) see Anita Spring, 'Putting women in the development agenda: agricultural development in Malawi', in *Anthropology of development and change in East Africa*, edited by David W. Brokensha and Peter D. Little (Boulder, Colorado: Westview Press, 1988, p. 13-42). See also Anita Spring, *Agricultural development in Malawi: a project for women in development* (Boulder, Colorado: Westview Press, 1989, 198p.); and Louis A. H. Msukwa, *A feasibility study on income generating activities for women in Karonga, Kasungu, and Mangochi districts: a final report* (Zomba: University of Malawi Center for Social Research, 1989. 103p.).

199 **Innovation adoption among female-headed households: the case of Malawi.**
G. H. R. Chipande. *Development and Change* (Beverly Hills), vol. 18, no. 2 (1987), p. 315-27. bibliog.

A survey of the main constraints facing female-headed farming households in Malawi including labour deficiencies due to male out-migration and inappropriate farming innovations that are labour- and outlay-intensive. For the effect on family life see Megan Vaughan, 'Which family? problems in reconstruction of the history of the family as an economic and cultural unit', *Journal of African History*, vol. 24, no. 2 (1983), p. 275-83.

200 **Men and women smallholder participation in a stall-feeder livestock program in Malawi.**
Anita Spring. *Human Organization* (Oklahoma City), vol. 45, no. 2 (Summer 1986), p. 154-62.

The increasing role of women in agriculture and household production is involving them in caring for cattle and other animals as men are driven away in search of wage labour in the modern economy. Yet even as the tasks of women are increasing, their visibility in production is not: planners have never targeted women for development programmes, in this case stall-feeding, and extension workers typically bypass women in favour of men.

201 **Nutrition education in Malawi.**
F. J. Weaver. In: *New developments in nutrition education*, edited by Sheila A. Turner, Richard B. Ingle. Paris: UNESCO, 1985, p. 175-80. bibliog.

A brief survey of the nutritional balance and nutrition education in Malawi. The data gathered indicated fully half the women cannot even grasp the concept of the existence of three basic food groups, and forty per cent do not provide nutritionally adequate meals for their families. These dietetic facts no doubt play a role in making children prone to sickness, contributing to the country's high mortality rates.

202 **The situation of children and women in Malawi.**
UNICEF, Government of Malawi.   Lilongwe: UNICEF, 1987. 82p.
maps. bibliog.
This is a detailed study of the aetiology and prevalence of child malnutrition, and of women's role as child-bearers, household provisioners and food producers. Their social status, and morbidity and mortality patterns are also examined.

203 **Tenacious women: clinging to *banja* household production in the face of changing gender relations in Malawi.**
Jean Davidson.   *Journal of Southern African Studies*, vol. 19, no. 3 (Sept. 1993), p. 399-421.
The author analyses the reasons women prefer individual household production activities rather than participation in gender-specific collaborative forms of production. This is largely a line of defence against their progressive marginalization by social modernization brought about 'by missionaries and colonial administrators. Tenaciously clinging to their land and *banja* production, these women try to maintain some control over an uncertain future' (p. 421).

204 **Using male research and extension personnel to target women farmers.**
Anita Spring.   In: *Gender issues in farming systems research and extension*, edited by Susan V. Poats (et al.).   Boulder, Colorado: Westview Press, 1988, p. 407-26. bibliog.
The author cites evidence that technology transfer and other processes are hindered when intra-household dynamics and the role of women in agriculture are ignored. There is a need to ensure that extension workers, mostly male, include in their surveys a diversity of farmers that includes women, since a large number of rural households are headed by them.

205 **Women farmers of Malawi: food production in the Zomba district.**
David Hirschmann, Megan Vaughan.   Berkeley, California: University of California Institute of International Studies, 1984. 142p.
map. bibliog.
A wide-ranging overview of Zomba district, where a high percentage of the poorer rural households are headed by women. Based on fieldwork and interviews with 70 respondents, the study identifies the preferred crops planted, the division of labour in these households and their income, the problems attending male out-migration, and the obstructive role of bureaucracy.

206 **Women in the estate sector of Malawi: the tea and tobacco industries.**
Megan Vaughan. Geneva: International Labour Office, 1986. 58p. bibliog.
Vaughan's monograph is part of ILO's documentation of the problems of poor women in the Third World. It demonstrates, on the basis of empirical research in 1984, the widely under-reported role of female workers on the tea and tobacco estates in southern Malawi.

207 **Women's participation in Malawi's local councils and district development committees.**
David Hirschmann. East Lansing, Michigan: Michigan State University, 1984. 17p. bibliog. (Working Paper no. 98).
A study of the socio-economic and attitudinal impediments that restrict women's access to two local structures. For an expanded version on this theme see David Hirschmann, *Women, planning and policy in Malawi* (Addis Ababa: United Nations Economic Commission for Africa, 1984. 54p.).

Eroding economy and declining school quality.
See item no. 245.

Urban Issues

208 **Capital relocation in Africa: the case of Lilongwe in Malawi.**
Deborah Potts. *Geographical Journal* (London), vol. 151, pt. 2 (July
1985), p. 182-96. maps.

This is a good analysis of Malawi's construction from scratch in the 1970s (with
significant South African fiscal, town planning and construction aid) of a 'modern'
new capital in Lilongwe in the central region. In line with similar actions elsewhere in
the Third World, the move was motivated by a desire to relocate from a crowded run-
down former capital with colonial connotations, providing a focus for national pride,
while forcing a shift in the development of a more central location in the country
(which, coincidentally, is President Banda's home region). The author argues that in
Lilongwe's case, despite the completed construction of the capital, its modern
government buildings and housing suburbs by the mid-1980s, the extreme reluctance
of many high officials and their staff to permanently relocate to Lilongwe (with
President Banda himself rarely visiting, let alone residing there) completely
undermines the ability of the new capital to act as a counterweight to the attractions
of Blantyre, the country's economic capital, which still remains the centre of gravity
of Malawi by a wide margin.

209 **The food supply of Lilongwe, Malawi.**
J. Lavrijsen, J. J. Sterkenburg. Utrecht: Geografisch Instituut
Rijksuniversiteit, 1976. 71p. bibliog.

The authors have studied the problems of supplying Lilongwe, the country's new
capital, with its much heightened basic food needs. The monograph pinpoints sources
of supply, main points of origin, marketing channels, the nature of the markets of
Lilongwe and their needs, consumer behaviour, and average annual expenses for food
and rent in Lilongwe.

210 **From vision to reality: the story of Malawi's new capital.**
Geraint Richards. Johannesburg: Lorton Publications, 1974. 63p.

Richard's illustrated outline includes city-planning details on the construction of Malawi's new capital a few miles from what was originally a small sleepy village. See also T. A. Blinkhorn, 'Lilongwe: a quiet revolution', *Finance and Development* (June 1971), p. 26-31.

211 **The growth of small-scale renting in low-income urban housing in Malawi.**
Thomas G. E. Pennant. In: *Housing Africa's poor*, edited by Philip Amis, Peter Lloyd. Manchester: Manchester University Press, 1990, p. 189-204.

An important contribution to the history of low-income housing in Malawi. The author analyses the history and problems of small-scale renting from local owners, the characteristics of owner-occupiers, and site and service housing, especially in Lilongwe where new quarters sprang up concurrent with the construction of the new capital but in inadequate numbers to cater for demand.

212 **Housing the urban labor force in Malawi: an historical overview, 1930-1980.**
Thomas G. E. Pennant. *African Urban Studies* (East Lansing), no. 16 (Spring 1983), p. 1-22.

The issue of urban housing became an object of study only in the 1970s. Until then it was a tacit assumption that housing would remain self-built and self-owned. Increasingly, however, subletting became the norm in Malawi. In this article Pennant surveys the sociology of renting households, especially in Lilongwe where the issue is at its most acute.

213 **The informal mechanisms for the financing and construction of housing in the sites and services schemes of Malawi: a case study of Blantyre city.**
Geoffrey L. du Mhango. *Journal of Social Science*, vol. 12 (1985), p. 114-32.

Based on a socio-economic survey of the activities of the Malawi Housing Corporation in 1979 in Blantyre and Mzuzu (in the north) this article underlines the predominant role of the informal sector in the construction of housing for the country's urban poor households. Fully 89 per cent of all houses were built either by informal contractors or by plot-owners themselves, the vast majority of whom (96.7 per cent) financed such construction from their own means.

214 **Market towns and services linkages in sub-Saharan Africa: a case study of Chipita, Zambia; Salima, Malawi and Chipinga, Zimbabwe.**
Sudhir Wanmali. *African Urban Quarterly* (Nairobi), vol. 6, no. 3/4 (Aug.-Nov. 1991), p. 267-77.

This article examines the nature of service sector activities in relation to agricultural development in their rural hinterlands in the smallholder foodgrain and cash-cropping areas of Malawi, Zambia and Zimbabwe. See also J. R. N. Mlia, 'Urbanization and rural development in Malawi', *Journal of Social Science*, vol. 7 (1978/79), p. 52-64.

215 **Performance of new capitals as regional policy measures: a case study of Lilongwe in Malawi.**
B. M. Kaluwa. *Journal of Social Science*, vol. 9 (1982), p. 67-86.

The author assesses the role of Malawi's newly constructed capital at Lilongwe in benefiting regional economic development in the central region where it is located. He concludes that in essence public employment has played a major role, with the partial relocation of government ministries' staff from Blantyre and Zomba to Lilongwe. But private employment and economic projects mounted in the vicinity of Lilongwe have remained relatively weak. Moreover, neither private nor public employment has manifested any strong upward growth trend after the initial relocation so that the future development of the capital is likely to be quite slow.

216 **Size relationships in the urban system of Malawi.**
D. W. Myburgh, J. A. van Zyl. *African Insight* (Pretoria), vol. 22, no. 2 (1992), p. 128-33.

In this article the authors assess the total scope of urbanization in Malawi, and offer a different perspective on its role within the context of Malawi's development plan.

217 **Towards a history of urban housing in Malawi.**
Thomas G. E. Pennant. *Journal of Social Science*, vol. 12 (1985), p. 91-113.

This is the history of colonial urban and housing policy until the 1960s. For additional urban issues and recent city-planning surveys in Malawi see also H. D. Kammeier, 'Planned urbanisation to complement rural development: the case of a small country, the Republic of Malawi', in *Equity and growth? Planning perspectives for small towns in developing countries,* edited by H. D. Kammeier and P. J. Swan (Bangkok: Asian Institute of Technology, 1984, p. 416-61); and H. Kerlen, 'Malawi district centres study: aspects of implementation and institutional framework', in *Equity and growth? Planning perspectives for small towns in developing countries,* edited by H. D. Kammeier and P. J. Swan (Bangkok: Asian Institute of Technology, 1984, p. 462-8).

218   Urban housing survey 1987: Blantyre and Lilongwe cities.
National Statistical Office.   Zomba: Government Printer, 1989. 52p.
In conjunction with the 1987 census the government conducted a detailed housing
survey in the country's two main cities, Lilongwe and Blantyre, the results of which
are reported herein, though some of the data were published in one of the volumes of
the 1987 census. For additional data see National Statistical Office, *Urban household
expenditure, 1979/80* (Zomba: Government Printer, 1983. 144p.).

The story of Malawi's capitals: old and new.
See item no. 122.

Social Issues

219 **Food production and malnutrition in Malawi.**
Wim Ettema, Louis Msuskwa.   Zomba: University of Malawi Centre
for Social Research, 1985. 63p. bibliog.

A critical nutritional survey of rural households in Malawi, that directly links the
widespread malnutrition in the country to the government's agrarian policies. The
author concludes that 'nowhere in government documents is improving malnutrition
stated as a direct objective of agricultural development policy . . . the current
agricultural policy may compound the problem of malnutrition, successful as it may
be in other respects. To this extent agricultural progress has been divorced from rural
development' (p. 57). The work ends with an annex of recommendations to alleviate
these problems. For a survey of the results of several policy reforms initiated in the
1980s see David E. Sahn (et al.), *Policy reform and poverty in Malawi* (Ithaca, New
York: Cornell University Food and Nutrition Policy Program, 1990. 254p. bibliog.).

220 **The impact of demographic changes on rural development in
Malawi.**
Graham Chipande.   In: *Population, food and rural development*,
edited by Ronald Lee (et al.).   Oxford: Clarendon Press, 1988,
p. 162-74.

This chapter assesses the reasons behind growing rural poverty in Malawi amid
declining farm-gate prices and rural real wages. The reason is seen as the inevitable
outcome of rapid population growth (3.2 per cent per annum) leading to land
pressure, male outward-migration, and the resultant low productivity in the
increasingly female-headed smallholder sector. Since farm credit and extension
services are also biased against such poor households there is a negligible likelihood
of improving smallholder productivity and ameliorating malnutrition and poverty.
Only a more even-handed balanced policy between the large estates and the smallholder sector is likely to improve conditions. For a comparable study focused on the
urban poor see Gillian Roe, *The plight of the urban poor in Malawi: results from a
baseline survey* (Zomba: University of Malawi Center for Social Research, 1992. 159p.).

221 **The Indian minority of Zambia, Rhodesia and Malawi.**
Floyd Dotson, Lilian O. Dotson. New Haven, Connecticut: Yale
University Press, 1968. 444p. bibliog.
In contradistinction to the Asian minorities in East Africa, very little has been written
about their counterparts in Malawi. Their status, privileges and rights to engage in
trade and commerce (their prime occupation) throughout the country were steadily
whittled down in Malawi by President Banda. This somewhat dated book is one of a
very few studies of the Indians in Central Africa.

222 **Malawi burial societies and social change in Zimbabwe.**
Robert B. Boeder. *Journal of Contemporary African Studies*
(Pretoria), vol. 1, no. 2 (April 1982), p. 339-48.
This article is a study of Malawi migrant workers in Zimbabwe and their voluntary
associations (usually referred to as burial societies) that serve as links between
tradition and modernity, their place of temporary residence and their homes in
Malawi. Such voluntary associations serve several other functions: they preserve
traditional values, help members to adjust to new environments, fiscally support those
unable to work, etc. Boeder notes that such organizations sprang up in Harare (then
Salisbury) as early as 1918 for Sena labourers from Malawi and Mozambique, and
that other ethnically oriented associations were created over the years in various
towns of the Malawian diaspora. For the repercussions of migrant workers abroad on
their families back home see also Boeder's 'The effects of labour emigration on rural
life in Malawi', *Rural Africana*, no. 20 (Spring 1973), p. 37-46.

223 **Malawi family formation survey, 1984.**
National Statistics Office. Zomba: Government Printer, 1987. 95p.
This is the first scientific survey of its kind ever conducted in Malawi, tapping
extremely important data of use to both governmental departments and international
donor agencies. The work is essentially a compendium, mostly of tables and raw
statistics relating to marriage ages of Malawian males and females, birth rates
correlated with age and education, fertility patterns, family size, birth intervals, the
prevalence (and knowledge, or lack of it) of birth control practices in Malawi
households, and the nutritional status of children.

224 **Production activities, food supply and nutritional status in
Malawi.**
Lila E. Engberg (et al.). *Journal of Modern African Studies*, vol. 25,
no. 1 (March 1987), p. 139-47.
An empirical and statistical study of rural patterns of nutrition in Malawi, broken
down by season and occupation, subsistence farming or tobacco growing.

225 **Rapid population growth and poverty generation in Malawi.**
William J. House, George Zimalirana. *Journal of Modern African
Studies*, vol. 30, no. 1 (1992), p. 141-61.
Jointly authored by the ILO Population Human Resources Adviser and the Head of
the Population and Health Resources Development Unit in the Office of the
Presidency in Malawi, this article strongly reiterates recent academic analyses.

Namely that the country's high demographic growth is exerting powerful pressures on the environment that cannot sustain such levels of population. Not only is poverty one natural outcome but, more importantly perhaps, environmental degradation is already seriously advanced, and natural non-renewable resources such as energy sources are rapidly being depleted. An earlier (briefer) article underlined how Malawi's early agrarian successes camouflaged the country's massive poverty and malnutrition. See Andrew Meldrum, 'Banda in a bind', *Africa Report*, vol. 32, no. 3 (May-June 1987), p. 47-9.

226   **Village segmentation and class formation in southern Malawi.**
      J. A. K. Kandawire.   *Africa* (London), vol. 50, no. 2 (1980),
      p. 125-45. bibliog.

This is an analysis of the factors behind class formation in rural Malawi. The author argues that 'there is evidence at the local level which shows that as land is increasingly becoming scarce, relative to population growth, village disputes over land illuminate the traditional structure of inequalities . . . [and] the inevitable result of the contradiction between population growth and land shortage is class formation' (p. 125).

The influence of the Livingstonia Mission upon the formation of welfare associations in Zambia.
See item no. 143.

Charging user fees for social services: education in Malawi.
See item no. 244.

Area handbook for Malawi.
See item no. 470.

Health and Medicine

227 **Before the winds of change.**
William Thomas Charles Berry. Suffolk, England: Halesworth Press, 1984. 120p. maps. bibliog.
In addition to being a personal biography, this is also the history of medical treatment in Malawi (and Gambia). The author was the Principal Medical Officer of the Department of Health and Social Security between 1936 and 1945. For more material on the state of health in Malawi see *Population and health in Malawi* (Zomba: Ministry of Health, 1984). For the nutritional and energy needs of small children in Malawi see E. L. Ferguson (et al.), 'The validity of 24-hour recall for stimulating energy, and selected nutrient intakes of a group of Malawian children', *Ecology of Food and Nutrition* (London), vol. 23, no. 4 (1989), p. 273-85.

228 **Blindness and visual impairment in southern Malawi.**
M. C. Chirambo (et al.). *Bulletin of the World Health Organization* (Geneva), vol. 64, no. 4 (1986), p. 567-72.
In light of the paucity of data about the prevalence and causes of blindness, a prevalence survey was conducted in the Lower Shire valley where blindness is common. The survey, which is reported in this article, indicated an incidence of 1.27 per cent of bilateral blindness, a figure that is in line with its occurrence in other African states. It was found that at least 60 per cent of this blindness is preventable or easily reversible.

229 **Chewa conceptions of disease: symptoms and etiologies.**
Brian Morris. *Society of Malawi Journal*, vol. 38, no. 1 (1985), p. 14-36.
Morris's article is a basic inventory of diseases as differentiated by the Chewa ethnic group into: those deemed 'natural'; those stemming from moral or ritual infringements; those commonly associated with witchcraft or sorcery; and those attributed to the role of spirits. These diseases are attended to by herbalists who 'have

74

little training in human biology, or little awareness of the natural causation of disease processes, [nevertheless] their empirical knowledge of body organs and disease symptoms is impressive' (p. 19) and many of their cures are potent enough to be helpful.

230 **Colonial microenvironments and the mortality of educated young men in Northern Malawi, 1897-1927.**
Bruce Fetter. *Canadian Journal of African Studies* (Toronto), vol. 23, no. 3 (1989), p. 399-415. bibliog.

An analysis of the rise of death rates during the first two decades of colonial rule, after which they began to decline. This rise is associated with urbanization and work conducted in the mines of South Rhodesia. The conclusions are supported by tables and diagrams.

231 **Ethnomedicine in four different villages in Malawi.**
Karl Peltzer. Zomba: University of Malawi, 1983. 30p. (Staff Seminar Paper, no. 30).

An empirical study of health-seeking patterns, the concept of disease and the healing practices of traditional healers (including those attending childbirth) in key Chewa, Yao, Lomwe and Tumbuka villages. The data are presented in a compact comparative manner, with tables outlining the methods of treatment of similar conditions in the four ethnically different villages as practised by both modern and traditional healers. See also the same author's *A model of African socialization: authority, group, body–mind environment* (Zomba: University of Malawi, 1986. 22p. (Staff Seminar Paper, no. 50); and his subsequent book, *Some contributions of traditional healing practices towards psychosocial health care in Malawi* (Frankfurt, Germany: Fachbuchhandlung für Psychologie, 1987. 341p.).

232 **A five-year medium term plan for the prevention and control of AIDS in Malawi (1989-1993).**
National AIDS Control Programme. Lilongwe: Ministry of Health, 1989. 128p.

For long a taboo subject in government circles, the progressive spread of AIDS in Malawi through the return of large numbers of Malawians from prolonged periods of work in neighbouring countries finally triggered the realization that epidemic proportions might be reached unless preventive and/or treatment policies were adopted. This government report is virtually the first such comprehensive overview of the dimensions of the disease in Malawi, and of the policies to be adopted to combat it.

233 **Government associations and the university: liaison in Malawi.**
Jerome D. Msonthi. In: *The professionalization of African medicine*, edited by Murray Last, G. L. Chavunduka. Manchester: University Press, 1986, p. 99-115.

In this chapter Msonthi analyses the herbalists and herbalists' organizations in Malawi, and the prevalent prices for different treatments. See also the same author's 'The herbalists' association of Malawi as a profession', *Society of Malawi Journal*, vol. 37, no. 2 (1984), p. 45-53; and 'Traditional birth attendants in Malawi: their role in primary health care and development', *Society of Malawi Journal*, vol. 36, no. 1 (1983), p. 40-4.

234 **Health services in a district hospital in Malawi.**
Eric R. de Winter. Assen, The Netherlands: Van Gorcum, 1972. 303p.

A description of community health-delivery activities in Nkhata Bay District Hospital in northern Malawi

235 **Herbalism and divination in southern Malawi.**
Brian Morris. *Social Science and Medicine* (Oxford), vol. 23, no. 4 (1986), p. 367-77.

An important study of ethnomedical practices in southern Malawi, stressing the distinctiveness of herbalists, diviners, and mythical causation, and the important role that various herbal remedies play in the treatment of certain illnesses. For more on this theme see the author's 'Medicines and herbalism in Malawi', *Society of Malawi Journal*, vol. 42, no. 2 (1989), p. 34-54, in which Morris strongly underlines the need for Westerners to grasp the concomitant belief among Malawians in *Mankhwala* (medicine), *Asing'anga* (traditional healers) and *Maula* (divination).

236 **Idioms of madness: Zomba Lunatic Asylum, Nyasaland.**
Megan Vaughan. *Journal of Southern African Studies* (Oxford), vol. 9, no. 2 (1983) p. 216-38.

This article is an intriguing description of aspects of colonial lunacy legislation in Malawi. Some of it clearly illustrates more about 'the insecurity and psychological vulnerability of the Europeans themselves' (p. 238). Very few Malawians were affected by the legislation in any case, since few ended up in the extremely primitive 'modern' Zomba asylum.

237 **Malawi leprosy control project.**
B. D. Molesworth. *Society of Malawi Journal*, vol. 21, pt. 1 (Jan. 1968), p. 58-69.

There are several specialist leprosy hospitals in Malawi, and significant research has been conducted on the disease in that country. This article describes one World Health Organization project in southern Malawi. For additional literature on leprosy see P. E. M. Fine (et al.), 'Seroepidemiological studies of leprosy in northern Malawi', *International Journal of Leprosy*, vol. 56, no. 2 (1988), p. 243-54; F. Baird, 'Leprosy vaccine trial for Malawi', *Africa Health*, vol. 8 (1990), p. 214-16; J. M. Ponninghaus, G. Boerrigter, 'Ten years' leprosy work in Malawi', *Leprosy Review*, vol. 57, no. 3 (1986), p. 221-36; J. M. Ponninghaus, P. E. M. Fine, 'Leprosy in Malawi', *Transactions of the Royal Society of Tropical Medicine and Hygiene*, vol. 82, no. 6 (1988), p. 801-944; J. M. Ponninghaus (et al.), 'An epidemiological study of leprosy in northern Malawi', *Leprosy Review*, vol. 58, no. 4 (1987), p. 359-75.

238 **Psychiatric problems in African children.**
J. Kalmanash. *Malawi Medical Bulletin*, no. 3 (1969), p. 25-31.

An inventory of the more prevalent psychiatric problems encountered in Malawian children, covering both those that are due to organic conditions and those resulting from socio-cultural conditioning frameworks. See also Alice R. Kamwendo, 'Developmental psychology research in Malawi', *Journal of Social Science*, vol. 12 (1985), p. 133-53. The author discusses the status of developmental psychology in Malawi, and the contributions it can make to various social problems if research activities are sustained.

239 **Register of tumour pathology, 1976-1980.**
M. S. R. Hutt. In: *Cancer occurrence in developing countries*, edited by D. M. Parkin. Lyon, France: Agency for Research on Cancer, 1986, p. 63-6.

Hutt includes data on the prevalence of cancer in Malawi, with distribution by sex, age and site. Of note is the fact that in 1968 the sole resident histopathologist left the country, and since then all diagnostic pathology has had to be conducted in London.

240 **The story of medicine and disease in Malawi: the 130 years since Livingstone.**
Michael King, Elspeth King. Blantyre: Montfort Press, 1991. 183p.

Replete with a chronology, illustrations and photographs (many historical), this is a fundamental survey of the evolution of medical care and facilities in Malawi since the early decades of colonial rule.

241 **Why poor children stay sick: the human ecology of child health and welfare in rural Malawi.**
Per Lindskog, Jan Lundevist. Uppsala, Sweden: Scandinavian Institute of African Studies, 1988. 111p.

With infant and child sickness and mortality rates in Malawi inordinately high, this extensive report focuses on these phenomena. The authors assess levels of medical knowledge among Malawian women, female and child nutrition levels, the kinds of illnesses and the treatments they are given once they occur, in an effort to pinpoint remedies to the situation in the country. See also Michael Fröhlingsdorf, 'Child spacing in Malawi', *Afrika: Review of German–African Relations*, vol. 3, no. 5/6 (1989), p. 19-23.

Draft environmental profile of Malawi.
See item no. 32.

A comparison of women's time-use and nutritional consequences in two villages in Malawi.
See item no. 195.

Nutrition education in Malawi.
See item no. 201.

Food production and malnutrition in Malawi.
See item no. 219.

Community theatre and public health in Malawi.
See item no. 427.

Education

242 A brief history of education in Malawi.
Kelvin N. Banda. Blantyre: Dzuka Publishing., 1982. 153p.

This is the first book-length treatment, by a Malawian, of the history of education from the establishment of mission education (1875-1926) to the present day. The book is a popular version of material that appeared previously, with neither footnotes nor references. For additional material on the early period of education in Malawi see especially Brian Rose, 'Education in Malawi', in *Education in Southern Africa*, edited by Brian Rose (London: Collier-Macmillan, 1970, p. 118-42); Roderick J. Macdonald, 'The socio-political significance of educational initiatives in Malawi, 1899-1939', *Transafrican Journal of History*, vol. 2, no. 2 (1972), p. 69-93; J. C. E. Greig, *Education in Northern Rhodesia and Nyasaland: the pre-independence period* (Oxford: Rhodes House Library, [n.d.]. 109p.); E. E. Charlton, *Educational planning in Malawi* (Paris: UNESCO, 1973. 98p.) and J. A. R. Kandawire, 'Education and rural development in colonial Nyasaland', *Journal of East African Research and Development* (Nairobi), vol. 4, no. 2 (1974), p. 11-22.

243 The case of non-formal vocational education for out-of-school youths in rural Malawi.
Paul Kishindo. *Development Southern Africa*, vol. 10, no. 3 (Aug. 1993), p. 393-400.

In an attempt to assist in the alleviation of chronic rural poverty as well as illiteracy in Malawi, the author argues in this article that literacy education should go hand-in-hand with apprentice vocational training.

244 Charging user fees for social services: education in Malawi.
Mateen Thobani. *Comparative Education Review* (Chicago), vol. 28, no. 3 (1984), p. 402-23. bibliog.

Thobani has produced an important critique of educational policy in Malawi, that includes a set of policy suggestions to alleviate certain chronic problems. The author criticizes the Malawian policy of marginal cost pricing for social services in general, and education in particular, as a measure to reduce recurrent expenditure. Unchanged low user-prices have resulted in serious overcrowding (up to 66 pupils per class) and poor primary education in Malawi, a situation which mainly hurts the poor. Higher fees at the secondary level, where there is a huge demand (only one out of nine pupils enter secondary schools), could fund growth so long as subsidies are established for the poorer students. At university level – where the cost of educating each student is 263 times that of educating a primary school pupil, a sum which accounts for 23 per cent of the national budget – full fees for room, board and tuition should be charged, with a loan scheme providing for repayment after graduation. A slightly different version of this article was published as 'Charging user fees for social services: the case of education in Malawi' (Washington, DC: World Bank, 1984. 35p. (Staff Working Papers, no. 572)). What was referred to as Thobani's 'neo-classical economics' approach to education was taken to task in a radical rebuttal in the same issue of the journal (with Thobani given a chance to respond) where the author, rejecting technocratic optimum-maximization approaches, argued for the examination of education from the perspective of equity issues. See Steven J. Klees, 'The need for a political economy of educational finance: a response to Thobani', *Comparative Education Review* (Chicago), vol. 28, no. 3 (1984) p. 424-40. Somewhat in the same vein is Jee-Peng Tan (et al.), 'User charges for education: the ability and willingness to pay in Malawi' (Washington, DC: World Bank, 1984. 101p. bibliog. (Staff Working Papers, no. 661)).

245 **Eroding economy and declining school quality: the case of Malawi.**
Bruce Fuller. *IDS Bulletin* (Brighton), vol. 20, no. 1 (Jan. 1989), p. 11-16.

Fuller explores the relationship between the economic adjustment policies of the Malawi government in the 1980s, its overriding emphasis on economic over social policies, and the decline in the quality of education in the country. Using tables to support his statements, the author notes that though Malawi has expanded its educational facilities dramatically, with primary enrolments going up by an average of 3.2 per cent per year, recurrent spending in the 1980s went up by only 0.6 per cent annually in real terms, with the result that spending per pupil fell by 2.6 per cent yearly. The outcome has been an inevitable 'declining availability of school places and eroding educational quality found within increasingly crowded classrooms' (p. 11). For two recent reports that focus on the specific problems faced by girls in schools, see K. Hyde's 'Instructional and institutional barriers to girls' achievements in secondary schools in Malawi: preliminary survey results' (University of Malawi Centre for Social Research, 1993. 48p.); and 'Gender streaming as a strategy for improving girls' academic performance: evidence from Malawi' (University of Malawi Centre for Social Research, 1993. 19p.).

246 **The evaluation of human capital in Malawi.**
Stephen P. Heyneman. Washington, DC: World Bank, 1980. 99p. bibliog. (Staff Working Papers, no. 420).

This report (supported by tables and diagrams) is a gloomy overview of the state of education in Malawi: in 1980 the country had the same percentage of pupils in primary schools as in 1911; the efficiency of 8th graders was comparable to American 4th graders, and the educational system was capable of absorbing only 3 per cent of all graduates into secondary schools. The author suggests a huge investment in education in order not to waste valuable human resources. See also the same author's

'Educational investment and economic productivity: evidence from Malawi', *International Journal of Educational Development*, vol. 4, no. 1 (1984), p. 9-15.

247 **Family effects on students' achievements in Thailand and Malawi.**
Morlaine E. Lockheed (et al.). *Sociology of Education* (Washington), vol. 62, no. 4 (1989), p. 239-56. bibliog.

An analysis of the role played by family background in students' achievements in the Third World. The authors use measures of social class broader than those conventionally used, arguing they are more suitable in analyses of developing countries. Cross-sectional data on 103 students from 21 schools in Malawi revealed that family background played a much higher role than had been assumed hitherto.

248 **The formal school as a traditional institution in an underdeveloped society: the case of Northern Malawi.**
Stephen Heyneman. *Paedagogica Historica* (Ghent), vol. 12, no. 2 (1972), p. 460-72.

Since the arrival of Scottish missionaries in Malawi, people in the north of the country have historically been far more avid seekers of education than their southern counterparts, with the result that northerners tend to be over-represented in the civil service. The author discusses the historical context of the cultural milieu surrounding the primary school in north Malawi, and argues that schools 'may have become internalized within the local society', thus not being viewed as a 'Western' institution, a fact that may account for their greater popularity there.

249 **Malawi University students: 1967-1971.**
Kathleen Myambo. *Society of Malawi Journal*, vol. 28, no. 1 (Jan. 1975), p. 40-53.

This article provides a rare glimpse of the composition of the student body at the University of Malawi, broken down by ethnic and regional origin, parental background and students' preferred future occupation. The data reveal the heavy over-representation of northern (40.9 per cent) and of Tumbuka (26.4 per cent) students. Fully 22.5 per cent hoped to land a civil service job, while 20.9 per cent had a teaching career as their primary vocational goal. For the state of legal studies in Malawi see Michael Wilkinson, 'Recent development in legal education in Malawi', *Indian Socio-legal Journal* (Bikaner), vol. 5, no. 1/2 (1979), p. 154-71.

250 **Moulding the ideal colonial subject: the scouting movement in colonial Malawi up to 1961.**
Isaac C. Lamba. *Transafrican Journal of History*, vol. 14 (1985), p. 63-77.

Lamba surveys the history and underlying philosophy of the Boy Scouts, Girl Guides and Boys' Brigades during the colonial era. Both the non-integrative nature of these movements and the rise of nationalism that was monopolized by Kamuzu Banda brought about a major displacement of these youth movements by the Malawi Young Pioneers. For an early look at that structure, later to become much more politicized as one of the main buttresses of the Banda regime, see A. W. Wood's 'Training Malawi's youth: the Young Pioneers', *Community Development Journal*, vol. 5, pt. 3 (July 1970), p. 130-8.

Education

251   **Piaget's theory of formal operational thinking and the teaching of history in Malawian secondary schools.**
Edrinnie E. Lora.   *Journal of Social Science*, vol. 8 (1980/81), p. 148-67.

The author attempts to assess the applicability in a Malawi context of Piaget's theory of formal operational thinking, based on research conducted in three Malawi secondary schools. The results suggest that 'the age for the beginning of formal operational thinking has to be modified' (p. 160) at least for Malawi, since the most reflective answers obtained were from pupils older than sixteen.

252   **Projections of primary and secondary school-going age population (1977-2012).**
W. M'Manga.   Zomba: University of Malawi Demographic Unit, 1990. 114p.

Based on statistics from Malawi's censuses, the country's high demographic growth rate, and other data, the author provides projections about the numbers of school-age children through to the year 2012. The projections indicate a burgeoning need for both primary and secondary education that should be of grave, and urgent, concern to educational planners because it is magnified by the already large numbers of youth not attending school, and the existing unacceptably high pupil–teacher ratios prevalent in Malawian classrooms. See also the two blander official reports by the Ministry of Education and Culture: 'Needs and priorities of the educational sector in Malawi' (Zomba: Government Printer, 1991, 17p.); and 'Problems of youth and education in Malawi' (Zomba: Government Printer, 1991. 16p.).

253   **Recruiting expatriate staff for the University of Malawi.**
R. J. Forbes, S. M. Nyirenda.   *West African Journal of Education*, vol. 23, no. 1-3 (1982), p. 233-40.

This is an empirically based study of the selection process by which the University of Malawi recruited expatriate staff, usually via the Inter-University Council in London. For the University's general policies on recruitment and localization see Gordon Hunnings, 'The role of expatriate staff at the University of Malawi', in *The future of the university in Southern Africa*, edited by David Welsh (Cape Town: David Philip, 1977, p. 125-28).

An annotated bibliography of education in Malawi.
See item no. 468.

An annotated bibliography of theses and dissertations held in Chancellor College library.
See item no. 469.

Politics

254 Banda.

Philip Short. London: Routledge & Kegan Paul, 1974. 357p. bibliog.

This is a sweeping and thorough 'unauthorized' biography of President Banda by a British journalist. The book is comprehensively and painstakingly researched, sympathetically written but not uncritical, with few controversial points. However, the book and Short himself were banned in Malawi on publication. Part of the reason for this was Short's negative assessments of Banda's authoritarian and idiosyncratic style – long before such views became commonplace – and the details he unearthed about Banda's early career and the reasons he puts forward for his relocating to the Gold Coast from London.

255 Censorship in Malawi.

Victor Ndovi. *Index on Censorship* (London), vol. 8, no. 1 (Jan.-Feb. 1979), p. 22-9.

Ndovi, a young journalist and BBC correspondent who was arrested in 1973 and released only in 1977, recounts in this interview the events leading to his imprisonment, and discusses the pervasive system of censorship in Malawi. Other brief items on censorship in Malawi have been published intermittently in this journal. For a list of the specific items actually banned in Malawi (these include the book *The Godfather*) see, for example, *Catalogue of banned publications, cinematographic pictures and records, from 1st August 1968 to 30th June, 1980* (Zomba: Government Printer, 1980. 28p.). A cumulative list is published every few years.

256 Economists in government: the case of Malawi.

B. D. Giles. *Journal of Development Studies* (London), vol. 52, no. 2 (Jan. 1979), p. 216-32.

This article argues that the relationship between economic rationality and decision-making is largely a problem of communications between economists, administrators and politicians. The manner in which economists are integrated into the Malawi government hierarchy is described and compared to the experience in neighbouring Zambia where they are largely excluded. The author was Chief Economist to the government of Malawi and head of a UNDP team to Zambia.

257 **Ethnicity, language and national unity: the case of Malawi.**
    Leroy Vail. In: *Working papers in Southern African studies*, edited
    by P. L. Bonner. Johannesburg: Ravan Press, 1988. vol. 2, p. 121-63.
A critical assessment of President Banda's anti-northern biases and pro-Chewa policies that prevented a consolidation of the tremendous national unity prevailing at the time of independence in Malawi, and instead now threaten tensions after his demise. The author reviews Britain's earlier strong discriminatory pro-Nyanja linguistic policy during the colonial era, before going on to document Banda's own inconsistencies, in speeches as well as in policies. He would argue for a non-ethnic approach, while acting at the same time to promote his Chewa people and purge southerners.

258 **Kamazu Banda of Malawi: a study in promise, power and
    paralysis.**
    John Lloyd Lwanda. Bothwell, Scotland: Dudu Nsomba
    Publications, 1992. 320p.
This recent work is a meticulous, extremely detailed and devastating analysis of President Banda's origins, rise to power, style of rule and policies, personal cronies and repressive thirty-year reign in office in Malawi. Stylistically somewhat disorganized, despite being divided into as many numbered subchapters as an official report, the material is not always presented either chronologically or thematically. Nevertheless, the book makes for fascinating reading. The author synthesizes a great deal of material some of which (such as the reasons for Banda's ignominious departure from London, and his professional difficulties in the Gold Coast) is rarely alluded to in any publications. Well documented, interspersed with quotes, and non-polemical, Lwanda's work emerges as one of the strongest indictments of an idiosyncratic and authoritarian potentate. The book concludes on an optimistic note with the events leading to the beginning of liberalization in Malawi and Banda's loss of control over the country he ruled for so long. The way in which the Banda regime elicits different assessments is visible in the thoughtful article by Beat Amman: 'Poverty, discipline and dignity in Malawi', *Swiss Review of World Affairs*, vol. 39, no. 10 (1990), p. 27-31. See also *Malawi beyond Banda* (Edinburgh: Edinburgh University Centre of African Studies, 1993). An Occasional Paper (no. 47) of the Centre, it carries two articles by Malawian religious leaders about the options in church–state relations in Malawi.

259 **Kwacha: an autobiography.**
    M. W. Kanyama Chiume. Nairobi: East Africa Publishing House,
    1975. 247p.
This autobiography of one of the young ministers who fell out with President Banda in the famous July 1964 cabinet crisis includes his own account of that event. Moving to Dar-es-Salaam, Chiume set up an opposition movement that was largely moribund. For a second account of the crisis by another of the young guard, see Henry Chipembere, 'Malawi in crisis: 1964', *Ufahamu* (Dar-es-Salaam), vol. 1, no. 2 (1970), p. 1-22.

Politics

260 **Malawi: faces of a quiet land.**
Paul Theroux. *National Geographic*, vol. 176, no. 3 (Sept. 1989),
p. 371-89.
A starry-eyed account by Theroux of his revisit of Malawi (he had served there with
the Peace Corps) which he found an island of peace in the midst of Southern Africa's
political turmoil and economic despair. See also Norman N. Miller, 'Malawi –
Central African paradox' (Hanover, New Hampshire: American Universities Field
Staff Reports, Africa no. 2, 1979, 12p.).

261 **Malawi: the politics of despair.**
David T. Williams.   Ithaca, New York: Cornell University Press,
1978. 339p. bibliog.
This book, though dated, remains by far the best single work on Malawi's recent
history, the rise to prominence of President Banda and his first decade in office. The
book is extremely well written, extensively researched and contains useful statistical
tables. It starts with the immediate pre-colonial era, discusses the intricacies of settler
politics (tending to gloss over economic inequities during the colonial era, which
scholars have since latched on to), and the 1950s attempt to force Nyasaland into the
ill-fated Central African Federation. The latter effort inexorably led, in the words of
Williams, to 'the rise of the phoenix', or Banda, whose 'habitually formidable and
sometimes sinister personality' (p. 15) was to come to dominate Malawi ever
afterwards. Williams's narrative is studded with penetrating insights into Banda's
unique style of governance, and he offers a balanced judgement about the early
decade of a controversial president. The book ends with a bibliographical essay that
assesses some of the more pertinent literature to that date.

262 **Malawi, March-July 1992: mass arrests of suspected government
opponents.**
Amnesty International.   London: Amnesty International, Sept. 1992.
14p.
A report on the wave of arrests in Malawi as the winds of change finally reached the
country, in due course unseating President-for-Life Banda. For an earlier report on
prison conditions in the country, see *Malawi: prison conditions, cruel punishment and
detention without trial* (London: Amnesty International, Feb. 1992. 17p.). See also
'Malawi', in *Academic freedom and human rights abuses in Africa* (New York:
Human Rights Watch, 1991, p. 35-40); and the more comprehensive indictment of
Banda's record of abuses of human rights in Richard Carver, *Where silence rules: the
suppression of dissent in Malawi* (New York: Human Rights Watch, 1990. 104p.
bibliog.).

263 **The new men revisited: an essay on the development of political
consciousness in colonial Malawi.**
Martin L. Chanock.   In: *From Nyasaland to Malawi: studies in
colonial history*, edited by R. J. Macdonald.   Nairobi: East African
Publishing House, 1976, p. 234-53.
The 'new men' were those trained in the early missionary stations to become pastors,
teachers and civil servants. Chanock focuses on one of the Native Associations
(precursor of political parties) to illustrate how political consciousness and anti-

85

Politics

colonialism were growing throughout the rest of society during the colonial era, a direct unanticipated outcome of missionary education. See also the same author's 'Ambiguities in the Malawian political tradition', *African Affairs*, vol. 74, no. 296 (July 1975), p. 326-46.

264 **The Nyasaland elections of 1961.**
Lucy Mair. London: Athlone Press, 1962. 87p.
This is a detailed study of the critical 1962 election in which Dr. Banda and his Malawi Congress Party (MCP) won a sweeping victory with an extraordinarily high electoral turnout, and subsequently pulled out Nyasaland from the much-hated Central African Federation. For the pre-independence election of 1964 that reconfirmed Banda as the absolute master of Malawi see H. B. Rowland, 'Nyasaland general elections of 1964', *Journal of Local Administration Overseas*, vol. 3, no. 4 (1964), p. 227-40. For the early evolution of the MCP see Roger Tangri, 'From the politics of union to mass nationalism: the Nyasaland African Congress, 1944-59', in *From Nyasaland to Malawi: studies in colonial history*, edited by R. J. Macdonald (Nairobi: East African Publishing House, 1976, p. 254-81). For the political views of the then still imprisoned leaders of the Nyasaland African Congress Party (soon to become the MCP) see Guy Clutton-Brock, *Dawn in Nyasaland* (London: Hodder & Stoughton, 1959. 192p.). There was a flood of literature in the 1950s and early 1960s about the Central African Federation. Of the better and more detailed analyses of the doomed federation, see: Thomas M. Franck, *Race and nationalism: the struggle for power in Rhodesia-Nyasaland* (New York: Fordham University Press, 1960. 369p.); and Patrick Keatley, *The politics of partnership* (London: Penguin Books, 1962. 528p. bibliog.).

265 **An outline of our government.**
Ndinda Stanley Jere, Donald Z. Mkandawire. Blantyre: Claim, 1987. 112p.
Written by a High Court judge and by the former principal of the Staff Training College, this book is a straightforward structural description of Malawi's constitution and governmental institutions, aimed at informing Malawians about their government. By way of contrast, another Malawian, living abroad, critically assesses the lack of democracy, public participation and power-sharing in these very institutions, that are merely instruments in the hands of an authoritarian personalist regime. See Mekki Mtewa, *Malawi democratic theory and public policy* (Cambridge, Massachusetts: Schenckman Books, 1986. 137p.). A rather interesting recent book, in German, assesses in depth the function of Malawi's National Assembly: Heiko Meinhardt, *Die Rolle des Parlaments im autoritaeren Malawi* (The role of Parliament in authoritarian Malawi) (Hamburg, Germany: Institut für Afrika-Kunde, 1993. 174p.). For a recent pamphlet, possibly the only one of its kind, focusing on the history of Malawian armed forces see James Njoloma, *The Malawi army* (Lilongwe: J. Njoloma, 1991. 29p.).

266 **Shouldering the refugee burden.**
Colleen Lowe Morna. *Africa Report* (July-Aug. 1988), p. 51-4.
A report, illustrated by photographs, on the paradoxical situation Malawi found itself in in the 1980s. Having supported the Renamo rebellion in neighbouring Mozambique (to the extent of allegedly allowing direct land transit to South African *matériel* and, allegedly, military advisers), Malawi had to pay a heavy price as it was flooded by

hundreds of thousands of refugees fleeing the resultant insecurity in that country. This influx of destitute refugees has strained the resources of Malawi, exacerbating the country's economic strains, with possible destabilizing consequences. See also Bruce Fetter, 'Malawi: everybody's hinterland', *African Studies Review*, vol. 25 (June-Sept. 1982), p. 79-116. For a report focusing specifically on the problems of women refugees in Malawi see Alastair Ager (et al.), *A case study of refugee women in Malawi* (Zomba: University of Malawi Center for Social Research, 1991. 68p.).

267 Struggling against the 'Bandastan'.

Chris Searle. *Race and Class* (London), vol. 21 (Spring 1980), p. 389-401.

An interview with the self-exiled Attati Mpakati, leader of the opposition Socialist League of Malawi, whose members President Banda's secret service had several times tried to assassinate in neighbouring countries. Mpakati criticizes Banda's policies of repressing the population, de-emphasizing social services throughout the country, and cooperating with South Africa. See also Attati Mpakati, 'Malawi: neocolonial profile', *World Marxist Review* (Prague), vol. 22, no. 6 (June 1979), p. 98-103; and Attati Mpakati, 'Malawi: the birth of a neocolonial state', *African Review*, vol. 3, no. 1 (1973), p. 33-68.

268 'Support' in Eastern Africa: some observations from Malawi.

Richard Hodder-Williams. In: *The politics of Africa: dependence and development*, edited by Timothy M. Shaw, Kenneth A. Heard. London: Longman, 1979, p. 153-81.

This is a very insightful examination of the concept and ingredients of political power and support in Malawi, aimed at better understanding President Banda's secure grip over society in the 1970s. The article is both an analysis of Banda's not inconsiderable base of support, and a methodological critique of the systems analysis approach to power favoured by political scientists. Hodder-Williams argues for the reinstatement 'of private motives as significant motives in political developments' (p. 175). For an earlier, equally astute analysis of Dr. Banda's power-base, see Hodder-Williams's 'Dr. Banda's Malawi', *Journal of Commonwealth and Comparative Politics*, vol. 12, no. 1 (1974), p. 91-114.

269 Tribalism in the political history of Malawi.

Leroy Vail, Landag White. In: *The creation of tribalism in Southern Africa*, edited by Leroy Vail. London: James Currey, 1989, p. 151-92. bibliog.

A seminal *tour de force* by the two well-known scholars of Malawi, who in a very heavily footnoted chapter dissect Banda's anti-Northern policies and emphasis on 'uniquely Chewa cultural attributes, not some sort of secular nationalism' (p. 182). In his drive to disenfranchise other groups Banda imposed Chewa as the sole language of Malawi, purged the University of its non-Chewa faculty and administrators, the civil service of most of its senior non-Chewa personnel, and 'transformed the ancient Nyau secret rites from symbols of backwardness to those of authenticity'. According to the authors this has fuelled 'a legacy of the past that will increase the likelihood of communal violence in the country at times of political transition' (p. 184).

Central African emergency.
See item no. 72.

From interest groups to party formation in colonial Malawi.
See item no. 84.

Malawi: a political and economic history.
See item no. 99.

The rise of nationalism in Central Africa: the making of Malawi and Zambia.
See item no. 119.

Press purge in Malawi.
See item no. 448.

Area handbook for Malawi.
See item no. 470.

Republic of Malawi Parliament biographies.
See item no. 504.

Administration

270 **Administration of Posts and Telecommunications 1891-1974.**
Colin Baker. *Society of Malawi Journal*, vol. 29, no. 2 (July 1976),
p. 6-33.
Baker recounts the history of Malawi's postal administration since its foundation in
1891 up to the year 1974. At that time Malawi had 59 post offices, 129 postal
agencies, 16,000 telephones and 100 telex connections.

271 **The administrative service of Malawi: a case study of Africanization.**
Colin Baker. *Journal of Modern African Studies*, vol. 10, no. 2
(1972), p. 543-60.
This article explores the process of Africanization in the Malawi civil service and,
more specifically, why President Banda was reluctant to speed up the localization
process as urged by his youthful cabinet ministers before the famous cabinet crisis of
1964. For two other articles by the same author on the reforms that in due course
were implemented see: 'Administrative reform in Malawi', *Quarterly Journal of
Administration*, vol. 6, no. 3 (1972), p. 273-85; and 'The development of agricultural
administration in Malawi', *Quarterly Journal of Administration*, vol. 6, no. 3 (1972),
p. 261-86. For Africanization issues relating to development committees, see R. A.
Miller 'District development committees in Malawi: a case study of administration',
Journal of Development Overseas, vol. 9 (1970), p. 129-42.

272 **Civil response to war: the Nyasaland civil service, 1914-1918.**
Colin Baker. *Journal of African Studies* (Los Angeles), vol. 11, no. 1
(Spring 1984), p. 25-34.
Baker examines the immediate, as opposed to the long-term, consequences of the
First World War on the civil service of Malawi, as a result of the proximity to the war
zone of German East Africa. The main role of the civil service at the time was to
support, secure and supply manpower, and to provide new civil servants for the soon-
to-be-occupied enemy colony.

273 **The evolution of local government in Malawi.**
Colin Baker. Ile-Ife (Nigeria): University of Ife Press, 1975. 60p.

A survey of local government in Malawi. Though Baker's time-frame is the entire period of 1891-1975, the bulk of the paper concerns itself with the Native Authorities prior to the Second World War, and there is nothing for the post-1964 independence period. See also Timothy Kiel Barnekov, *An inquiry of native administration in Nyasaland* (Syracuse, New York: Syracuse University Program of Eastern African Studies, 1967. 129p. (Occasional Paper, no. 48)); and R. W. Robins, 'Development of rural local government in Nyasaland', *Journal of African Administration*, vol. 13 (1961), p. 148-51.

274 **The genesis of the Nyasaland civil service.**
Colin Baker. *Society of Malawi Journal*, vol. 41, no. 1 (1988), p. 30-44.

This is an exploration of the origins of the civil service and the police force of Malawi by one of the country's prime historians. In 1893 the entire civil service comprised 168 individuals, all of whom are listed in an appendix.

275 **The relationship between politics and administration: a political neutrality dilemma for bureaucrats in Malawi.**
Isaac B. Bothomani. *Saipa*, vol. 21, no. 1 (1986), p. 18-30.

Though theoretically distinct, politics and public administration are intrinsically intertwined. In many countries the inevitable tug-of-war and/or conflict that may develop between political and administrative hierarchies can be resolved through consultations and deliberations. This has been particularly difficult, if not impossible, however, in Malawi, where President Banda has dominated all aspects of decision-making and even the minutiae of public administration, regarding any disagreement as evidence of personal disloyalty if not treason. Bothomani focuses on the dilemmas this has posed for Malawian administrations.

276 **Staff continuity in Nyasaland.**
Colin Baker. *African Affairs*, vol. 75, no. 302 (Oct. 1976), p. 475-87.

The author traces the permanence of the colonial administration's staff, noting that that between 1900 and 1969 the average civil servant's stay in his or her district was 17 months, though longer in northern districts where health and climate conditions were better. See also John McCracken, 'Experts and expertise in colonial Malawi', *African Affairs*, vol. 81, no. 322 (Jan. 1982), p. 101-16.

277 **Towards more effective control of public expenditure in Malawi.**
Chinchamata Chipeta. *Journal of Social Science*, vol. 11, no. 1 (1984), p. 84-99.

Noting some problems encountered in reconciling public accounts in Malawi, the author argues for closer examination of public expenditure, through internal and external audits and greater administrative controls.

278 **Training for localisation of the public service in Malawi.**
M. J. Bennion. *Journal of Local Administration Overseas*, vol. 5, no. 1 (1966), p. 23-8.

At independence a large percentage of Malawi's civil service (and not just in the upper echelons) as well as middle-ranking and higher officers in the police and armed forces were expatriates. Though President Banda declared early on that the quality and competence of personnel was more important to him than the nationality of the incumbent, localization in due time acquired a momentum of its own. This article assesses the problems of localizing the large numbers of expatriates in the Malawi civil service.

Coercion and control in Nyasaland: aspects of the history of a colonial police force.
See item no. 76.

A history of the Malawi police force.
See item no. 89.

Malawi: a political and economic history.
See item no. 99.

Seeds of trouble: government policy and land rights in Nyasaland, 1946-1964.
See item no. 120.

Women's participation in Malawi's local councils and district development committees.
See item no. 207.

An outline of our government.
See item no. 265.

The Malawi government directory.
See item no. 493.

Legal System and Constitution

Despite exceptions and some serious recent backsliding, Malawi has been relatively free of the massive routine embezzlement and theft from public services which is common elsewhere in the continent. The author explores the phenomenon in Malawi, the penal law governing it, and how Malawi courts have handled cases coming before them.

The author argues in this article that the statutes of general application are no longer applicable in Malawi, and that the legislature needs urgently to make some clearcut declaratory provisions on the issue.

This is an overview of Malawi's judiciary and the two parallel systems of law in existence, their jurisdictions and the tensions and conflicts between them, followed by a discussion of elements of jurisprudence in the Malawi legal system. For traditional law in criminal offences in north Malawi see C. J. M. Fleming, 'Crime and punishment in northern Malawi', *Society of Malawi Journal*, vol. 30, no. 1 (Jan. 1977), p. 6-14. bibliog. See also the author's earlier comprehensive and fascinating three-part study of north Malawi's traditional law of contract, criminal offences (against the person, dignity and property) in 'The law of obligations in northern Malawi', *Society of Malawi Journal*, vol. 27, no. 1 (July 1974) and vol. 28, no. 1/2 (Jan. 1975). bibliog.

282   **Criminal procedure and evidence in Malawi.**
David Newman.   Zomba: University of Malawi Department of Law,
1982. 358p.
This hefty volume is a study of criminal procedure and the law of evidence in
Malawi. For an overview of the changing system of traditional criminal law in the
country see L. J. Chimango, 'Traditional criminal law in Malawi', *Society of Malawi
Journal*, vol. 28, no. 1 (Jan. 1975), p. 25-39. For the gap between the modern penal
code and traditional law, exacerbated in 1969 by President Banda's transfer of
jurisdiction from the former to the latter (after a modern court threw out, on the
grounds of lack of evidence, the famous 'ritual murders' case), see Paul Brietzke,
'Murder and manslaughter in Malawi's traditional courts', *Journal of African Law*
(London), vol. 18, no. 1 (Spring 1974), p. 37-56.

283   **Customary family law in Malawi: adherence to tradition and
adaptability to change.**
Boyce P. Wanda.   *Journal of Legal Pluralism*, no. 27 (1988),
p. 117-34.
A study of contemporary customary law and practice with respect to marriage, the
family, and divorce in Malawi. For the traditional system in north Malawi see
C. J. W. Fleming, 'The natural family and the legal family in North Malawi', *Society
of Malawi Journal*, vol. 29, no. 2 (July 1976), p. 34-45. bibliog.

284   **The design and implementation of customary land reforms in
central Malawi.**
Clement Ng'ong'ola.   *Journal of African Law* (London), vol. 26,
no. 2 (1982), p. 115-32.
A discussion of the reforms in land law implemented in 1967 that shifted customary
lands into the private domain. The author argues that the reforms have not yet
produced the expected developmental benefits that private ownership was supposed to
produce.

285   **An introduction to the law of business organisations.**
Vince Johns.   Zomba: University of Malawi, 1982. 296p.
This is a detailed overview of the various binding statutes and regulations in Malawi
relating to limited and unlimited companies, articles of association, directors and
partners, finances and auditing, shares and laws of dissolution, together with copies of
the actual forms needed for registration. See also Matembo Nzunda, 'New company
law for Malawi', *Journal of African Law* (London), vol. 33, no. 1 (1989), p. 1-18.

286   **Land law in Malawi.**
J. D. A. Brooke-Taylor.   Zomba: University of Malawi, 1977. 2 vols.
A comprehensive exposition of the laws governing land in Malawi, with particular
attention to land tenure, equity and statutes of usage, concurrent possession,
inheritance law, leases, tenancies and rights of creditors over land, as well as
registration law. The author was the Solicitor of the Supreme Court of England and
Wales, and Lecturer in Law at the University of Malawi. For a brief overview of
salient land law features a decade later, by Malawi's Commissioner of Lands in the

Legal System and Constitution

Office of the President, see A. T. B. Mbalanje's 'Land law and policy in Malawi', in *Land policy and agriculture in eastern and southern Africa* (Tokyo: United Nations University, 1986, p. 52-9).

287 **Land reform and land dispute resolution in Malawi: the work of the Lilongwe Local Land Board.**
Clement Ng'ong'ola. *Journal of Eastern Research and Development* (Nairobi), no. 16 (1986), p. 105-21.
Malawi's land reforms were introduced to correct problems linked to the system of matrilineal land tenure then obtaining in part of the country. It was assumed that land was still held in common, and that a system stressing individual landholdings would spur land development and a land market. Based on an examination of the Lilongwe Land Board's activities, the author concludes that the expected results have not materialized, but that instead a class of land disputes hitherto unknown in Malawi has increasingly appeared. For the system before the reforms see H. J. Lamport-Stokes, 'Land tenure in Malawi', *Society of Malawi Journal*, vol. 23, no. 2 (July 1970), p. 59-88.

288 **Law, custom, and social order: the colonial experience in Malawi and Zambia.**
Martin Chanock. Cambridge: Cambridge University Press, 1985. 286p. bibliog.
This widely acclaimed book is a survey of the history (and criticism) of modern and customary law in the two countries in an attempt 'to reunite the subject of law with the economic, social, and political history of colonialism' (p. 4). The book concludes with an extensive bibliography.

289 **The law of land, succession, movable property, agreements and civil wrongs.**
J. O. Ibik. London: Sweet and Maxwell, 1971. 209p.
This is the classic, but by now somewhat dated, restatement of Malawi's basic customary private and property law, organized by sections and by ethnic group, including the relevant Statutes and Orders. The book is written by the Nigerian who served for several years as Customary Law Commissioner in Malawi.

290 **The law of marriage and divorce.**
J. O. Ibik. London: Sweet and Maxwell, 1970. 214p. bibliog.
The classic post-independence restatement of Malawi's traditional marriage and divorce law, outlined by ethnic group.

291 **Legal aid services in Malawi.**
Bruce P. Wanda. *African Law Studies*, no. 11 (Dec. 1974), p. 37-70.
Written by a law lecturer at the University of Malawi, this lengthy article is a study of the history and evolution, staffing, financing and administration of legal aid services in Malawi.

292 **Malawi.**
In: *Constitutions of new states*, edited by Leslie Wolf-Phillips. New
York: Praeger, 1965, p. 114-35.
The full text of Malawi's 1964 independence constitution. The text is also found in
Simon Roberts, 'The constitution of Malawi, 1964', *Journal of African Law*, vol. 8,
no. 3 (1964), p. 178-84. The constitution is critically analysed in Mekki Mtewa, 'The
Malawi constitution reconsidered', *Political Science Review*, vol. 22, no. 2/3 (1983),
p. 201-19.

293 **Malawi Parliament: practice and procedure.**
L. M. Khofi. Zomba: Government Printer, 1974. 46p.
A guide to the structures and constitutional functions of Malawi's Parliament,
together with parliamentary procedure.

294 **The State, settlers, and indigenes in the evolution of land law and
policy in colonial Malawi.**
Clement Ng'ong'ola. *International Journal of African Historical
Studies* (Boston), vol. 23, no. 1 (1990), p. 27-58.
A study in land law policy. The thrust of this article is that colonial land legislation in
Nyasaland was largely determined by the manner in which Harry Johnston
adjudicated land claims shortly after the proclamation of a British protectorate. This
resulted in legal land transfers from Africans to European settlers in contravention of
customary law and without adequate protection of African rights, all leading to future
conflicts between settlers and natives.

Foreign Relations

295 **Aid and dependence: British aid to Malawi.**
Kathryn Morton.   London: Overseas Development Institute, 1975.
150p.

This is an overview of Malawi's economy at independence and the kinds and levels of
British aid to the fledgling economy, without which, the author suggests, Malawi
would not have survived.

296 **Dependency and choice: Malawi's links with South Africa.**
Steve Kibble.   Leeds: University of Leeds, African Studies Unit,
1988. 60p. (Leeds Southern African Studies, no. 8).

When Malawi attained independence it was one of Africa's least developed countries,
landlocked and hence dependent upon neighbouring countries for its links with the
outside world, with little indigenous development capital, and with up to 100,000 of
its citizens working in the mines of South Africa and sending money home, These
remittances were a major source of foreign exchange. President Banda's assumption
of power in Malawi added another ingredient, that of choice, to these objective
dependency relations on South Africa, that led to even closer economic collaboration
between the two countries. This mix of objective and subjective factors is the subject
of Kibble's monograph on Malawi–South Africa relations.

297 **Foreign policy of African states: politics of dependence and
confrontation.**
Suresh Chandra Saxena.   New Delhi: Deep and Deep, 1982. 227p.
bibliog.

This is a study of the foreign policy of African states, with particular attention to, and
case-studies of, Botswana and Malawi. The foreign postures of both are examined
along a range of regional, continental and global issues, and the obvious conclusion is
reached – that Malawi is pro-Western. See also James Mayall's early article,
'Malawi's foreign policy', in *The World Today* (Oct. 1970), p. 435-45.

298 **Malawi and the EEC: the first seven years.**
A. Hewitt. In: *EEC and Third World: a survey*, edited by
Christopher Stevens. London: Hodder & Stoughton, 1984, p. 100-42.
A comprehensive overview of Malawi's first seven years of independence, and the
country's diplomatic, cultural, political and economic relations with the EEC and its
component members. For a somewhat similar work see the same author's *Malawi's
first eight years of cooperation with the EEC: the results of the Lomé Conventions*
(London: Overseas Development Institute, 1983. 68p. bibliog.). For the Canadian
contribution to Malawi's development see L. A. H. Msukwa, R. A. Nickerson,
'Fuelwood and polewood in Malawi', in *With our own hands: research for Third
World development. Canada's contributions through the I.D.R.C.* (Ottawa: I.D.R.C.,
1986, p. 173-86).

299 **The Malawi connection.**
Allen Isaacman. *Africa Report* (Nov.-Dec. 1986), p. 51-4.
Isaacman discusses revelations that the Malawi government was supporting South
Africa in its destabilization efforts in Mozambique through the support of the Renamo
rebellion. Paradoxically, as a result of such policies, Malawi (one of the smallest and
poorest countries in southern Africa' (p. 16) was flooded with half a million
Mozambican refugees fleeing unsettled conditions in their own country: see 'Malawi:
stretched to the limit', *Refugees* (Geneva), no. 55 (July-Aug. 1988, p. 16-19). For an
annotated compendium of the literature on refugees in Malawi see Vote D. Somba,
'Refugee problem in Malawi: annotated bibliography of articles on refugees in
Malawi from national newspapers, October 1986-March 1989' (Zomba: University of
Malawi Library, [1989]. 27p.).

300 **Malawi foreign policy and development.**
Carolyn McMaster. New York: St. Martin's Press, 1974. 246p.
An early, but to date the sole monograph on Malawi's foreign policy. The book
stresses the degree to which foreign policy was essentially President Banda's personal
preserve, and outlines (in particular) Malawi–United Kingdom development efforts.

301 **Malawi labour migration and international relations in Southern
Africa.**
Robert B. Boeder. *Africa Insight* (Pretoria), vol. 14, no. 1 (1984),
p. 17-25.
In this article, illustrated by photographs, the author argues that Malawi's foreign
policy 'has been closely related to well-established political and economic facts of
life in southern Africa, especially Malawi's historic role as a labour reservoir for
South Africa and Zimbabwe' (p. 17) and that economic cooperation rather than
destabilization has been a successful policy for South Africa. For a couple of early
examinations of Malawi–South African relations see David C. Preiss, 'The bridge and
the laager: South Africa's relations with Africa, with specific reference to Malawi'
(Johannesburg: South African Institute of International Affairs, 1973. 16p.); and
Gerhard Max Erich Leistner, 'Malawi, South Africa and the issue of closer economic
cooperation' (Pretoria: Africa Institute of South Africa, 1968. 7p.).

302 **Malawi's growing links with South Africa: a necessity or a virtue?**
Henry B. Masauko Chipembere. *Africa Today*, vol. 18, no. 2 (1971),
p. 27-47.

This is an early assessment of President Banda's decision to pursue a continuation of
close economic relations with South Africa, in face of both the political opposition to
such a policy within his first cabinet and regional condemnation.

303 **The Malawi–Tanzania boundary dispute.**
James Mayall. *Journal of Modern African Studies*, vol. 11, no. 4
(1973), p. 611-28.

Mayall outlines the problems plaguing Malawi–Tanzania relations that resulted in
long periods during which the Tanzanian border was closed to Malawians, and Dar-
es-Salaam was a place of refuge for President Banda's foes. The problems stemmed
in part from an unusual boundary that limited Tanzanian sovereignty to the shoreline
of Lake Malawi (and not along the middle of the Lake as is common), and also from
Banda's contempt for President Nyerere and early efforts to secure a corridor through
Tanzania to the Indian Ocean. The sharply different personalities of Banda and
Nyerere, their completely different world-outlooks and ideologies (especially with
respect to developmental approaches, South Africa and Portugal) precluded any
rapprochement until the late 1980s.

304 **Notes on Malawi–Mozambique relations 1961-1987.**
David Hedges. *Journal of Southern African Studies* (Oxford),
vol. 15, no. 4 (Oct. 1989), p. 617-44.

This over-arching article examines Malawi–Mozambique relations at different times,
and attempts to explain the motivations governing the foreign policy at each period
and on both sides. The author maintains that until President Banda's entrenchment in
office Malawi had no coherent plan to modify colonial policy; in the transitional
period 1961-65 there was a desire to expand the Malawi Congress Party's power into
part of Mozambique in tandem with Portugal's desire to set up a friendly buffer state
between the rump of Mozambique and Tanzania; between 1965 and 1971 Malawi
linked up with South Africa and adopted a variety of conservative postures *vis-à-vis*
neighbouring states; when Mozambique attained independence under a radical
ideology Malawi started expanding its armed forces, and the period until 1987 saw
increasingly sharp regional conflicts with overt and covert Malawian support for
South Africa's policies aimed at destabilizing Maputo. For Malawi's first decade of
relations with Portugal (during which the latter dominated Mozambique) see Robert
D. Henderson, 'Relations of neighbourliness – Malawi and Portugal, 1964-74',
Journal of Modern African Studies, vol. 15 (Sept. 1977), p. 425-55.

Shouldering the refugee burden.
See item no. 266.

Area handbook for Malawi.
See item no. 470.

Refugee problem in in Malawi.
See item no. 503.

Economy

305 **A brief history of the tobacco industry in Nyasaland.**
W. H. J. Rangeley. *Nyasaland Journal*, vol. 10, pt. 1 (Jan. 1957),
p. 62-83; vol 10, pt. 2 (July 1957), p. 32-51; vol. 11, pt. 2 (July 1958),
p. 24-7.
Written by a Malawi-born European, who was to become Commissioner of the
Southern Province, these articles trace the history of the country's important tobacco
industry since its introduction in the 1890s. See also M. L. Golola, 'The introduction
of tobacco as cash crop in the central region of Malawi, 1919-1930', *Makerere
Historical Journal* (Kampala), vol. 2, no. 1 (1976), p. 39-55. For two technical
analyses see T. W. Tanton, J. B. Abington, 'Factors affecting yields of dark fire-cured
tobacco in Malawi', *Experimental Agriculture*, vol. 15 (1979), p. 353-9; and J. B.
Abington, T. W. Tanton, 'Effects of variety, fertilizer and environment on fire-cured
tobacco in Malawi', *Experimental Agriculture*, vol. 15 (1979), p. 153-60. See also
J. Sinoya Nankumba, *A case study of tenancy arrangements on private burley tobacco
estates in Malawi* (Morrilton, Arkansas: Winrock International Institute for
Agricultural Development, 1989. 16p.).

306 **Cattle in Malawi's southern region.**
R. Schmidt. *Society of Malawi Journal*, vol. 22, no. 2 (July 1969),
p. 57-72.
This is one of the very few articles on Malawi's cattle herds, animal husbandry and
the dairy industry in Malawi.

307 **Changes in income distribution in poor agricultural nations:
Malawi and Madagascar.**
Frederic L. Pryor. *Economic Development and Cultural Change*
(Chicago), vol. 39, no. 1 (Oct. 1990), p. 23-45.
A very important exploration and comparison of economic growth in Malawi and
economic decline in Madagascar, in both instances accompanied by widening income

differentials. In both cases, Pryor argues, policy failures – all theoretically correctable, and in some instances very easily so – triggered major income differentials. Based on the two case-studies the author reaches several conclusions which have great relevance for other developing countries. Foremost among these is the need to design policies, especially with respect to the rural and agrarian sectors, that stress and lead to both growth and equity.

308 **Crafts and small enterprises in the economic periphery of Malawi.**
Udo Witulski. *Africa Insight* (Pretoria), vol. 16, no. 3 (1986), p. 149-56.

In this article Witulski assesses the dimensions, significance, and viability of the mushrooming small-crafts industry in Malawi.

309 **Economic crisis in Malawi.**
Thomdika Mkandawire. In: *Recession in Africa*, edited by Jerker Carlsson. Uppsala, Sweden: Scandinavian Institute of African Studies, 1983, p. 28-47.

This article examines the factors that undermined the economy of Malawi in 1978-82. Among these were the disruption of commodity evacuation routes in Mozambique, a decline in terms of trade, and soaring costs of transportation. At the same time the country's historic neglect of smallholder agriculture produced excess susceptibility to global commodity prices for the few estate sector products, while low expenditure on education necessitated the import of costly manpower. All of these factors aggravated the crisis. For the insidious negative effect on all economic progress in Malawi caused by the country's rapid demographic growth see Futures Group, *Malawi: the effect of population factors on social and economic development* (Washington, DC: Futures Group, 1981. 60p.); and Graham H. R. Chipande, 'The impact of demographic changes on rural development in Malawi', in *Population, food and rural development*, edited by Ronald D. Lee (et al.) (Oxford: Clarendon Press, 1988, p. 162-74).

310 **Economic developments in Malawi since independence.**
Simon Thomas. *Journal of Southern African Studies* (London), vol. 2, no. 1 (Oct. 1975), p. 30-51.

This is a very balanced assessment of Malawi's early economic policies and pattern of development. The author concludes that 'if the success of government policies is to be judged by the achievements of the government's objectives, then Banda has, indeed, been very successful ... [but] because of his inability to change traditional agriculture radically while preserving stability, Banda has sacrificed long term development for short term economic growth' (p. 51).

311 **The effectiveness of structural adjustment lending: initial evidence from Malawi.**
Jonathan Kydd, A. Hewitt. *World Development*, vol. 14, no. 3 (March 1986), p. 347-65. bibliog.

This article is an analysis of the first two structural adjustment programmes in Malawi, the specific policy reforms demanded by the World Bank, and the degree to which they were implemented in Malawi. The authors generally laud both the conditions imposed on Malawi and the regime's responses, which accounted for their relative success, but offer several criticisms of the World Bank approach. This analysis is replicated in two other masterful articles: Jonathan Kydd, Adrian Hewitt, 'Limits to recovery: Malawi after six years of adjustment', *Development and Change* (The Hague), vol. 17, no. 3 (1986), p. 531-55. bibliog.; and A. Hewitt, J. Kydd, 'Malawi: making effective use of aid resources', *IDS Bulletin* (Brighton), vol. 17, no. 2 (1986), p. 77-84. For the World Bank's report see World Bank, *Malawi: Growth and structural change. A basic report* (Washington, DC: World Bank, 1982).

312 **Fishing and the colonial economy: the case of Malawi.**
J. McCracken. *Journal of African History*, vol. 28, no. 3 (1987), p. 413-29.

McCracken focuses on the evolution of fishing and its role in the political economy of colonial Nyasaland. Over one-fifth of Malawi's surface is covered by water, and so it possesses more fishing grounds than other similarly landlocked countries. The author points out that during the late 19th century fishing played a major role in the economy of Malawians, but by the 1950s European companies accounted for over half of the fish caught in Lake Malawi.

313 **Food self-sufficiency in Malawi: are successes transferable?**
J. Gus Liebenow. In: *Drought and hunger in Africa: denying famine a future*, edited by Michael H. Glantz. Cambridge: Cambridge University Press, 1987, p. 369-92. bibliog.

Liebenow argues that Malawi is only one of a handful of states to stress agriculture in its development plans, and to consistently attain food self-sufficiency and even export substantial amounts of foodstuffs to neighbouring countries – all a direct outcome of President Banda's agricultural policies. The political stability in Malawi, low rural–urban drift, tight control on urban salaries and civil service growth, may be the key to success elsewhere.

314 **The informal financial sector in Malawi.**
C. Chipeta, M. L. C. Mkandawire. *African Review of Finance and Banking* (Milan), vol. 2 (1992), p. 121-57.

The informal banking sector in Malawi is as large as the formal banking system. In this comprehensive study the authors outline its scope, nature, organization, services and interest rates, and explain its origins and the reasons for its growth. Despite the fact that it clearly fulfils an obvious need, closer links with the country's formal institutions would be of use to both. This important phenomenon is also surveyed in another article: B. R. Bolnick, 'Moneylenders and informal financial financial markets in Malawi', *World Development* (Cambridge), vol. 2, no. 1 (Jan. 1992), p. 57-68. See also David Hulme, 'Replicating finance programmes in Malawi and Malaysia', *Small Enterprises Development*, vol. 4, no. 4 (Dec. 1993), p. 4-15.

Economy

315 Informal sector in Lilongwe: a survey of informal activities in
garages, metal fabricating, tinsmithing, and woodworking.
A. A. Aboagye. Addis Ababa: Jobs and Skills Programme for Africa,
1986. 125p.

In many countries in Africa the informal sector is the largest, most vibrant and
meaningful entrepreneurial sector in the country. This Economic Commission for
Africa survey reports on the scope and activities of the informal service and
manufacturing sector that sprang up after the relocation of the country's capital to
Lilongwe. The report concludes that given the oligopolistic structure of Malawi's
urban industries and the quasi-monopoly of the country's major conglomerates, the
informal sector is not given adequate room to operate. See Mapopa Chipeta, 'Status
of the informal sector in Malawi', *Southern African Political and Economic Monthly*
(Harare), vol. 3, no. 11 (Sept. 1990), p. 9-14.

316 Land and labor in rural Malawi.
Rural Africana, edited by Melvin Page. Special Issues, nos 20, 21
(Spring, Summer 1973).

These two issues of *Rural Africana* are devoted to Malawi, each including articles
focusing on issues of economic development in rural Malawi by scholars such as
Chanock, Schoffeleers and Boeder.

317 Malawi.
Christopher Adam, William Cavendish, Percy S. Mistry.
In: *Adjusting privatization: case studies from developing countries.*
London: J. Currey, 1992, p. 352-75.

Assuring the privatization and liberalization of African state economies is one of
several main preoccupations of the World Bank in the last ten years. Though Malawi
has in general been a bastion of free enterprise, the national economy has been
dominated by a number of large state or quasi-state conglomerates such as ADMARK
and Press Holdings (the latter owned 'in trust for the Malawi nation' by President
Banda) that have effectively stifled private initiative on the part of small
entrepreneurs or farmers, and siphoned away most available commercial finance for
new private ventures. This chapter, which is full of valuable statistical tables, surveys
the nature and negative effects of these conglomerates, and suggests ways in which
the country's economy can be given a healthier injection of private entrepreneurial
spirit. For recent privatization trends in Malawi see Robert E. Christiansen, Lee Ann
Stackhouse, 'The privatization of agricultural trading in Malawi', *World Development*, vol. 17, no. 5 (1989), p. 729-40.

318 Malawi: an alternative pattern of development.
Edinburgh: University of Edinburgh Centre of African Studies, 1984.
642p. (Seminar Proceedings, no. 25).

This book contains sixteen papers presented at a seminar held at the Centre, 24-25
May 1984, with the participation of some of the foremost scholars on Malawi, and
dealing with either the colonial heritage or the contemporary era. Among the papers
one should note: Kings M. Phiri, 'Production and exchange in precolonial Malawi',
(p. 3-32); John McCracken, 'Share-cropping in precolonial Malawi' (p. 33-66);
Megan Vaughan, 'The politics of food supply: colonial Malawi in the 1940's'

(p. 67-92); Matthew Schoffeleers, 'Economic change and religious polarization in an African rural district' (p. 187-242); John Iliffe, 'The poor in the modern history of Malawi' (p. 243-92); Jonathan Kydd, 'Malawi in the 1970's: development policies and economic change' (p. 293-380); Robert Christiansen, 'Financing Malawi's development strategy' (p. 407-70); and J. A. K. Kandawire, 'Forms of organization for rural development in Malawi' (p. 527-46).

319 **Malawi at the crossroads. The post-colonial political economy.**
Edited by Guy C. Z. Mhone. Harare: SAPES Books, 1992, 380p.
The first book edited by a Malawian and with contributions exclusively by Malawians. It contains twelve articles focusing on either the (exploitative) heritage of the past, or suggesting socio-economic options based on social equity for the future, as the Banda regime drew to an end. The articles are: Guy Mhone, 'The political economy of Malawi: an overview' (p. 1-33); Mapopa Chipeta, 'Political process, civil society and the State' (p. 34-50); Jonathan Kaunda, 'National development planning in Malawi' (p. 50-89); Chinyamata Chipeta, 'Economic policy framework' (p. 90-134); Exley Silumba, 'Foreign trade policies and performance in Malawi, 1965-1990' (p. 135-70); Richard Mkandawire, 'The land question and agrarian change in Malawi' (p. 171-87); Gordon Kamchedzera, 'Land tenure relations, law and development in Malawi' (p. 188-204); Ben Kaluwa, 'Malawian industry: policies, performance and problems' (p. 205-40); Austin Ngwira, 'The impact of small-scale rural non-farm agro-industries on employment and household' (p. 241-65); Christon Moyo, 'Education policy and development strategy in Malawi' (p. 265-98); Pachero Simukonda, 'The non-governmental sector in Malawi's socio-economic development' (p. 298-349); and Tijanjana Maluwa, 'The legal regime and the protection of refugees in Malawi' (p. 349-71).

320 **Malawi fisheries: an assessment and overview.**
Kenneth R. McKaye, Jay. R. Stauffer. Lilongwe: USAID, 1985. 77p.
A USAID report of the state of the fisheries in Malawi. Although 70 per cent of animal protein is produced by fish captured in Malawi waters, and two-thirds of the population consumes the fish, the overall catch has declined by 40 per cent in six years. This situation demands a solution. For earlier reports on fishing and the fishing industry see J. A. Pinegar, I. J. Clucas, *Report on a visit to Malawi: fish processing and preservation* (London: Tropical Products Institute, 1974. 43p.); A. J. P. Mzumara, 'The fisheries department of Malawi: organisation, policy and management', *Journal of Social Science*, vol. 7 (1978/79), p. 108-14; R. R. Coutts, 'The distribution of artisanal fishing craft in Lakes Malawi and Malombe', *Journal of Social Science*, vol. 7 (1978/79), p. 115-22.

321 **Malawi tea.**
The Tea Association. Blantyre: Blantyre Print, 1974. 64p.
This history of the cultivation of tea and all aspects of its marketing and export is replete with numerous tables and photographs. Tea, planted on a commercial scale in the 1890s, but recording a profit only in 1908, had by 1924 surpassed one million pounds sterling in exports, and in the 1980s became the country's main export commodity. For the early history of Malawi's tea see G. G. S. J. Hadlow, 'The history of tea in Nyasaland', *Nyasaland Journal*, vol. 13, pt. 1 (Jan. 1960), p. 21-31; and J. A. Hutson, 'An outline of the early history of the tea industry in Malawi', *Society of Malawi Journal*, vol. 37, no. 1 (Jan. 1978), p. 40-6. On the modern biotechnology

applied to increase productivity on Malawi's plantations see D. James, 'Cloning of tea in Malawi', in *New technologies and development*, edited by A. S. Bhalla (et al.) (Boulder, Colorado: Lynne Rienner, 1988, p. 258-68); and R. W. Palmer-Jones, 'Control of the distribution of tea yields in Malawi', *Experimental Agriculture* (Cambridge), vol. 13, no. 3 (July 1977), p. 225-33.

322 **The market for dried fruits and vegetables in Malawi, Tanzania and Zambia.**
Brian MacGarry.   Harare: MacGarry, 1988. var. pag.

This consultancy study was conducted for the SADCC Food Industry Advisory Unit. It identifies specific existing fruit and vegetable products that could be dried, and markets that could absorb such produce, in an effort to assure farmers of food security and additional cash income in export markets not tied to seasonal variations.

323 **Measures to assist the Least Developed Countries: the case of Malawi.**
A. Jennings.   *World Development*, vol. 14, no. 12 (Dec. 1986), p. 1463-88.

The author argues in this article that the international community failed to fulfil fiscal and aid commitments made to Malawi at the 1981 UN Conference on Least Developed Countries notwithstanding the fact that Malawi introduced and implemented the measures called for.

324 **Oxfam Malawi country review.**
Louis A. H. Msukwa.   Zomba: University of Malawi Center for Social Research, 1986. 61p. bibliog.

This is an evaluation of Malawi's development policies and strategies, and the role of non-governmental organizations in the country's development. Possible areas of Oxfam participation and involvement are specified at the end of the monograph.

325 **Peasants, migrants and plantations. A study of the growth of Malawi's economy.**
Leroy Vail.   *Journal of Social Science*, vol. 11, no. 1 (1984), p. 1-36.

Starting from the assumption that Malawi's economic underdevelopment is not predetermined, but the product of concrete decisions and policies taken in the past, Vail outlines some reasons and implications for future decision-making. He argues that internal contradictions still exist with respect to the agrarian sector, with a bias in favour of estate farming and against peasant farmers, and these will continue to pose challenges in the future if they are not resolved.

326 **Policy reform and adjustment in an economy under siege: Malawi, 1980-1987.**
Jonathan Kydd.   *IDS Bulletin* (Brighton), vol. 19, no. 1 (Jan. 1988), p. 32-41. bibliog.

A critical look at Malawi's recent economic performance under the World Bank's structural adjustment programmes. The author notes that since external factors played a major role in creating Malawi's fiscal difficulties, the World Bank treated Malawi with kid gloves, and demanded inadequate cuts in recurrent spending. Lack of IMF 'zeal' (p. 41) was also due to a realization that more stringent austerity measures would have precipitated 'conflict between donor organizations, as this would involve cutting back capacity created by recent aid projects' (p. 41). See also *Structural adjustment programmes in SADC: experiences and lessons from Malawi, Tanzania, Zambia and Zimbabwe*, edited by A. M. Mwanza (Harare: SAPES, 1992. 216p.) and Kenneth Meyers, 'Emerging Malawi', in *Problems of developing countries in the 1990's* (Washington, DC: World Bank, 1990, p. 207-28. (Discussion Paper, no. 98)).

327   **The political economy of poverty, equity and growth: Malawi and Madagascar.**
Frederic L. Pryor.   Washington, DC: World Bank, 1990. 470p.
bibliog.
This is the best comprehensive analysis of Malawi's economy: a massive, deep, perceptive and very readable study of the political economies of Malawi (p. 21-193) and Madagascar (p. 349-401). The two countries were paired largely because of their similar economic indicators. This eminently balanced work – in a subdiscipline often marked by polemics and diametrically different conclusions – is organized around comprehensive studies of the two countries (which are the meat of the book), each with identical internal structure and marshalling incredible amounts of specific data. That is followed by a comparative analysis which, while of lesser interest to students of Malawi, has been lauded as an outstanding contribution to cross-country analysis methodology. Pryor notes that although the 'rosy view in the economic literature based on outdated [early] national accounts data' needs to be revised downwards, Malawi's economic performance has nevertheless been 'successful but not spectacular' (p. 43), a fact that must be given great importance and analytical attention for the lessons it carries for other countries, since at independence the country was not given any chances of economic success. The book ends with a massive and very authoritative bibliography with only a few omissions.

328   **Pricing policies in Africa with special reference to agricultural development in Malawi.**
James Kadyampakeni.   *World Development*, vol. 16, no. 11 (Nov. 1988), p. 1299-315. bibliog.
The author of this survey of the role of agricultural pricing policies in Malawi, set against a cluster of other factors, concludes that the most important variable that led to developmental success was the maintenance of a balance between urban wages and the prices paid to rural farmers for their crops. In most states the balance between the two has been against rural smallholders, but not so in Malawi. The author defends the country's much-criticized marketing board, ADMARK, as 'the most effective policy instrument of government in maintaining the rural–urban balance in the internal terms of trade, in treating peasants equally from all regions, in structuring prices so that modest food prices have not been combined with declining food production and with protecting peasants from the gyrations of international prices' (p. 1310).

Economy

329 **The private sector and economic development of Malawi.**
Jerome Wolgin (et al.). Washington, DC: Agency for International
Development, 1983. 46p.

An AID evaluation of the contribution and success of former AID efforts to
strengthen the role of the private sector. The report carries its main conclusion in the
very first sentence – 'the private sector is alive and well in Malawi and owned by the
Government' (p. vi). Eleven specific 'lessons' illustrated by Malawi's success are
outlined in the report, with the main emphasis on the contribution of committed
public policy and external assistance to the development of the private sector.

330 **Project appraisal and the multiplier: the case of the Viphya pulp
mill project in Malawi.**
B. D. Giles, A. Jennings. *Oxford Economic Papers* (Oxford), vol. 34,
no. 2 (July 1982), p. 390-402.

This is a project appraisal of what became Malawi's largest enterprise, the Viphya
pulp mill in northern Malawi, and the multiplier effect, triggering development in
related sectors. For another project appraisal see Michael Johnny, *Project
performance of IRD-programmes in Sierra Leone and Malawi* (Hamburg, Germany:
Verlag Weltarchiv, 1986. 180p.).

331 **Reflections on the long-term perspective study for sub-Saharan
Africa, with particular reference to Malawi.**
Gilbert B. Chirwa. In: *The long-term perspective of sub-Saharan
Africa.* Washington, DC: World Bank, 1990. vol. 1, p. 44-59.

Based on current economic indicators and sectoral analysis, this contribution assesses
the long-term economic prospects of Malawi.

332 **The region of Zomba and Machinga, Malawi.**
Dov Weintraub, Julia Margulies. In: *Basic social diagnosis for IRRD
planning: conceptual framework, case studies and some generalisations*,
edited by Dov Weintraub, Julia Margulies. Aldershot, England:
Gower, 1986, p. 63-90.

This article outlines some basic constraints on economic development in the two
districts targeted for study in Malawi. The two development sociologists (from the
Hebrew University in Israel) offer several specific suggestions on how to remove
them. A similar thrust can be observed in Dov Weintraub, 'Interpreting traditions in a
developmental planning context: a Malawian case study', in *Comparative social
dynamics: essays in honor of Samuel Eisenstadt*, edited by Eric Cohen (et al.)
(Boulder, Colorado: Westview Press, 1985, p. 164-75).

333 **Rural development under indigenous and non-indigenous money:
a case study.**
Chinyamata Chipeta. *Society of Malawi Journal*, vol. 38, no. 2
(1985), p. 37-48.

Chipeta discusses some of the reasons for the still highly prevalent use of indigenous
'money' – cattle and foodstuffs, especially maize and millet – in Rumphi district,

from the point of view of the employer and the employee. A survey sample revealed that up to 67 per cent of the families interviewed paid or were paid with these commodities instead of with cash.

334 **Some African experience with regional planning implementation with particular reference to Malawi.**
     Hugh McClintock. *Public Administration and Development*
     (London), vol. 5, no. 4 (1985), p. 289-308.

This article discusses the limited effectiveness of planning in Malawi. McClintock makes the comparison with Kenya, generally in rural areas, but with particular reference to the administrative machinery within which planning operates. The experience suggests that planning policies must be consistent with regional planning activities of other governmental agencies as well as with national pricing policies.

335 **Some highlights of Malawi's experience with financial liberalization.**
     Financial News Analysis (Dakar: African Centre for Monetary
     Studies), vol. 5, no. 1 (Jan. 1992). 15p.

A detailed assessment of Malawi's faithful application of economic austerity and financial liberalization as called for by global donor agencies. As a result the original budget crisis was eliminated, surpluses were recorded, and inflation fell sharply. For a critical examination of the policy of export diversification in Malawi see Ali Ridwan (et al.), *Is export diversification the best way to achieve export growth and stability?* (Washington, DC: World Bank, Southern Africa Department, 1991.44p.).

336 **Statement of development policies, 1987-1996.**
     Department of Economic Planning and Development. Zomba:
     Government Printer, 1987. 197p.

The second official statement of national planning objectives, setting out the means by which these will be pursued. The report first reviews the socio-economic givens and former attainments, and then sets out policies and goals in all fields for the next decade.

337 **Structural adjustment, agricultural development and the poor: some lessons from the Malawian experience.**
     Uma Lele. *World Development*, vol. 18, no. 9 (1990), p. 1207-19.
     bibliog.

This is a perceptive discussion of the 'dualism-within-dualism' in the Malawian economy, and its consequences on World Bank structural adjustment programmes (SAPs) that did not take it adequately into account. Indeed, such programmes, aimed at fine-tuning the macro-economic balance, exacerbated existing wage disparities with adverse impact upon the poor, and thus in essence further inhibited economic growth. This explains the limited impact of the SAPs, despite an always well-managed economy and good adjustment to the World Bank programme. Nevertheless, by relying on inoperative market incentives, recovery has been held back. The author, then working for the World Bank, argues for a two-sector approach to development with respect to poor countries such as Malawi. See also Wycliffe Chilowa, *Structural adjustment and poverty: the case of Malawi* (Fantoft, Norway: C. Michelsen Institute, 1991).

338 **The structural adjustment programme in Malawi: a case of successful adjustment?**
Edited by Ben Kaluwa. Harare: SAPES, 1992. 332p.

Malawi's adjustment efforts have been characterized by a high degree of policy continuity, by market orientation and free trade policies. However domestic demand has contracted, there has been no significant shift in structural variables, and fundamental social dimension issues have not been addressed. See also Carolyn Winter, 'Structural adjustment lending: boon or blow for Malawi', *Journal of Contemporary African Studies* (Pretoria), vol. 4, no. 1/2 (Oct. 1984-April 1985), p. 103-18.

339 **Structural change in Malawi since independence: consequences of a development strategy based on large-scale agriculture.**
Jonathan Kydd, Robert Christiansen. *World Development*, vol. 10 (1982), p. 355-75.

In this important article the authors assess the nature of the major structural changes in the Malawian economy since independence, and identify the key policies pursued by the government to attain these changes. The most important of these policies was a stress on rapidly expanding large-scale agriculture, the transfer of labour into wage employment, and a concomitant decline in the importance of peasant smallholder production. The long-term implications of these are examined. See also Leroy Vail, 'The state and the creation of colonial Malawi's agricultural economy', in *Imperialism, colonialism and hunger: East and Central Africa*, edited by Robert I. Rotberg (Lexington: D. C. Heath, 1983, p. 39-87).

340 **Subnational planning in transition: the case of Malawi.**
J. R. N. Mlia.   In: *Subnational planning in southern and eastern Africa*, edited by A. H. J. Helmsing, K. H. Wekwete.   Aldershot, England: Avebury, 1990, p. 131-46. bibliog.

This article is an assessment of the changes in regional and local planning since independence and especially in the last decade, placed within an historical context. The author pinpoints the main factors that have contributed to these recent changes, especially in the regional rural growth service centres project, which could be expected to benefit Malawi's large rural populations both directly and significantly.

Mineral exploration in Malawi.
See item no. 25.

National atlas of Malawi.
See item no. 26.

Malawi: a political and economic history.
See item no. 99.

The myth of the capitalist class.
See item no. 104.

The pattern of internal migration in response to structural change in the economy of Malawi.
See item no. 185.

Aid and dependence: British aid to Malawi.
See item no. 295.

Dependency and choice: Malawi's links with South Africa.
See item no. 296.

Area handbook for Malawi.
See item no. 470.

Agriculture

341 **Agricultural change and continuity in Malawi.**
Martin L. Chanock. In: *The roots of rural poverty in Central and Southern Africa*, edited by R. Palmer, N. Parsons. Berkeley, California: University of California Press, 1977, p. 396-409.

Chanock's seminal article powerfully underlines his belief that despite numerous policy initiatives and changes after independence, many were of these not particularly successful, and that the main economic policy and agrarian thrust of the Banda government has shown a direct continuation of the emphasis seen during the colonial era. The crops grown in the country, the reliance of Banda's regime upon – and their favouring of – export-oriented large estates, and social policies aimed at keeping farmers linked to these large plantations, are all little different from colonial policies during the pre-independence era. This has had grave implications for the large numbers of smallholders who after have been left to fend for themselves. See also J. A. K. Kandawire, 'The structure of the colonial system as a factor in the underdevelopment of agriculture in colonial Nyasaland', *Journal of Social Science*, vol. 4 (1975), p. 35-45; and Horst Dequin, *Agricultural development in Malawi* (Munich, Germany: Ifo-Institut für Wirtschaftsforschung, 1970. 248p.).

342 **Agriculture and food policy in Malawi: a review.**
Guy C. Z. Mhone. In: *The state of agriculture in Africa*, edited by Thandika Mkandawire, Nnaceur Bourenane. London: Codesria, 1987, p. 59-86. bibliog.

This is a radical polemical interpretation of Malawi's export-oriented agrarian thrust and economic policy. The author argues that despite the regime's populist rhetoric regarding food self-sufficiency, it 'does not have a positive policy directed at improving the welfare of the masses, and that in fact, the logic of the society's socio-economic and political structure demands the exploitation of the masses' (p. 79). He takes to task the work of the most respected objective scholars on Malawi – Kydd and Christiansen – and refers to their balanced, and selectively critical, assessments, as 'hairsplitting' (p. 85), arguing that Banda's economic policies are merely aimed to 'prop up a fascist capitalist state' (p. 79).

343 Agriculture and related developments in Malawi.
Journal of Social Science, vol. 13 (1986).

This Special Issue includes ten papers on agricultural issues delivered at a social sciences conference for Southern African Universities in July 1985, and at another conference in April 1986. See also the papers on Malawi's agriculture presented at a Gaborone (Botswana) 1982 conference that were published in *Land policy and agriculture in Eastern and Southern Africa*, edited by J. W. Arntzen (et al.) (Tokyo: United Nations University Press, 1986. 150p.); and Kenneth Good, 'The direction of agricultural development in Zambia, Zimbabwe and Malawi', in *Industrial development in Zambia, Zimbabwe and Malawi*, edited by Zbigniew A. Konczacki (London: Frank Cass, 1990. vol. 2, p. 127-58).

344 An analysis of supply response among cotton growers in Malawi.
Duncan M. Chembezi, Abner W. Womack. *Agricultural Systems* (Barking, England), vol. 23, no. 2 (1987), p. 79-94. bibliog.

The production of cotton, a traditional smallholder crop, has stagnated in Malawi in recent years with the acreage under the crop declining. Much of the blame for this has been levelled at low producer prices. An econometric analysis reveals that producers are responsive to price incentives, but their response is inelastic. See also Jane Harrigan, 'Malawi: the impact of pricing policy on smallholder agriculture 1971-1988', *Development Policy Review* (London), vol. 6, no. 4 (1988), p. 415-33; and James Kadyampakeni, 'Pricing policies in Africa with special reference to Malawi', *World Development*, vol. 16, no. 11 (1988), p. 1299-316. For a report that points out the discrepancies between low farmers' yields and research-based crop expectations, a result of omissions in research recommendations and poor policy implementation in Malawi, see John Farrington's 'Research-based recommendations versus farmers' practices: some lessons from cotton-spraying in Malawi', *Experimental Agriculture* (London), vol. 13, no. 1 (Jan. 1977), p. 9-15. bibliog. See also Carol Dickerman, Peter C. Bloch, *Land tenure and agricultural productivity in Malawi* (Madison: University of Wisconsin, [n.d.]. 56p. (LTC paper no. 143)).

345 Aspects of agricultural extention in Malawi: an overview.
E. S. Malindi. *Journal of Social Science*, vol. 13 (1986), p. 7-25.

This is a discussion of extension work and the problems of agricultural extension activities in Malawi, presented by a member of the Ministry of Agriculture in Lilongwe. For a USAID report on Malawi's extension service see John M. Curtis (et al.), *An assessment of agricultural extension and training in Malawi* (Washington, DC: Agency for International Development, 1982. 94p. bibliog.).

346 **Commodity production, subsistence, and the state in Africa: Peasant cotton agriculture in the Lower Tchiri (Shire) Valley of Malawi, 1907-51.**
Elias C. Mandala. In: *Geographic perspectives in history*, edited by Eugene D. Genovese, Leonard Hochberg. London: Basil Blackwell, 1989, p. 281-314.
A reinterpretation of colonial economic policy and agriculture with respect to cotton in Malawi. The author concludes that the government 'was autonomous only with respect to the means of achieving its goals . . . [striking] an alliance with the peasantry only because of the failure of European settlers to satisfy the demands of metropolitan British capital' (p. 314).

347 **Contract farming in Malawi: smallholder sugar and tea authorities.**
J. S. Nankumba, B. Kalua. *Eastern Africa Economic Review* (Nairobi), (Aug. 1989), p. 42-58.
A study, based on fieldwork in 1986-88, of the performance of two authorities with monopolies over the production of major cash crops in Malawi. The authors assess their performance and come up with several policy recommendations that they suggest could both improve peasant productivity and satisfaction with the activities of the monopolies. For the operation of Malawi's largest sugar estate see John Amer, A. MacGregor Hutcheson, 'The Nchalo sugar estate: a major agricultural development in Malawi', *Society of Malawi Journal*, vol. 24, no. 1 (1967), p. 7-34. See also I. Livingstone, 'Agricultural development boards in Malawi', in *Tropical boards in tropical Africa* (London: Kegan Paul, 1985, p. 169-92).

348 **Customary land, the state and agrarian change in Malawi: the case of the Chewa peasantry in the Lilongwe Rural Development Project.**
R. Mulombodji Mkandawire. *Journal of Contemporary African Studies* (Pretoria), vol. 3, no. 1/2 (Oct. 1983-April 1984), p. 109-28.
This article analyses the consequences and implications of the 1969 shift from customary land law to freehold title as manifested in the Lilongwe Rural Development Project (RDP), the first area in which the new legislation was implemented. The article describes traditional patterns of land tenure, questions the new legislation's assumptions that productivity had been low under customary tenure and would improve under the new legislation, and describes the new conflicts arising since the legislation was introduced. See also the same author's subsequent article on a somewhat similar theme, where he argues that the new legislation was based on an imperfect appreciation of Chewa concepts of land rights that are adaptable to changing economic circumstances: 'Markets, peasants and agrarian change in post-independence Malawi', *Journal of Contemporary African Studies* (Pretoria), vol. 4, no. 1/2 (1984/5) p. 89-102. For a general discussion of the approach of Malawi's rural growth centres see R. T. Ghambi, 'Rural growth centres: the Malawi example', in *Equity with growth? planning perspectives for small towns in developing countries*, edited by H. D. Kammeier, P. J. Swan (Bangkok: Asian Institute of Technology, 1984, p. 676-86). See also D. W. Nothale, 'The customary system of land tenure and agricultural development in Malawi', *Journal of Social Science*, vol. 11, no. 2 (1984), p. 64-76.

349 **Early attempt at aquaculture in Malawi and implications for future projects.**
Owen J. M. Kalinga. *Journal of Asian and African Studies* (Leiden), vol. 3/4 (July-Oct. 1993), p. 145-61. bibliog.
In this article Kalinga, better known for his pioneering historical work on the Ngonde, assesses government policy with respect to the cultivation of fish in Malawi. Basing his arguments on fieldwork he contends that the thrust failed largely because it produced frustration in farmers who were not provided with extension workers, and without such help aquaculture was impractical for them.

350 **Economic development through estate agriculture: the case of Malawi.**
Frederic L. Pryor, Chinyamata Chipeta. *Canadian Journal of African Studies* (Toronto), vol. 24, no. 1 (1990), p. 50-74.
The authors examine the estate system of agriculture in Malawi, its historical origins and development, the way estate owners view their problems, and the impact of the estate system on the smallholder. The article is based upon a survey of estate owners in Malawi. For the history of Lomwe and Ngoni workers on these estates see H. H. K. Bhila, 'The role of the Ngoni and Lomwe in the growth of the plantation economy in the Shire highlands 1890-1912', *Journal of Social Science,* vol. 5 (1976), p. 28-43.

351 **Economic transition among the Poka of northern Malawi from subsistence to cash cropping.**
John U. Ogbu. *Journal of African Studies* (Los Angeles), vol. 5, no. 2 (Summer 1978), p. 151-72.
This is a study of the Poka-Tumbuka on the eastern slopes of the Nyika plateau, and of the reasons why initial efforts to promote coffee cultivation among them were not successful – cultivation was not profitable – and why later, after an economic upturn, their inadequate reserve capital prevented them from shifting to growing the crop. This is explained by the fact that it is three years before coffee plantations yield returns.

352 **Establishing rural service and growth centres: with seven case studies from Malawi.**
Heinz-Ulrich Thimm (et al.). Hamburg, Germany: Verlag Weltarchiv, 1986. 367p. bibliog.
A study of the problems of integrated rural development with case-studies from seven rural growth centres. All are written, with one exception, by Malawian teachers at the Banda College of Agriculture in Lilongwe. The study commends the regime for avoiding the pitfalls of urban-based development, arguing that 'the present situation that more than 80% of the people live in rural areas should be considered as an asset of Malawi, and not a sign of backwardness' (p. 359). See also Hugh McClintock, 'Some African experience with regional planning implementation with particular reference to Malawi', *Public Administration and Development,* vol. 5, no. 4 (1985), p. 289-308.

353 **Factors influencing the length of working day in Malawi agriculture.**

J. Farrington. *Eastern Africa Journal of Rural Development* (Kampala), vol. 8, no. 1/2 (1975), p. 61-79.

This study, based on statistical data for 1970-71, attempts to ascertain the main variables influencing the length of the working day in the peasant agriculture of Malawi. The analysis is presented by function and type of activity, age, sex and social/familial status.

354 **Facts for planning rural development: some lessons in the administration of data collection from Malawi.**

D. A. G. Green, N. Maddock. *Agricultural Administration and Extension* (Barking, England), vol. 24, no. 1 (1987), p. 33-48.

In this article, the authors argue that despite the collection of large amounts of information about Malawi's agriculture aimed at providing a basis for planning for the National Rural Development Programme, serious reservations exist about its utilization, timeliness or relevance, and about whether there is any communication whatsoever between data-gatherers and -users. Proposals are made to ameliorate these situations. Another article documents how the collection and transmission of information were affected by bureaucratic behaviour during an agricultural disaster: see David L. Pelletier, Louis H. Msukwa, 'The role of information systems in decision-making following disasters', *Human Organization* (Oklahoma City), vol. 49, no. 3 (1990), p. 245-54. See also D. P. Shaw, 'The need for more overt integrated rural planning: the case of Malawi', *Geoforum* (Oxford), vol. 19, no. 2 (1988), p. 213-25.

355 **Fertilizer situation and markets in Malawi.**

Lewis B. Williams, John H. Allgood. Muscle Shoals, Alabama: International Fertilizer Development Center, 1990. 25p.

The authors report on the use of fertilizer in Malawi. The use of fertilizer is in its infancy in the country, but it is growing at the rate of 6 per cent per year, and 43,000 tons were used in 1988. The smallholder marketing system subsidizes small farmers and the government is committed to its growth, with the result that the outlook for the spread of fertilizer and improved agriculture is bright. See also D. H. Ng'ong'ola, D. A. G. Green, 'An economic analysis of smallholder fertilizer use in the Lilongwe Rural Development Project, Malawi', *Welsh Studies in Agricultural Economics* no. 6 (1987), p. 85-92.

356 **Individualism is the antithesis of indirect rule: cooperative development and indirect rule in colonial Malawi.**

Joey Power. *Journal of Southern African Studies*, vol. 18, no. 2 (June 1992), p. 317-47.

Starting from the position that 'the introduction of cooperatives and indirect rule to colonial Malawi during the 1930s was part of an exercise in imperial social engineering designed to thwart class formation' (p. 317), Power assesses the reasons why virtually all cooperatives in Malawi's southern province failed during the colonial era. One of the main reasons, he suggests, is that they could not become viable in a non-African-controlled economy.

357 Maize research in Malawi: lessons from failure.
Jonathan Kydd. *Journal of International Development* (Manchester), vol. 1, no. 1 (Jan. 1989), p. 112-44. bibliog.
A review of Malawi's thirty-four years of maize research which the author concludes has been disappointing. There has been inadequate funding and continuity, a fact which may explain the several widespread food crises in the country. Kydd argues that with a fast-growing population, increased land pressures, and child malnutrition levels among the highest in the world, Malawi can no longer be viewed as the success story it was once touted to be. For an earlier more rosier report see J. Gus Liebenow, *Malawi's search for food self-sufficiency* (Hanover, New Hampshire: Universities Field Staff Reports, 1982. 3 parts. bibliog.). For a technical report on maize yields correlated with rainfall patterns see D. MacColl, 'Studies on maize at Bunda, Malawi', *Experimental Agriculture* (Cambridge), vol. 25, no. 3 (July 1989), p. 357-66, 367-74.

358 Malawi rural enterprises and agro-business development institutions: project paper.
United States Agency for International Development. Washington, DC: AID, 1985. 2 vols.
This is an overview of Malawi's agriculture, agrarian credit corporations and finances, and the nature of US–Malawi cooperation and agricultural assistance.

359 Malawi's agricultural economy and the evolution of legislation on the production and marketing of peasant economic crops.
Clement Ng'ong'ola. *Journal of Southern African Studies* (Oxford), vol. 12, no. 2 (April 1986), p. 240-61.
This article consists of an overview of all legislation passed during the colonial and post-colonial era relating to the production and marketing of peasant crops. The author argues that although less legislation exists in the post-colonial era, the fact that a marketing monopoly was established indicates a continuity of policies from colonial days. In a two-page annex there is a listing of all important cropping and marketing legislation in Malawi. Important policy changes with respect to the role of the state in food marketing began to take place in the late 1980s. Preliminary assessments of their effect can be found in Wycliffe Chilowa, *Liberalization of agricultural produce marketing and household food security in Malawi* (Fantoft, Norway: C. Michelsen Institute, 1991. 26p.); Vanessa Scarborough, *Domestic food marketing liberalisation in Malawi: a preliminary assessment* (Ashford, England: Wye College, Department of Agricultural Economics, 1990. 50p.); and Vanessa Scarborough, *Agricultural policy reforms under structural adjustment* (Ashford, England: Wye College, Department of Agricultural Economics, 1990. 39p.).

360 Malawi's 'captured' peasantry: an empirical analysis.
David Hirschmann. *Journal of Developing Areas* (Macomb), vol. 24 (July 1990), p. 467-88.
An important contribution to the debate sparked by Goran Hyden's seminal general work (based on Tanzania) about Africa's 'uncaptured' (by the state) peasantries – that is, farmers who by choice remain outside the influence of the state and the mainstream economy, forming a basic stumbling-block to efforts aimed at

modernization of the economy and society. Hirschmann shows that in Malawi at least there is 'a peasantry that is considerably more rather than less captured' (p. 486) and that is greatly affected by state policies. Indeed, when state policies hit at peasant interests the end result is often catastrophic to the state itself, underlining the symbiosis of state–peasant interests rather than their separateness. See also the important article by Dharam Ghai, Samir Radwan, 'Growth and inequality: rural development in Malawi, 1964-78', in *Agrarian politics and rural poverty in Africa*, edited Dharam Ghai, Samir Radwan (Geneva: International Labour Office, 1983, p. 71-97. bibliog.).

361 **Mchinji: a farm management and socio-economic survey of smallholder farmers in Mchinji district, Malawi.**
Malawi Planning Division. Lilongwe: Ministry of Agriculture, 1986.
139p. bibliog.

This is a comprehensive agro-economic survey, including detailed statistics on a variety of dimensions, of the economy of Mchinji district and on the smallholder agricultural farms there, their productivity and problems. See also Carol W. Dickerman, Peter C. Bloch, *Land tenure and agricultural productivity in Malawi* (Madison: University of Wisconsin, 1991. 56p.).

362 **Planters, peasants and the colonial state: the impact of the Native Tobacco Board in the central province of Malawi.**
John McCracken. *Journal of Southern African Studies*, vol. 9, no. 2 (1983), p. 172-92.

McCracken makes an important contribution to the controversial field of colonial agrarian policy. He illustrates, at least with respect to tobacco, that 'the state in colonial Malawi operated as an arbiter between various types of interest, unable to support any one too fully, in the knowledge that the triumph of a particular interest group would lead to the collapse of the whole' (p. 192). More specifically, he illustrates how in the Native Tobacco Board a handful of estate owners were able to dominate pricing and marketing policies, while on the other hand most district officers were active proponents of native production if only out of anxiety to be able to collect their hut tax quotas from the resultant incomes of the farmers.

363 **The rural economy in Malawi: a critical analysis.**
A. Kapote Mwakasungura. Fantoft, Norway: C. Michelsen Institute,
1986. 120p.

This work takes a critical look at Malawi's developmental strategy of large-scale individual farming and the World Bank's Integrated Rural Development projects in the country. These, the author argues, have not benefited the majority of the country's farmers. See also Neil Spooner, 'Does the World Bank inhibit smallholder cash cropping?', *IDS Bulletin* (Brighton), vol. 19, no. 2 (1988), p. 66-70.

Agriculture

364 **Smallholder constraints to agricultural production in Blantyre Agricultural Development Division.**
Edited by J. H. A. Maida. Lilongwe: Ministry of Agriculture, 1986. 162p.

A collection of articles presented at a workshop conducted in 1986 in order to ascertain the reasons for the visible constraints on increased crop production of small farms in the Blantyre region, and to pinpoint what can be done by extension workers to increase productivity. The individual contributions refer to issues ranging from problems of soil degradation and conservation, better and more extension services, the need for the greater use of fertilizers, etc. Contrary to the title of the book, the geographical scope ranges from Karonga at the northern extremity of the country to Mulanje in the south.

365 **Socio-economic aspects of rural development in Malawi: a report on some survey findings.**
David H. Humphrey. *Eastern Africa Journal of Rural Development* (Kampala), vol. 8, no. 1/2 (1975), p. 46-60.

Humphrey's report is based on a survey analysis of 275 farmers in eleven villages in Malawi that tried to ascertain the constraints on development lodged in cultural values and beliefs. Though the sample is dated (the research was conducted in 1971), since cultural values change only slowly with time, this research throws some interesting light on the problems of development in a transitional society. See also Chinyamata Chipeta, 'Rural development under different family economic forms in Malawi', *Journal of Eastern African Research and Development* (Nairobi), no. 16 (1986), p. 1-19; and K. Bell, 'Rural development in Malawi', *Journal of Social Science*, vol. 11, no. 2 (1984), p. 77-111. bibliog.

366 **Success with group lending in Malawi.**
Walter Schaefer-Kehnert. *Development Digest* (Washington), vol. 20, no. 1 (Jan. 1982), p. 10-15.

This article reports on the Lilongwe Land Development Programme that was set up to lend funds to small groups of farmers, and that has turned out to be very successful, with high rates of repayment of loans. For a more extensive analysis of this project see S. Nankimba, 'Malawi: agricultural credit in the Lilongwe Land Development Programme', in *Project performance of IRD-programmes in Sierra Leone and Malawi* (Hamburg, Germany: Verlag Weltarchiv, 1986, p. 127-80). See also C. Enders, B. Kasch, 'Some notes on the agricultural credit system in Malawi: case study in the Ntcheu rural development project', *African Review of Money, Finance and Banking*, no. 1 (1987), p. 15-25.

367 **Village water supply in the decade: lessons from field experience.**
Colin Glennie. New York: J. Wiley, 1983. 152p. bibliog.

A technical but very readable step-by-step guide (illustrated with many plates) to programming and organizing the laying out of water-supply systems in rural areas. Glennie based it on his Malawi experience.

117

Agriculture

Malawi in maps.
See item no. 20.

National atlas of Malawi.
See item no. 26.

Colonialism, capitalism and ecological crisis in Malawi.
See item no. 30.

Malawi.
See item no. 32.

Population growth and environmental degradation in Malawi.
See item no. 34.

Directory of plant names in Malawi.
See item no. 41.

The origins and development of agriculture in southern Africa.
See item no. 67.

Economics and ethnicity: the Italian community in Malawi.
See item no. 80.

Land and politics in Malawi 1875-1975.
See item no. 94.

Peasants, planters and the colonial state.
See item no. 113.

Seeds of trouble: government policy and land rights in Malawi.
See item no. 120.

Thangata – forced labor or reciprocal assistance?
See item no. 125.

Ubureetwa **and** *thangata*: **catalysts to peasant political consciousness in Rwanda and Malawi.**
See item no. 126.

White farmers in Malawi: before and after the depression.
See item no. 127.

Work and control in a peasant economy.
See item no. 129.

Working conditions and worker responses in Nyasaland tea estates.
See item no. 130.

Land and labor in rural Malawi.
See item no. 184.

The role of the Ngoni and Lomwe in the growth of the plantation economy in the Shire highlands.
See item no. 188.

Bureaucracy and rural women.
See item no. 191.

Capitalism, kinship and gender in the lower Tchire (Shire) valley of Malawi.
See item no. 192.

Women farmers of Malawi.
See item no. 205.

Women in the estate sector of Malawi.
See item no. 206.

The impact of demographic changes on rural development in Malawi.
See item no. 220.

Peasants, migrants and plantations.
See item no. 325.

Pricing policies in Africa with special reference to agricultural development in Malawi.
See item no. 328.

Structural change in Malawi since independence.
See item no. 339.

Annotated bibliography of agriculture in Malawi.
See item no. 467.

Malawi agricultural research directory.
See item no. 490.

Trade and Commerce

368 **Annual statement of external trade.**
National Statistics Office. Zomba: National Statistics Office, 1990.
49p.
This annual, composed mostly of tables, is a compendium of statistics and data about
Malawi's foreign trade. The publication had the same title prior to independence. For
an overview and analysis of Malawi's early patterns of trade (1891-1960) see Colin
A. Baker, 'Nyasaland, a history of its export trade', *Nyasaland Journal*, vol. 15, pt. 1
(Jan. 1962), p. 7-35.

369 **Income distribution and foreign trade: the case of Malawi.**
F. Johnson, T. Magnac. In: *External trade and income distribution*,
edited by François Bourguignon, Christian Morrison. Paris:
Organisation for Economic Cooperation and Development, 1989,
p. 123-54.
An impressive and important exploration, buttressed by extensive data and statistics,
of the relationship between income distribution in Malawi and the structure of the
country's exports, and including some revision of the general assumptions and
conclusions rife in the literature on this topic. The analysis reveals that there is very
little connection between the two. Export activities are not an important cause of
income inequality; inequality among estate workers (primarily in the tea and tobacco
sectors) is likewise small due to competition in the labour market, while the
manufacturing sector is too small to have any impact on income inequality. The basic
income gap is more similar to the kind normally found between workers in the
traditional and the modern sectors. Some structural market features, commodity price
distortions and differential access to credit markets play a role, but income inequality
in Malawi is of the universal agrarian–industrial, traditional–modern sectors kind.
The authors also point out that the paucity of quantitative indicators prevents more
complex answers to the issue of whether export growth would have been higher in the
absence of strong government support for the estate sector.

370 **Malawi's export crop boom: a re-appraisal.**
Jonathan Kydd. *IDS Bulletin* (Brighton), vol. 19, no. 2 (April 1988),
p. 71-80. bibliog.
Written by one of the prime analysts of Malawi's economy, this is a re-assessment of
Malawi's stunning agricultural export boom between 1966 and 1979, a period that
also saw a concomitant stagnation of the income of rural Malawians. Kydd speculates
that possibly the pursuit of a peasant-centred land, marketing, pricing and taxation
policy – and not policies overwhelmingly supporting estate agriculture – might have
attained realistically higher mass levels of income and employment. Exactly such a
policy is currently being pursued under World Bank conditionalities, but under
immensely more adverse external economic conditions.

371 **The privatization of agricultural trading in Malawi.**
Robert Christiansen, Lee Ann Stackhouse. *World Development*,
vol. 17, no. 5 (May 1989), p. 729-40.
This is an important study of the privatization of smallholder agricultural marketing
in recent years in Malawi. Despite a host of problems, including major disruptions in
the supply of maize, the implementation of the programme of privatization was
successful. However, some basic issues still have to be definitively resolved,
including the relationship between the private sector and ADMARK, the parastatal
marketing organ, and the whole question of food security in the country.

372 **Some observations on the market-place exchange system of
Malawi.**
P. A. Lindkog. *Society of Malawi Journal*, vol. 34, no. 1 (1981),
p. 45-55.
This article is a preliminary examination of a neglected aspect of Malawi trade –
market relations and the growth of market-place exchanges in the Shire Highlands.

Business information on Malawi.
See item no. 475.

Doing business in Malawi.
See item no. 480.

Malawi buyer's guide.
See item no. 491.

Industry

373 The cloning of tea in Malawi.
D. James, R. Lalkaka, T. Malik.   In: *New technologies and development: experiences in technology blending*, edited by A. S. Bhalla, Dilmus James.   Boulder, Colorado: Lynne Rienner, 1988, p. 258-68.

This article outlines the utilization of high-tech procedures, backed by UN funding, in the important tea industry of Malawi.

374 Constraints, conduct, and performance of Malawian manufacturing firms.
Ben M. Kaluwa.   Zomba: University of Malawi Economics Department, 1987. 66p. bibliog.

An important monograph that pinpoints the factors that constrain the productivity and profitability of enterprises in Malawi. The author's analysis is based on data obtained from responses to a custom-designed questionnaire sent to all substantial manufacturers in the country. Among the author's findings one can note that excess capacity was found to be fairly high (38 per cent of firms reported it) mostly traceable to competition from imports, government restrictions on pricing, and weak domestic markets. Input supply bottlenecks due to communications problems were also identified as affecting firms and their pricing policies and profitability.

375 Craft development in Malawi, 1981-1983.
James McKendry.   Farnham, England: J. Hepworth, 1983. 28p.

This is the Final Report of a Craft Advisor to the Malawi Export Promotion Council following a 30-month study project financed by the European Economic Community. The report identifies specific craft products suitable for export, advises on craft industry development, and makes recommendations on the educational, training and marketing policies that must be implemented to develop this sector of the economy.

376 **Industrial and trade directory.**
Zomba: Associated Chambers of Commerce and Industry, 1990. 174p.
This publication appears more or less annually and is an inventory of all business
enterprises in Malawi and their sphere of operations.

377 **Industrial development in Zambia, Zimbabwe and Malawi: the**
primacy of politics.
Marcia M. Burdette. In: *Studies in the economic history of Southern*
Africa, edited by Zbigniew A. Konczacki (et al.). London: Frank
Cass, 1990, vol. 2, p. 75-126.
This is a survey of industrial development in the three countries (with rather less on
Malawi), underlining how (in general) industrial policy thrusts are primarily
determined by political considerations. This was especially true in the case of
Malawi, where it was President Banda's personal decision to follow an agrarian path,
rather than pursue industrialization.

378 **Malawi.**
In: *Electricity in rural development*. Blantyre: Southern African
Development Conference, 1987, p. 1-10.
The availability of large-scale hydro-electric power is a relatively new phenomenon
in Malawi,. The first water turbine and generator in the country entered into service at
Nkula Falls on the Shire River in 1966, after 24 years of deliberations. The section on
Malawi in this book constitutes an overview of current electricity supply and demand,
for industrial, commercial and private use, and provides projections of electrical
output and needs in the future. For the history of electricity in Malawi see the earlier
article by A. E. Archibald: 'Hydro-electric power development on the Shire River',
Society of Malawi Journal, vol. 31, no. 2 (July 1978), p. 6-16.

379 **Malawi.**
Richard Scobey. In: *Energy, environment and development in*
Africa: SADCC country studies, part 1. Uppsala, Sweden:
Scandinavian Institute of African Studies, 1984, p. 171-86.
This section in the volume on the SADCC countries is an inventory of all energy
resources and energy consumption in the country, commercial as well as non-
commercial (i.e., firewood). See also F. C. Chikunkhunzeni, 'The study of Malawi
with special reference to fuel and power: H. E.P., coal, oil and firewood', *Malawian*
Geographer, vol. 26 (1987), p. 7-20.

380 **Managerial motivation in Kenya and Malawi.**
Peter Blunt, Merrick Jones. *Journal of Modern African Studies*,
vol. 24, no. 1 (1986), p. 165-75.
An investigation, based on empirical data, as to what 'organisational structures and
reward systems should be designed to attribute the same priorities to, and therefore
satisfy a set of managerial needs arranged in a universally applicable hierarchical
order' (p. 166). The data reveal 'a high degree of similarity among African managers
in Kenya, Liberia and Malawi concerning the importance they attach to security needs

which for them are pre-eminent, unlike their counterparts in North America and Western Europe' (p. 174).

381 Resource-based industrial development: past experience and future prospects in Malawi.
Ian Livingstone. *Industry and Development* (Vienna), no. 10 (1984), p. 75-125.

A valuable, comprehensive overview and inventory of Malawi's resources, existing industries, and industrial possibilities in agriculture, agro-industry and agro-processing, livestock resources, fisheries, forest products and manufacturing, and the prospects of their being developed in the future in light of the country's constraints. The latter are primarily Malawi's weak infrastructure, low local rural purchasing power, capital constraints, poor communications and, because of *the country's geographical location, high shipping costs to and from the ports on the Mozambique coast.

382 Small-scale industry in Malawi.
Wim Ettema. *Journal of Modern African Studies*, vol. 22, no. 3 (Sept. 1984), p. 487-510.

In this article Ettema provides a survey of existing small-scale industry in Malawi, based on a 1983 database of 1,816 small businesses. Forty per cent of these were open-air enterprises, and the majority concentrated in the fields of maize mills, carpentry, building, welding, garages and brick-making. Since 35 per cent of the secondary sector in Malawi is engaged in small-scale industry, it forms an important source of employment in a country suffering from chronic unemployment. The author outlines the characteristics of the entrepreneurs, the gender of the owners of the enterprises (only 12 per cent were owned by women, mostly in beer-brewing and pottery), their level of education, gross monthly earnings, amenities (most without water, electricity or telephones), fields and styles of operation, degree of success, and the structural constraints on small-scale industry in Malawi.

383 Training the African manager: the role of the expatriate manager in Malawi.
John M. Parkinson, Peter J. Rutherford. *Journal of Contemporary African Studies* (Pretoria), vol. 6, no. 1/2 (April-Oct. 1987), p. 25-47.

Like other countries in Africa, Malawi is highly dependent on expatriates for managerial and technical skills. To attain Africanization, aggressive management development schemes need to be implemented in which senior expatriates play a major role. This article outlines several pitfalls that have commonly been encountered in the drive to Africanize Malawi's managerial cadres.

Project appraisal and the multiplier: the Viphya pulp mill project in Malawi.
See item no. 330.

Communications

384 **The airmail history of Nyasaland.**
A. J. Hawken. *Society of Malawi Journal*, vol. 33, no. 2 (July 1980), p. 25-32.

This is an interesting account of the evolution of the airmail postal service in colonial Nyasaland.

385 **The district road improvement and maintenance programme: better roads and job creation in Malawi.**
Steiner Hagen, Colin Relf. Geneva: International Labour Office, 1988. 96p. bibliog.

A descriptive analysis of the development, achievements, and current structure and organization of the District Road Improvement and Maintenance Programme (DRIMP) in Malawi since the late 1970s. The authors suggest that Malawi's experience may of be of use to other Third World leaders contemplating similar programmes, and also of practical interest to engineers involved in road projects, or instructors mounting training programmes or seminars dealing with road construction or maintenance.

386 **Inventory of designated roads in Malawi.**
Blantyre: Road Planning Unit of the Ministry of Works and Supplies, 1990. var. pag.

This is a periodically updated inventory of Malawi's road system. Composed mostly of tables and illustrations, and paginated individually by region, the almanac gives the length, official route number, and other details of all major and minor roads in Malawi. For how the original road system developed in the 1890s (only paved and modernized after independence by President Banda) see Colin Baker, 'Malawi's early road system', *Society of Malawi Journal*, vol. 24, no. 1 (Jan. 1971), p. 7-21. For data on the increasing traffic densities on roads not originally expected to cope with such heavy loads see *Growth of road traffic densities in Malawi* (Lilongwe: Office of the President and Cabinet, Transport Planning Unit, 1985, 88p.).

387 **The Limbe Post Office.**
Barbara Lamport-Stokes. *Society of Malawi Journal*, vol. 40, no. 2 (1987), p. 11-29.

This detailed study should be of great interest to postal history philatelists, tracing as it does the origins and growth of the Limbe Post Office. The article is illustrated with examples of the postmarks used over the years to cancel outgoing mail. Another useful publication for philatelists, is *Post Office guide* (Blantyre: Postmaster General, 1983. 349p.). The latter is a comprehensive manual to the Post Office's services throughout the country, and includes lists of all postal branches and postal schedules.

388 **Malawi's transportation problems.**
James G. Kadyampakeni. *African Insight* (Pretoria), vol. 17, no. 1 (1987), p. 52-7.

A succinct analysis of the major problems Malawi was faced with as a consequence of the insecurity of its rail links to the Indian Ocean ports. The situation caused massive import/export bottlenecks and delays, and costly evacuation of produce via the lengthy overland route to South African ports.

389 **Nyasaland and the Shire Highlands railway.**
J. D. Rees. Zomba: Society of Malawi, 1986. 54p. Reprint of the 1908 ed.

A reprint, with a new introduction, of the original prospectus for intending new settlers prepared by the British Central Africa Company on the memorable occasion (in 1908) when the arrival of the first of the Shire Highlands Railway trains arrived in Limbe. The railway was the precursor of the expanded Malawi Railways that are still based in Limbe. The booklet is replete with period memorabilia such as warnings against the sale of alcohol 'to any native', and various advertisements (including one for Nobel-Glasgow explosives). It describes conditions in the colony, and what new settlers should expect.

390 **Nyasaland at the aviation cross-roads: Adam Cobham's flying boat visit, 1928.**
Colin Baker. *Society of Malawi Journal*, vol. 44, no. 1 (1991), p. 9-33.

This article recounts a little-known incident – Cobham's 1928 seaplane stop in Vau in North Nyasaland on his way from England to Cape Town. The article is illustrated with plates that reveal the very primitive nature of aviation at that time and in that part of the world. For a study of another oddity in the history of communications of Malawi see the same author's 'Sir Geoffrey Colby and the "Solent" flying-boat service to Nyasaland, 1949-59', *Journal of Modern African Studies*, vol. 26, no. 1 (March 1988) p. 165-70. The latter reports on the flying-boat service that operated for one year on the Southampton–Johannesburg route via a stop at Cape MacLear on Lake Malawi, 'a vital, if incremental step' towards placing Malawi on the aviation map (p. 170). Aviation began to make progress in Malawi in 1933 when Blantyre's Chileka airport was inaugurated: for that development see J. A. Florence, 'The growth of civil aviation in Nyasaland', *Nyasaland Journal*, vol. 11, pt. 2 (July 1958), p. 14-23.

391 **Sir Alfred Sharpe. Early railway development in Malawi.**
Robert B. Boeder. *Society of Malawi Journal*, vol. 33, no. 2 (July 1980), p. 43-50.

This is a brief outline of the construction of the Shire Highlands railway to Beira in Mozambique, that eliminated the major bottlenecks that had hitherto developed at the Shire River rapids and affected traffic to and from the coast. For the post-independence construction of the 100-mile spur that linked the rail systems of Malawi and Mozambique, thus giving Malawi a second Indian Ocean outlet at Nacala, see A. MacGregor Hutcheson's 'New developments in Malawi's rail and lake services', *Society of Malawi Journal*, vol. 22, no. 1 (Jan. 1969), p. 32-45.

392 **A structural analysis of Malawi's road network: an application of graph theory.**
Ezekiel Kalipeni. *Journal of Social Science*, vol. 10 (1983), p. 84-99. maps.

In this article the author applies graph theory to the study of the development of Malawi's transportation geography. The implications lead to recommendations to invest in the 'transport of the nodes of the Central Region, and in order to develop the North to invest in new roads there as well' (p. 97).

393 **Transport developments in Malawi, 1964-1974.**
John Perry. *Journal of Social Science*, vol. 3 (1974), p. 48-73.

During Malawi's first decade of independence the country completely transformed the primitive communications system it inherited from colonial days, by initiating a major paving programme of the north–south arteries, and by constructing a second railroad track to the coast at Nacala. In an earlier study Perry surveys the history of transportation in Malawi from colonial days: 'The growth of the transport network of Malawi', *Society of Malawi Journal*, vol. 22, no. 2 (July 1969), p. 23-37.

394 **Transportation of tea.**
Transport Planning Unit, Office of the President. Lilongwe: Transport Planning Unit, 1985. 50p.

This is an account of tea trade and tea transportation in Malawi. Tea is one of Malawi's most valuable commodities, and its prompt and safe transport to Indian Ocean ports for export overseas is a matter of priority to both producers (many of them European) and to the state which has a financial stake in tea exports. A variety of problems have plagued Malawi's tea exports, however: the slow and unreliable evacuation of produce via the old, decaying track to the coast at Beira; FRELIMO's war of liberation against Portugal in Mozambique, that threatened the railway; later, and more seriously, Renamo's revolt against the radical regime that emerged in independent Maputo. That revolt played havoc with Malawi's lifelines, disrupting them for over a year at a time, and forcing very costly tea evacuations by road via Zambia to Durban, South Africa, as well as the accumulation of stockpiles in Limbe itself.

Communications

The making of an imperial slum. Nyasaland and its railways 1895-1935.
See item no. 97.

Nyasaland mails and stamps.
See item no. 111.

Administration of Posts and Telecommunications, 1891-1974.
See item no. 270.

Languages and
Linguistics

395 **Chichewa guide for visitors.**
M. V. B. Mangoche, H. H. Mpanga.   Limbe: Dzuka, 1990. 60p. map.
A popular compact English–Chichewa dictionary and vocabulary, mostly intended for visitors.

396 **A cyclopaedic dictionary of the Mang'anja language spoken in British Central Africa.**
David Clement Ruffelle Scott.   Edinburgh: Foreign Mission Committee of the Church of Scotland, 1892. 737p.
The classic, and most comprehensive, Mang'anja dialect dictionary. A more compact version of this work was published posthumously, with updating and editing by Alexander Hetherwick, also of the Church of Scotland in Blantyre, as *Dictionary of the Nyanja language* (London: Religious Tract Society, 1929. 612p.). Both works include Nyanja–English vocabularies only. For one early (short) Nyanja–English–Nyanja dictionary and Nyanja grammar study see Alexander Riddel, *A grammar of the Chinyanja language as spoke at Lake Nyassa* (Edinburgh: J. Maclaren & Son, 1880. 150p.).

397 **A dictionary of Yao language.**
G. M. Sanderson.   Zomba: Government Printer, 1954. 167p.
For long in print in Zomba, this is the classic Yao–English–Yao dictionary. See also the author's earlier work, originally published in 1916, that includes part of the above dictionary as well as a phonology and grammar of Chiyao: *A Yao grammar* (London: Society for the Promotion of Christian Knowledge, 1922. 211p.). For additional studies of the language see W. H. Whiteley, *A study of Yao sentences* (Oxford: Clarendon Press, 1966); Edward Steere, *Collections for a handbook of the Yao language* (London: Society for the Promotion of Christian Knowledge, 1971. 105p.); K. Mbega, W. H. Whiteley, 'Formality and informality in Yao speech', *Africa*, vol. 31, no. 2 (April 1961), p. 135-46; and A. Mtenje, 'The role of redundancy and default rules of Chiyao phonology', *Journal of Humanities*, no. 3 (Dec. 1989), p. 1-21.

398   **A note on tonal mobility in Chichewa.**
Francis Moto.   *Journal of Humanities*, no. 1 (April 1987), p. 65-74.

An outline of the morphological structure of Chichewa verbs, their classification according to tone and two of the most commonly applied tonal rules, followed by an examination of how these factors affect the movement of tones. For another examination of tonality by the same author see his 'Aspects of tone assignment in Chichewa', *Journal of Contemporary African Studies* (Pretoria), vol. 3, no. 1/2 (Oct. 1983-April 1984), p. 199-209. See also A. D. Mtenje's two articles: 'Tone shift principles in the Chichewa verb', *Lingua* (Amsterdam), vol. 72, no. 2/3 (1987), p. 169-209; and 'Arguments for an autosegmental analysis of Chichewa vowel harmony', *Lingua* (Amsterdam), vol. 66, no. 1 (1985), p. 21-52. bibliog. For a number of additional linguistic studies on Chichewa see M. L. Trithart, *Relational grammar and Chichewa subjectivisation rules* (Bloomington: Indiana University Linguistics Club, 1977. 102p.); G. G. Corbett, A. Mtenje, 'Gender agreement in Chichewa', *Studies in African Linguistics*, vol. 18, no. 1 (1987), p. 1-38; and J. Bresnan, S. A. Mchombo, 'Topic, pronoun, and agreement in Chichewa', *Language*, vol. 63, no. 4 (1987), p. 741-82.

399   **On the inadmissibility of feature-changing rules in phonological theory: evidence from Chiya.**
Al Mtenje.   *Journal of Contemporary African Studies* (Pretoria), vol. 8/9, no. 1/2 (1989/90), p. 79-108.

This is a linguistic discussion of the multiple Chiyao phonological rules to support the author's contention that 'feature-changing rules be completely excluded from phonological theory' (p. 108). See also W. H. A. Whiteley, *A study of Yao sentences* (London: Oxford University Press, 1966).

400   **Patterns of language-use in Malawi: a socio-linguistic investigation in the Domasi and Malindi areas of southern Malawi.**
Edrinnie Kayambazinthu.   *Journal of Contemporary African Studies* (Pretoria), vol. 8/9, no. 1/2 (1989/90), p. 109-31.

The author analyses the prevalence of first- and second-language usage in a Yao region in southern Malawi. The work is buttressed by tables and statistical data, and illustrates the context and purpose of each language.

401   **A short English–Nyanja vocabulary.**
Thomas Price.   Lusaka: National Educational Company of Zambia, 1975. 127p.

This compact dictionary is a reprint of an original version first published in 1957.

402   **The student's English–Chichewa dictionary.**
Zambesi Mission.   Blantyre: CLAIM, 1978. 173p.

This is the classic staple English–Chichewa dictionary. Former editions were published under the title *English–Nyanja dictionary*. A more comprehensive earlier edition was published by the Zambesi Mission as *English–Cinyanja dictionary* (Blantyre: Zambesi Mission Press, 1955. 381p.).

403   **Tumbuka–Tonga English dictionary.**
William Y. Turner.   Blantyre: Hetherwick Press, 1952. 284p.

This is a comprehensive dictionary of the two mutually understandable north Malawi languages, by a former Livingstonia missionary. For a linguistic study of Tumbuka see Leroy Vail, 'The noun classes of Tumbuka', *African Studies*, vol. 30, no. 1 (1971), p. 35-59.

Literature

404   **Censoring the African poem: personal reflections.**
Jack Mpanje.   In: *Criticism and ideology: second annual African Writers' Conference*, edited by Kirsten H. Peterson, Per Wastberg. Uppsala, Sweden: Scandinavian Institute of African Studies, 1988, p. 104-11.

This article, reprinted also in the *Index on Censorship* (London), vol. 18, no. 9 (1989), p. 7-9 and 11, is the text of Mpanje's 1986 speech at the Second African Writers' Conference held in Stockholm. In it he offers his views on the stultifying nature of the oppressive censorship of the press and on all creative writing in President Banda's Malawi. Mpanje, Malawi's most celebrated author and poet, was in 1988 the winner of the International Award for Poetry for a collection of poetry that was banned in his own country. In 1987, while head of the Department of Language and Literature at the University of Malawi, he was arrested and jailed for sedition. Amnesty International adopted him as their Prisoner of Conscience, but he was released only in 1992 as the winds of liberalization finally reached Malawi.

405   **Chimombo's use of the M'Bona myth in the *Rainmaker*.**
Anthony Nazombe.   *Journal of Humanities*, no. 1 (April 1987), p. 37-53.

A literary examination of the manner in which Chimombo uses themes, symbolism and even names drawn from the Chewa creation myth and Mbona cult of Malawi, in his poetic and dramatic works. For another literary dissection of a recent Malawian work see Mpalive-Hangson Mssika, 'Sexual politics in Malawian popular fiction: the case of Aubrey Kalitera's *Why father, why*', *Kunapipi* (Aarhus), vol. 11, no. 3 (1989), p. 23-33. In connection with this review see also Aubrey Kalitera's other works: *Mother, why mother* (Blantyre: Power Pen Books, 1983) and *Daughter, why daughter* (Blantyre: Power Pen Books, 1983).

406 **District officer.**
Michael Kittermaster. London: Constable, 1957. 197p.
This novel, set in colonial Malawi, was written by an expatriate who worked in the colony, and whose father had been its governor in the 1930s. The theme centres around the romantic entanglements of district commissioners. The same author has written another novel: *Katakala* (London: Constable, 1957. 212p.).

407 **I will try.**
Legson Kayira. London: Longman, 1965. 251p.
The autobiography of a remarkable Malawian who undertook a 2,500-mile trek across Africa in search of an American education. The main part of the book recounts his experiences during the first two years when he made his way to Khartoum in Sudan. He was eventually able to attain his dream, and attended the University of Washington.

408 **Land of fire: oral literature from Malawi.**
Matthew Schoffeleers, A. A. Roscoe. Lilongwe: Likuni Press, 1985. 241p.
A collection of eleven folktales collected from the Sena, Chewa, Yao, Lomwe, Nanyanja and Tumbuka ethnic groups, that has been acclaimed as the most substantial collection of Malawi oral literature. The folktales in and of themselves are not particularly unusual; what is unique is the elaborate commentary provided by Schoffeleers (an esteemed Dutch religious anthropologist and priest) and Roscoe (a professor of English, formerly in Malawi and currently in New Zealand) that follows each one of them, thus underlining the value of interdisciplinary approaches in African Studies.

409 **The looming shadow.**
Legson Kayira. London: Longman, 1968. 143p.
Written by a young man who walked across Africa and ended eventually in the United States of America where he went to university, this is a novel of village life and intrigue in Malawi where a feud between two villagers erupts and develops into accusations of witchcraft and attempted murder. The theme is handled with dexterity and detached amusement. Kayira's book has been analysed in Thomas H. Jackson's 'Legson Kayira and the uses of the grotesque', *World Literature Written in English* (Arlington, Texas), vol. 22, no. 2 (1983), p. 143-51. Kayira has also published another novel entitled *Jingala* (London: Longman, 1969. 160p.), that recounts a family conflict in a remote village where the son of a retired tax-collector wishes to become a priest. See also *The detainee* (London: Heinemann, 1974).

410 **Malawian oral literature: aesthetics of indigenous arts.**
Steve Chimombo. Zomba: University of Malawi Centre for Social Research, 1998. 304p. bibliog.
This work is written by one of Malawi's most acclaimed playwrights, whose themes tend to be embedded in Chewa oral legends of origin. It is a comprehensive history, literary analysis and criticism of Chewa folklore, social life and customs. See also the author's 'The dupe in a modern context', *Baraza*, vol. 3 (1985), p. 48-68; and 'Folkstory analysis: basic approaches', *Kalulu*, vol. 1, no. 1 (1976), p. 35-51.

Literature

411 **Night of darkness and other stories.**
Paul Zeleza. Limbe: Montfort Press, 1976. 217p.
A collection of twenty-two short stories dealing with such disparate themes as conflict between the individual and society, problems of individual choice, and psychology.

412 **Nine Malawian plays.**
Edited by James Gibbs. Limbe: Montfort Press, 1976. 171p.
A collection of nine Malawi plays that have been performed throughout that country. Included are plays by Innocent Banda, Spencer Chunga, Chris Kamlongera, Hodges Likwembe, Joe Mosiwa, Enoch Mvula and James Ng'ombe. See also *Theatre in Malawi* (Zomba: University of Malawi Department of English, 1976. 102p.).

413 **No bride price.**
David Rubadiri. Nairobi: East African Publishing House, 1967.
180p.
This is a riveting story of a newly promoted Principal Secretary who runs foul of his Minister and is framed by him on a false charge. A subtheme brings in the conflicts and tensions between Indians and Africans in East Africa. The author, a university professor, was Malawi's first Ambassador to the United Nations. For some more recent novels by Malawians see Tito Banda, *A bitter disapproval* (Limbe: Montfort Press, 1987); Tito Banda, *Sekani's solution* (Limbe: Monfort Press, 1979); Dede Kamkondo, *Silvo and the cruel thief* (Limbe: Popular Publications, 1989. 47p.); and Dede Kamkondo, *The children of the lake* (Limbe: Popular Publications, 1987. 103p.).

414 **No easy task.**
Aubrey Kachingwe. London: Heinemann, 1966. 240p.
This is Kachingwe's first novel. It is the story of political and emotional awakening of a young journalist set against the background of a tug-of-war within a British colony with a settler minority, teetering towards independence.

415 **O Earth, wait for me.**
Frank Mkalawile Chipasula. Johannesburg: Ravan Press, 1984. 84p.
A collection of poems by a self-exiled north Malawian living in the United States. See also his earlier collection of poems: *Visions and reflections: a collection of poems* (Lusaka: National Education Company of Zambia, 1972. 51p.). For other poems by Malawians see *Mau: 39 poems from Malawi* (Blantyre: Hetherwick Press, 1972. 36p.).

416 **Oral literature research in Malawi: a survey and bibliography.**
Steve Chimombo. *Research in African Literatures* (Austin), vol. 14, no. 4 (Winter, 1987), p. 485-98.
This article reviews the intense revival of interest in the oral literature of Malawi, and concludes with a compendium of literature published on this theme.

417 **The quiet chameleon: modern poetry from Central Africa.**
Adrian Roscoe, Mpalive-Hangson Msiska.   New York: Hans Zell,
1992. 240p. bibliog.

A very readable introduction to the poetry of Malawi, Zambia and Zimbabwe. The
authors look into the writings of some of Malawi's poets, including the rich irony of
Jack Malanje, the country's best known poet, the reflective verse of Felix Mnthali, the
passionate voice of Frank Chipasula and others. Key texts are closely analysed to
identify distinctive themes and writing strategies. See also Angus Calder, 'Under
Zomba plateau: the new Malawian poetry', *Kunapipi* (Aarhus), vol. 1, no. 2 (1979),
p. 59-67; A. Nazombe, *The haunting wind: new poetry from Malawi* (Limbe: Dzuka,
1990. 128p.); *Kulankula: interviews with authors from Malawi and Lesotho*, edited
by Bernth Lindfors (Bayreuth, Germany: Eckjard Breitinger, 1989. 75p.). For Ngonde
poetry, see Robo J. Mwaipape's 'Ngonde poetry', *Odi*, vol. 1, no. 1 (1972), p. 14-19;
and for a general introduction of Malawi's literature see Adrian Roscoe, *Uhuru's fire:
African literature east to south* (Cambridge: Cambridge University Press, 1977).

418 **The Rainmaker.**
Steve Chimombo.   Limbe: Popular Publications, 1978. 51p.

This is a much-acclaimed classic, and perhaps the best-known Malawian play. Full of
haunting symbolism drawn from the Chewa myth of origin, the plot parallels that of
the Mboni rain-cult oral tradition epic. For more recent work by Chimombo see his
The basket girl (Limbe: Popular Publications, 1991. 136p.).

419 **'Shreds and tatters': Lipenga's short stories.**
Steve Chimombo.   *Journal of Humanities*, no. 3 (Dec. 1989),
p. 109-27.

An analysis of Lipenga's collected short stories *Waiting for a turn* which, according
to Chimombo, rather than being 'shreds and tatters' as Lipenga himself describes
them, are actually powerfully connected by 'verbal devices of rhythm' (p. 109). For
some of Lipenga's short stories see the collection contained in Ken Lipenga's *Waiting
for a turn* (Limbe: Montfort Press, 1981. 112p.).

420 **Singing in the dark rain: poets, novelists and censorship in
Malawi.**
James Gibbs.   *Index on Censorship* (London), vol. 17, no. 2 (1988),
p. 18-22.

An overview of the oppressive censorship in Malawi, that in its first seven and a half
years of existence banned over 840 books, 100 periodicals and 16 films. The books
included not only works critical of President Banda, or items that might be offensive
to the puritanical and ultra-conservative leader, such as pornography and Marxism,
but also studies of President Nkrumah's overthrow in Ghana, birth control tracts,
accounts of the political problems of contemporary Africa, George Orwell's *Animal
farm*, and publications of the Watchtower Movement. The article also discusses the
status of poets and novelists in Malawi in light of the implicit threat over their heads
every time they attempt to publish something that might be deemed as subversive.

421 **Tales of old Malawi.**
E. Singano, Adrian A. Roscoe.   Limbe: Montfort Publications, 1974.
72p.
This is a collection of folktales edited and introduced by Roscoe, at the time a professor of English at the University of Malawi. See also Peter J. Khomani, 'Substance and form in seven Sena Folk tales', *Kululu*, vol. 1, no. 1 (1976), p. 61-71. For an interesting collection from the turn of the century see Robert S. Rattray, *Folklore stories and songs in Chinyanja* (New York: Negro Universities Press, 1969).

422 **'Whiskers, Alberto' and 'The township lambs' – towards an interpretation of Jack Mapanje's poem 'We wondered about the mellow peaches'.**
James Gibbs.   *Journal of Commonwealth Literature* (London),
vol. 22, no. 1 (1987), p. 31-46.
A literary analysis of one of Jack Mapanje's poems by a scholar at Belgium's University of Liège. Gibbs' analysis is that Mapanje's poems dovetail with political events in Malawi, and especially the suppression of free speech in the country. For a broader analysis of Mpanje's work by a compatriot poet see Steve Chimombo, 'The chameleon in lore, life and literature – the poetry of Jack Mapanje', *Journal of Commonwealth Literature* (London), vol. 23, no. 1 (1988), p. 102-15.

Creative writing in Malawi: a bibliography.
See item no. 479.

One hundred years of Chichewa writing.
See item no. 501.

Art

423 **Basketry masks of the Chewa.**
L. B. Faulkner. *African Arts*, vol. 21, no. 3 (1988), p. 28-31.
Not particularly known for their indigenous arts, and rarely mentioned in African art
literature, the Chewa nevertheless have a tradition of basketry and carved masks. The
latter are usually mentioned only in the vernacular literature since they are used in
Nyau secret society initiation rites, and are constructed in deeply wooded areas
forbidden to outsiders. This article, which is accompanied by illustrations, discusses
the construction and uses of Chewa masks.

424 **Images of Malawi: a collection of paintings and prose.**
Monica Peverelle. Blantyre: Central Africana, 1991. [n.p.].
An unpaginated collection of Peverelle's coloured sketches of Malawi scenes,
accompanied by extracts from her notebooks on the country and its people.

425 **Masks of Malawi.**
Barbara Blackmun, Matthew Schoffeleers. *African Arts*, vol. 5, no. 4
(1972), p. 36-41.
This article describes the masks used by the Chewa in their Nyau secret society
initiation dances. It is accompanied by both colour and black-and-white photos. There
is a separate society, rites and dances, for women, called *chiwoda*. For a brief
description of their dances see Alifeto Chilivumbo, 'Malawi's lively art form', *Africa
Report*, vol. 16, no. 7 (Oct. 1971), p. 16-18.

426 **Phoka pottery from northern Malawi.**
R. O. Heckroodt. *Society of Malawi Journal*, vol. 38, no. 2 (1985),
p. 20-8.
A description of contemporary pottery-making by the Phoka people along the north
Rumphi river in the country's northern region. The techniques used, and the nature
and symbolism of the decorations on the pottery, are described with the aid of
fourteen black-and-white photographs.

Nyau in Kotakota District.
See item no. 155.

Theatre

427 **Community theatre and public health in Malawi.**
David Kerr. *Journal of Southern African Studies* (Oxford), vol. 15,
no. 3 (1989), p. 469-85.
Kerr reports on an experiment, initiated in 1985, to link the performing arts and
primary healthcare communication in two districts in southern Malawi. The
participating groups were the Primary Health Care Unit of Liwonde and the
University of Malawi Theatre for Development. A series of performances were held,
leading to mutual discussions on a variety of issues such as sites of village wells and
the activities of the village health committees. Music, dances and healing have always
been linked together in African societies. For one dance therapy for the ill see Alifeto
Chilivumbo, '*Vimbuza* and *mashawe*: a mystic therapy', *African Music Society
Journal,* vol. 5 (1972), p. 6-9.

428 **An example of syncretic drama from Malawi's Malipenga.**
Christopher F. Kamlongera. *Research in African Literatures*
(Austin), vol. 17, no. 2 (Summer 1986), p. 197-210.
Malipenga, a form of dance-drama, is a new mode of theatre found in rural areas in
central and northern Malawi. It both complements popular theatre and expands on it
with new aspects of European–African cultural blends. This article examines the
origins of Malipenga in Malawi and its salient characteristics. See also *Theatre in
Malawi 1970-1976,* edited by James Gibbs (Zomba: University of Malawi English
Department, 1979).

429 **An experiment in popular theatre in Malawi: the University
Travelling Theatre to Mbalachanda, July 1981.**
David Kerr. *Society of Malawi Journal,* vol. 35, no. 1 (1982),
p. 34-51.
This is a report on the itinerary of the University of Malawi theatre ensemble's visit
to Mbalachanda, one of ten projected Rural Growth Centres administered directly by

the Office of the President and the Malawi Cabinet, as part of a project bringing theatre to the countryside. The article also describes the four plays performed there, and the reactions of the audiences.

430   **Theatre and social issues in Malawi: performers, audiences, aesthetics.**
      David Kerr.   *New Theatre Quarterly* (Cambridge), vol. 4, no. 14 (1988), p. 173-80.

Kerr, the artistic director of the Chikwakwa Theatre in Zomba between 1974 and 1980 notes that most of those involved in theatre in Africa have usually rejected both the outward trappings, and underlying ethos, of what they regard as 'colonialism-inspired' theatre, and, in their quest for greater authenticity, have paradoxically accepted élite-inspired notions of 'popular' theatre. Kerr describes one such experiment that was both adopted, and assimilated, by villagers in Malawi. See also David Kerr, 'Unmasking the spirits: theatre in Malawi', *Drama Review* (Cambridge, Massachusetts), vol. 31, no. 2 (1987), p. 115-25.

431   **Theatre for development in Africa, with case studies from Malawi and Zambia.**
      Christopher Kamlongera.   Bonn, Germany: Education Science and Documentation Centre, 1989. 278p.

An ambitious analysis of the post-1970 emergence of the phenomenon called 'theatre for development'. The author provides a comprehensive aesthetic, sociological and historical evaluation of popular theatre practice in Malawi and Zambia. The thrust of the book is wider, however, in that the material on Malawi and Zambia (chapters 7 and 8) aims primarily to illustrate the utility and possible problems of such experiments throughout Africa.

Music and Dance

432 **Donald Kachamba's kwela music.**
Gerhard Kubik. *Society of Malawi Journal*, vol. 32, no. 2 (July 1979), p. 45-59. bibliog.

This is an introduction, accompanied by illustrations, to the work of Kachamba. Though of Blantyre origins, he is thought of as a Ngoni artist. The author, an Austrian musicologist, recounts the history of his music on the occasion of Kachamba's cutting two LP records. For other analyses of Malawian music forms see the two articles by Wim van Zanen: 'The equidistant heptatonic scale of the Asena in Malawi', *African Music* (Roodeport, South Africa), vol. 6, no. 1 (1980), p. 107-25; and 'Malawian pango music from the viewpoint of information theory', *African Music* (Roodeport, South Africa), vol. 6, no. 3 (1983), p. 90-106.

433 **Ethno-musicological research in southern parts of Malawi.**
Gerhard Kubik. *Society of Malawi Journal*, vol. 21, no. 1 (Jan. 1968), p. 20-32.

This article is a report on a comprehensive musicological survey of traditional music and musical instruments in Malawi, undertaken by a team under the Austrian musicologist Kubik. It resulted in copious field notes, recordings of indigenous music and films. For one analysis of the songs sung during the traditional Nyau secret society rites see James J. Msosa, 'How poetic are Nyau songs?', *Kalulu*, vol. 2 (June 1977), p. 18-30. See also George T. Nurse, 'Popular songs and natural identity in Malawi', *African Music*, vol. 3, no. 3 (1964), p. 101-6; and A. K. Som, 'Acoustics of Malawian xylophone', *Eighth International Congress on Acoustics* (London), 1974, p. 330-40.

434   **The Kachamba Brothers' Band: a study of neo-traditional music in Malawi.**
Gerhard Kubik.   Manchester: Manchester University Press, 1975.
75p. bibliog.

This volume, illustrated with eight pages of plates and accompanied by facsimile music portfolios, is a translation of a German text written by the Austrian musicologist and originally published in Vienna. The book was also published earlier, in 1974, in its English translation and title, by the Institute of African Studies of the University of Zambia in Lusaka. The book is a study of the origin and evolution of the Kachamba band and music, its role within the context of 'new' Southern African music, and its musicological links with contemporary music trends such as *Kwele*, *Jive* and *Simanje-manje*. The author describes in great detail the instruments in use, as well as the songs that appeared in the two LP records that were cut by the band in 1972. See also some of the other works by the same author: *Malawian music: a framework for analysis* (Zomba: University of Malawi, 1987. 93p. bibliog.); and 'The Southern African periphery: banjo traditions in Zambia and Malawi', *Die Welt der Musik: The World of Music* (Berlin), vol. 31, no. 1 (1989), p. 3-30.

Architecture

435 Blantyre historical guide.
Paul A. Cole-King. Blantyre: Christian Literature Association in Malawi, 1973. 26p.

A guide to the history of Blantyre and, through old photographs, to its architecture. It was written by the country's then Director of Antiquities. For a smaller pamphlet, a guide to Malawi's national monuments and historic buildings, see *Heritage of Malawi* (Lilongwe: Monuments Advisory Council, 1984. 16p.). See also Barbara Lamport-Stokes, *Blantyre: glimpses of the early days* (Blantyre: Society of Malawi, 1989. 152p.).

436 Blantyre's early buildings.
John Lamport-Stokes. *Society of Malawi Journal*, vol. 36, no. 2 (1983), p. 27-41.

This article, accompanied by twenty-one black-and-white plates, is an inventory and description of Blantyre's earliest buildings. For thirty plates of historic buildings in Malawi see also David Brian Roy, *The Malawi collection* (Zomba: Malawi Institute of Architects, 1984. 30p.). Much of this information, and many of the photographs, are difficult to find elsewhere.

437 Historic buildings of Malawi.
David Brian Roy. *Society of Malawi Journal*, vol. 38, no. 1 (1985), p. 80-7.

This is a brief study, accompanied by plates, of six sixty-year-old historic buildings in Malawi.

438   **Huts to houses.**
Marjorie A. Saunders.   *Society of Malawi Journal*, vol. 37, no. 2
(July 1984), p. 54-8.
An interesting, if brief, account of the changed building styles and methods in one specific Ngoni district, as observed by the author over her thirty years of residence in Malawi.

Archives and Libraries

439 Archivists and scholars in Central and Eastern Africa: a personal reflection on their inter-dependence.

Kings Phiri. *Journal of Contemporary African Studies* (Pretoria), vol. 3, no. 1/2 (Oct. 1983-April 1984), p. 211-19.

This article, written by a Malawian historian, is an examination of the mutuality of basic interests, and the relations between archival workers and archival researchers in the humanities, in Central Africa in general, and in Malawi in particular.

440 Directory of Malawi libraries.

Stanley M. Made, Therese M. Brown. Zomba: University of Malawi Library, 1976. 111p.

Dated (but still useful) compendium of all libraries in Malawi, both at the University and in the various governmental ministries, colleges, schools, and elsewhere. The material is very conveniently organized with one page for each entry. The information provided for each library includes street and postal addresses, phone number, year established, name of the librarian, hours of operation, the size of the collection, and whether it is accessible to the general public. A somewhat more compact and updated second edition of this work was published in 1990: Joseph J. Uta, *Directory of Malawi libraries* (Zomba: University of Malawi Library, 1990. 42p.).

441 An inventory of S&T library facilities available in Malawi.

J. H. A. Maida. Blantyre: Office of the President, Department of Research and Environmental Affairs, 1991. 27p.

A detailed and very up-to-date inventory of all science and technology (S&T) library resources in the country. The specific information provided on each includes the year of establishment of each resource centre; its precise location and facilities; the total holdings and estimated annual additions; the classification system used; financial resources; personnel; and main clientele.

145

442   **The National Archives of Malawi and the problem of migrated archives.**
Steve B. Mwiyeriwa.   *African Research and Documentation*, no. 30 (1982), p. 32-4.

This brief article outlines the nature, dimensions and problems of missing materials in the Malawi Archives.

443   **The National Archives of Malawi: research opportunities for foreign scholars.**
Steve S. Mwiyeriwa.   *Journal of Contemporary African Studies* (Pretoria), vol. 3, no. 1/2 (Oct. 1983-April 1984), p. 221-7.

A brief survey of the origins, holdings and maintenance of Malawi's National Archives. Despite being one of the best-managed repositories of documentation in the region, the Centre remains plagued by problems stemming from the relative absence of technical services for both the archivists working there, and scholars wishing to use its facilities.

444   **The national library service.**
G. P. Rye.   *Society of Malawi Journal*, vol. 29, no. 1 (Jan. 1976), p. 35-45.

This is a survey of Malawi's public library service, its outreach activities and services.

Publishing

445 **Dr. Banda's banned books.**
Harriet McIlwraith. *Index on Censorship*, vol. 8, no. 6 (1979),
p. 56-8.
A review of the system of press censorship in Malawi, focusing on the kinds of
publications and specific titles (e.g., *The Godfather*) deemed socially harmful and
hence barred from entry into the country. Customs officers at the country's airport
used routinely to check arriving passengers' luggage meticulously, more for such
subversive literature than for other kinds of contraband.

446 **Early efforts at creating African literature: its distribution, local
authorship and library service in Northern Rhodesia and
Nyasaland.**
Augustine W. C. Msiska. *Libri* (Copenhagen), vol. 36, no. 3 (1986),
p. 240-6.
This brief article surveys the history of publishing in Malawi, including the origins of
African literature, its publication, promotion, and distribution, and the emergence of
library services in what is today Zambia and Malawi. The author notes how,
following early uncoordinated publishing activities by individual missionaries, a
number of 'literature committees' sprang up, leading eventually to the Joint
Publications Bureau of Northern Rhodesia and Nyasaland that coordinated publishing
in the two colonies.

447 **History and development of printing and publishing in Malawi.**
Clemence R. Namponya. *Libri* (Copenhagen), vol. 28, no. 2 (1978),
p. 176-81.
In this article Namponya provides a history of book publishing in Malawi, with stress
on the colonial era. Specific individual newspapers that emerged, and other
publications that were published during the early days, are identified. Namponya
concludes that early publishing activity in colonial Nyasaland was 'essentially the

Publishing

history of the efforts of the missionaries at evangelization and of the government at administering the colony' (p. 167).

448   **Press purge in Malawi.**
      Index on Censorship, vol. 2, no. 4 (1973), p. 53-7.

The freedom of the press has never been entrenched in Malawi. The Presidential Office is empowered to act – and not slow to do so – in banning both the local publication of any material judged as either subversive or 'socially harmful', and the entry of books, newspapers, periodicals or movies deemed likewise unacceptable. This article is one of the first published on press restrictions in Malawi.

449   **Printing presses and publishing in Malawi.**
      Steve S. Mwiyeriwa.   *African Book Publishing Record*, vol. 4, no. 2 (April 1978), p. 87-97.

Mwiyeriwa provides a very useful survey of the Malawian publishing trade, including their editorial, pricing and marketing policies and arrangements. The author, an archivist with the National Archives in Zomba, undertakes a valuable case-by-case analysis of each of the eighteen presses which existed in the country at the time of writing, and ends his article with an appendix listing them and their postal addresses.

Publications

450 **The African.**
Lilongwe: Likuni Press, 1949- .
Published by the White Fathers, *The African* started in 1949 as a fortnightly and appeared in three languages: English, Chichewa and Tumbuka.

451 **Central African Planter.**
Zomba, 1895- .
This publication is of historical interest in that it was the first newspaper in Nyasaland, and indirectly the progenitor of more recent newspapers. It commenced publication in 1895, its name a reflection of the dominant interest of the small European settlement in the colony as well as of its founder. The paper underwent several metamorphoses, changing its name (and coverage) in 1897 to the (fortnightly) *Central African Times*. In 1909 the newspaper became the *Nyasaland Times* and twice subsequently changed its frequency of publication. In 1964 it changed its name to the *Malawi Times*.

452 **Government Gazette.**
Zomba: Government Printer, 1964- .
This is the official government gazette of Malawi that in July 1964 superseded the *Nyasaland Gazette* (and other previous titles). It publicizes all governmental ordinances.

453 **Hansard.**
Zomba: Government Printer. irregular.
This publication, irregularly published, is the official verbatim transcript of the debates of Malawi's National Assembly. Though freedom of speech is severely circumscribed, and all deputies until the 1990s were members of the country's single party, the debates contain from time to time veritable gems which, though regarded as innocuous (by whoever edits the transcripts), provide deep insights into the preoccupations of the country's parliamentarians.

454 **Journal of Social Science.**
Zomba: University of Malawi. annual.
This annual is, after the *Society of Malawi Journal*, the second-best source of research material about Malawi, published mostly by Malawians at the local University.

455 **Kululu.**
Limbe. irregular.
This irregularly issued publication, edited by scholars from the University of Malawi, is inter-disciplinary in its coverage of (primarily) cultural and oral literature issues.

456 **Mala Bulletin.**
Zomba. 1978- . 2 issues per year.
The bi-annual bulletin, since 1978, of the Malawi Library Association, contains articles mostly of interest to librarians and researchers.

457 **Malawi Law Reports.**
Oxford: Law Reports International. annual.
This is an annual that is published very much in arrears (e.g., volume 9, 1978/9, was published only in 1991). Its thick tomes contain cases heard by the High Court of Malawi. The subject matter is indexed, as are all individual cases that arc cited.

458 **Malawi News.**
Blantyre: Blantyre Printing and Publishing Press. 1959- . weekly.
Since December 1959, and until the recent press liberalizations of the 1990s that brought about a proliferation of publications (some of which have already folded up) this was the main weekly newspaper of Malawi, and the official organ of the ruling Malawi Congress Party.

459 **Malawi Times.**
Zomba, 1964- .
Successor, in 1964, of the privately published *Nyasaland Times*.

460 **Odi.**
Limbe, 1972- . quarterly.
Since 1972 this has been the quarterly publication of the Writers Group at the University of Malawi. *Odi* is a literary, bi-lingual (English and Chewa) journal that publishes reviews, short stories and plays. Most of Malawi's top authors and and playwrights have on occasion been published in it.

461 **Society of Malawi Journal.**
Blantyre: Society of Malawi, Historical and Scientific. 1965- .
2 issues per year.
The bi-annual continuation since July 1965 of the earlier *Nyasaland Journal* (founded in 1946), whose numbering it continued. This journal is Malawi's most valuable source of articles and research findings by local and expatriate scholars on a very wide variety of topics, though always steering clear of political or controversial issues. Most of these articles are not subsequently republished outside the country.

462 Star Magazine.
Blantyre: Blantyre Printing and Publishing Press. 1975- . monthly.
This is a flashy (for sedate Malawi) monthly journal, geared mostly to a feminine readership. Appearing first in August 1975, the journal was the second indigenous attempt to 'fill the vacuum . . . [with] a popular magazine that can provide information and entertainment' (quoted from the editorial of the first issue). The journal was so popular that in July 1977 a supplement, *Star Stories* (appearing every two months), was launched.

463 Vision of Malawi.
Blantyre: Department of Information. quarterly.
Intermittent (though officially a quarterly) publication of the Malawi Department of Information. It replaced the previously titled *This is Malawi*.

464 Youth News.
Limbe: Malawi Young Pioneers. 1972- . quarterly.
Since 1972 this has been the quarterly publication of the Malawi Young Pioneers, the youth organ of the Malawi Congress Party. The Young Pioneers, a bulwark of the Banda regime, were recently disbanded, and the publication terminated.

Reference Works and Bibliographies

465 Africa Confidential.
London. fortnightly.

This extremely expensive eight-page newsletter on Africa has carved itself an enviable niche as an utterly indispensable serious research tool, providing detailed in-depth reports by extremely knowledgeable anonymous expert informants resident in the countries concerned. Each issue carries between four and six articles of one or two pages, with the last page devoted to short vignettes, equally valuable, on a number of countries. While in any particular year there may appear, perhaps only six 'full' articles on Malawi, the detail contained in each (especially with respect to personalities) is simply not available in any other publication.

466 Africa Research Bulletin.
Exeter, England. monthly.

Published in two series that cover all of Africa (one on primarily political issues, the other on economic matters), well-indexed, comprehensive in coverage, these monthlies are widely acknowledged as by far the best sources of up-to-date primary documentation on the continent. Essentially, the publications extensively extract African news items, and condense news and articles on Africa appearing during the preceding month in a wide array African and continental newspapers and weeklies. Where necessary, they are translated into English. The source extracted always appears at the foot of each entry.

467 Annotated bibliography of agriculture in Malawi, 1930-1980.
Clemence R. Namponya. Zomba: University of Malawi Research and Publications Committee, 1985. 312p.

This book contains a briefly annotated but very comprehensive bibliography of 1,391 books, articles and reports relating to Malawian agricultural issues. The compiler was the Librarian of the Bunda College of Agriculture in Malawi.

468   **An annotated bibliography of education in Malawi.**
      Ray Jackson.   Zomba: University of Malawi Library, 1976. 57p.

A bibliography compiled by the Chairperson of the Department of Education at the University of Malawi. It includes some 450 items, most on Malawian educational issues, some in typescript form. The bibliography expands on earlier bibliographies, the most recent of which was: Jonathan M. Daube, *Education in Malawi: a bibliography* (Limbe: University of Malawi, 1970. 15p.).

469   **An annotated bibliography of theses and dissertations held by Chancellor College library.**
      Augustine W. C. Msiska.   Zomba: Chancellor College Library, 1988. 101p.

Despite being marred by intermittent errors, this is still a valuable resource guide to academic research on Malawi and neighbouring states. The volume lists 289 dissertations, by both expatriates and locals in Malawi, and Malawians and foreigners abroad, held by the University library. The dissertations are divided into twenty categories. The directory is striking for the total absence of research on post-independence Malawi political themes (forbidden in a country where the University did not even have a Political Science department) and the large percentage of dissertations conducted on other African states.

470   **Area handbook for Malawi.**
      Harold D. Nelson.   Washington, DC: US Government Printing Office, 1975. 353p. maps. bibliog.

A very comprehensive compilation of information on the history, society, economy, religious and cultural life, political evolution and structures of Malawi. It is part of a series of handbooks covering many countries of the world. Some of the volumes in this series have been updated over the years, but not the Malawi one. Though considerably dated by now in several fields, if one keeps that in mind this book remains one of the better single-volume reference works on Malawi, and a starting point for more specific readings and research on the country.

471   **Bibliographies for African Studies, 1970-1986.**
      Yvette Scheven.   London: Hans Zell, 1988. 615p.

This is a very comprehensive bibliography of bibliographies on Africa. The book is organized by themes/subjects followed by country rubrics and is well indexed at the end by author/country/topic. Though the country section for Malawi amounts to only three pages (p. 447-9) with nineteen entries, the work is well worth consulting since there is more in it than meets the cursory eye, and some of the bibliographies listed for neighbouring countries are of use to students of Malawi.

472   **A bibliography of Malawi.**
      Edward E. Brown, Carol A. Fisher, John B. Webster.   Syracuse, New York: Syracuse University Press, 1965. 161p.

This was one of the first comprehensive bibliographies on Malawi, and is still of use for research on the pre-colonial and colonial eras. It includes some 3,000 unannotated items divided into twenty-four categories. An attempt to have the bibliography updated periodically resulted in only one additional publication: John B. Webster,

Reference Works and Bibliographies

Paulus Mohome, *A supplement to a bibliography of Malawi* (Syracuse, New York: Syracuse University Program of Eastern African Studies, 1969. 62p. (Occasional Bibliography, no. 13)). Though the latter is primarily a chronological update of the parent volume, it also includes several items missed originally.

473 **A bibliography of oral literature in Malawi, 1860-1986.**
Steve Chimombo. Zomba: University of Malawi, 1987. 32p.
Written by the well-known Malawian author, this is an important bibliography of Malawi folktale literature, oral traditions, narratives, proverbs, folksongs and riddles. This work was intended to be the first of an annual publication. It commences with a brief introduction on oral literature research in Malawi, and then continues with listings organized under four categories: folktales, proverbs, popular songs, and 'devinettes'.

474 **Books about Malawi.**
National Library Service. Blantyre: National Library, 1969. 23p.
This bibliography includes a selection of the most significant early publications on Malawi.

475 **Business information on Malawi.**
Blantyre: National Bank of Malawi, 1984. 2nd ed. 48p.
The second edition of a business and commerce handbook to Malawi that is intermittently updated. It contains concisely packed information on the geography of the country, currency, banking system, business conditions, taxation and other useful information pertinent to visiting businessmen. The booklet is illustrated with maps, tables and photographs.

476 **Catholic directory of Malawi, 1983-1986.**
Lilongwe: Catholic Secretariat of Malawi, 1985. 124p.
A detailed directory of the Catholic establishment of Malawi, with their addresses and telephone numbers. Included are lists of hostels, convents, bookstores, and the names of all officers and the number of staff in each diocese by district and parish.

477 **Contributions from Bunda: a list of papers and publications from Bunda College of Agriculture.**
Clemence R. Namponya. Lilongwe: Bunda College of Agriculture, 1978. 33p.
This is a bibliography, mostly on agricultural topics, of papers, reports and research conducted at Malawi's school of agriculture.

478 **A comprehensive author and subject index to the *Society of Malawi Journal*, 1948-1978.**
Gadi G. Y. Mgomezulu. *Society of Malawi Journal*, vol. 32, no. 2 (1981), p. 1-84.
As the title indicates, this is a 30-year index (under forty-two subject classifications, including book reviews and obituaries) of Malawi's most valuable journal that has

published original research both by local Malawians and expatriates, much of which has not appeared in print elsewhere. Since few libraries overseas have an entire press-run of the *Journal*, the index is invaluable to those who cannot physically examine it but might discover through the index items to be photocopied via inter-library services.

479 **Creative writing in Malawi: a bibliography.**
Steve Chimombo. *Research in African Literatures* (Austin, Texas), vol. 18, no. 3 (Fall 1987), p. 336-9.
A useful compendium of all books, plays, collections of short stories and oral literature, published in English, Chichewa and other local languages.

480 **Doing business in Malawi.**
New York: Price, Waterhouse Center for Transnational Taxation, 1984. 23p.
This pamphlet, periodically updated, is an information guide for businessmen exploring commercial transactions with, or industrial possibilities in, Malawi. It includes concise information on legislation and regulations pertaining to foreign investments and trade, and data on the taxation system of the country.

481 **Historical dictionary of Malawi.**
Cynthia Crosby. Metuchen, New Jersey: Scarecrow Press, 1992. 2nd ed. 229p. bibliog.
One of the most important reference works on Malawi, this is part of a 50-volume series that covers just about every African country. The book contains a chronology and introductory essay, biographical and other entries on every aspect of the country, its history, political, social and religious personalities, the economy, towns and ethnic groups, etc. The work concludes with a bibliography of over 800 unannotated books and articles, classified under broad topics.

482 **Investing in Malawi.**
Malawi Development Corporation. Blantyre: Malawi Development Corporation, 1989. 265p.
A comprehensive compendium of all legislation and ordinances governing investments in Malawi, as well as foreign trade and exchange regulations, general economic and business conditions, and a listing of business enterprises in the country. For some recent changes in taxation law in the country see Zmarak Salizi and Wayne Thirsk, *Tax reform in Malawi* (Washington, DC: World Bank, 1990. 45p.).

483 **Know Africa.**
London: Africa Books, 1991. 2 vols.
This massive second edition of one of the basic reference works on Africa contains in the first volume (subtitled 'Africa today') a well-organized and comprehensive chapter on Malawi's history, economy, politics and recent socio-economic evolution. The equally large second volume (Africa's Who's Who'), contains alphabetically arranged biographies of the most important personalities in Africa, including Malawians. The bibliographies are not arranged under nationality (though the

nationality of each individual is noted). Some of these biographies are not easily available elsewhere, but around half are of Nigerians, and many are very dated.

484 Malawi.
Robert B. Boeder. Oxford: Clio Press, 1979. 1st ed. 165p.

This first edition of the current book is still very valuable to students of Malawi interested in some of the earlier literature on the country that has not been included in this volume. The book contains 557 numbered and annotated items, 50 theses and roughly 450 other items that are mentioned in the annotations. Boeder, who at one time lectured at the University of Malawi, has himself written several important monographs and articles on that country.

485 Malawi.
In: *Africa south of the Sahara*. London: Europa Publications, bibliog. annual.

This annual publication covers all the countries of Africa, and is one of the prime reference works on that continent. Each country section comprises a series of essays (written by different authors) on 'Physical and social geography', 'Recent history', 'The economy', statistical tables, other basic information, and a 'Directory' with data on the country's structures, leaders and diplomatic representation. Though punctually published, some of the data within are not fully up to date.

486 Malawi.
In: *Africa contemporary record*, edited by Colin Legum. New York: Africana Publishing Co., annually 1966-89.

This invaluable reference work on Africa is unfortunately currently discontinued, but the back volumes are still an important source of information about Malawi. The thick tomes consist of a section of thematic articles on regional or continental issues, followed by a country-by-country account of the socio-economic developments during the preceding year, and statistical data. The chapters on Malawi were always comprehensive and reliable.

487 Malawi – 25 years of independence.
J. Kalley (et al.). *Southern Africa Update* (Johannesburg: University of Witwatersrand Library), vol. 5, no. 1 (April 1990), p. 2-68.

A bibliography of 745 items – a handful of which are briefly annotated – subdivided into twenty-three subject areas. The bibliography is among the most comprehensive on Malawi, though its length is inflated in several categories (in the absence of substantive books or articles) by various one-page news items from, for example, the monthly *Africa Research Bulletin*.

488 Malawi: an official handbook.
Blantyre: Ministry of Information. annual.

Though an annual, this publication is intermittently published, and summarizes basic facts about the country and its social and economic development.

489 **Malawi: an outline guide for expatriate contract employees.**
Ian E. Knight. London: Royal Commonwealth Society, 1983. 17p.
This pamphlet, in its sixteenth revised edition, contains useful information about the
country for intending first-time expatriate residents. Customs, prices, availability of
housing, commodities and facilities are among some of the topics covered. A
somewhat similar pamphlet, distributed by a voluntary group of resident American
women, exists for Americans arriving in Malawi for the first time.

490 **Malawi agricultural research directory.**
Lilongwe: Chief Agricultural Research Office, 1988. 72p.
This publication is a directory of all projects, researchers and institutions involved in
agricultural research in Malawi. Pagination varies.

491 **Malawi buyer's guide.**
Blantyre: Malawi Export Promotion Council, 1987. 100p.
This periodically published volume (technically an annual, and at times quite short) is
a register of all government ministries and commercial and industrial enterprises in
Malawi with possible relevance to foreign importers. The listings provide names,
addresses and telephone numbers. The book is liberally interspersed with
advertisements, photographs, illustrations and maps. The same export promotion
organization also publishes a catalogue of Malawi handicrafts available for export:
Craft buyers' guide. Catalogue of Malawi made handicrafts, edited by Chatonda S.
Mhone (Blantyre: Malawi Export Promotion Council, Small Enterprise Development
Organization, 1990. 68p.). There is yet another periodically updated listing of
Malawian commercial and industrial enterprises: *Industrial and trade directory,*
edited by S. J. Mpasy (Blantyre: Malawi Chamber of Commerce and Industry, 1991).

492 **Malawi entrepreneur's handbook.**
USAID. Lilongwe: USAID, 1990. 162p.
Part of a recent series of handbooks by the Rural Enterprise and Agro-business
Development Institutions Project of USAID, this is a reference manual for small
Malawi entrepreneurs or intending entrepreneurs. Two other manuals in this series
exist: USAID, *Promoting small and medium scale manufacturing of products from
the minerals and rocks of Malawi* (Lilongwe: USAID, 1990. 130p.); and *Agro-
industrial opportunities in Malawi: how to start your own business* (Lilongwe:
USAID, 1990. 162p.). The volumes have been, apparently, very sought-after in
Malawi. They all provide, in simple language, basic business know-how to aid new
entrepreneurs to detect opportunities, adopt acceptable quality-control standards, and
to successfully market their products.

493 **The Malawi government directory 1990.**
Zomba: Government Printer, 1990. 145p.
A directory of every administrative officer in Malawi by department, and including
departmental address and phone number. It is periodically updated. There also exists
a *Staff list* (Zomba: Government Printer, 1987), a somewhat similar periodically
updated register of all senior officers in the Malawi government and administration.

Reference Works and Bibliographies

494 **Malawi national bibliography.**
National Archives of Malawi. Zomba: Government Printer. annual.
This bibliography has been published annually since 1968. It has contained in recent years around 20 pages, listing some 130-40 mostly locally published books, pamphlets, and the first issues of new periodicals deposited, as required by law, in the National Archives Library. The annual is usually published one year in arrears.

495 **Malawi statistical yearbook.**
National Statistical Office. Zomba: Government Printer. annual.
Though officially an annual this publication has, at most times, been published in arrears, at times considerably so. It provides the latest data on all aspects of Malawi, including the economy, forestry, fishing, population and trade. See also the National Statistical Office's *Compendium of agricultural statistics* (Zomba: Government Printer, 1977. 90p.).

496 **Malawi yearbook.**
Blantyre: Department of Information.
Officially an annual publication on all aspects of Malawi, but the volumes have been erratically published.

497 **Malawiana theses.**
Kwathu Kwabwino Likagwa. Zomba: University of Malawi Library, 1983. 31p.
Originally submitted in part-fulfilment of research for the Malawi Library Association Certificate, this is a useful unannotated compilation of some 335 academic dissertations on Malawi written for degree requirements both in Malawi and at foreign universities.

498 **National inventory of scientific publications.**
J. H. A. Maida. Blantyre: Office of the President, Department of Research and Environmental Affairs, 1991. 233p.
A comprehensive listing of all scientific publications and reports, published or unpublished, found in all libraries and/or ministries in Malawi. The material is grouped under the governmental Ministry or University division holding it. The term scientific is used very loosely, however, since the inventory covers also literary works, poetry and drama. A companion volume inventoried priority areas for research; see J. H. A. Maida, *National inventory of research projects and priority areas of research* (Blantyre: Office of the President, Department of Research and Environmental Affairs, 1991. 225p.). Another publication has also been published under the same auspices, stressing agricultural research: *National register of research publications, 1965-1975* (Zomba: Government Printer, 1976. 43p.). See also Augustine W. C. Msiska, *A bibliography of plans, reports and surveys on Malawi held by the University Library* (Zomba: University of Malawi Library, 1973. 22p.). For holdings on agriculture see *DAR library system union catalogue* (Lilongwe: Department of Agricultural Research Library System, 1987. unpaged). See also *Union list of periodicals: Bundu College of Agriculture, Chancellor College, Kamuzu College of Nursing, Polytechnic, University of Malawi Library* (Zomba: The libraries, 1983. 133p.).

Reference Works and Bibliographies

499 National inventory of scientists and engineers in Malawi.
J. H. A. Maida. Blantyre: Office of the President, Department of
Research and Environmental Affairs, 1991. 483p.
This is a directory listing all scientific and engineering personnel in Malawi.

500 National register of research publications 1965-1975.
National Research Council. Lilongwe: National Research Council,
1975. 43p.
A listing of some 400 research papers and reports prepared during Malawi's first
decade of independence. They are listed by institution of origin.

**501 One hundred years of Chichewa writing 1875-1975: a selected
bibliography.**
S. M. Made, M. V. B. Mangoche Mwebe, Ray Jackson. Zomba:
University of Malawi, 1976. 87p.
An unannotated bibliography of some 1,000 items written in Chichewa. See also
S. Mwiyerima, *Vernacular literature of Malawi, 1854-1975* (Zomba: National
Archives, 1976).

502 Reference works for Malawian studies: a select and annotated list.
John W. East. *MALA Review*, vol. 3, no. 1 (July 1982).
This is an introductory annotated listing of sixty works, most published in Malawi,
organized under thirteen subject categories. MALA is the organ of the Association of
Malawian Librarians.

**503 Refugee problem in Malawi: annotated bibliography on refugees
in Malawi from national newspapers October 1986 – March 1989.**
Vote D. Somba. Zomba: Chancellor College Library, 1989. 27p.
With Malawi periodically flooded by hundreds of thousands of refugees fleeing civil
war or harsh economic conditions in Mozambique, this bibliography focuses on items
relating to this problem published in the local national press. Since tight press
censorship existed in Malawi until recently, the material presented largely represents
officially accepted views.

504 Republic of Malawi Parliament biographies.
Blantyre: Department of Information, 1986. 72p.
Despite becoming obviously outdated because of the multi-partyism of the 1990s, this
is still a very valuable publication for anyone undertaking serious research on
Malawi. The volume contains a concise biography, almost every one accompanied by
a photograph, of all elected and nominated MPs in the June 1983 elections in Malawi.
Apart from its intrinsic historical value, and the fact that much of the information is
simply not available in any other source, a number of the personalities still revolve
around the pinnacle of power today. It is, on the other hand, surprising that such a
publication was issued at all, since the Malawian parliament under President Banda
has at all times been completely bereft of any power or authority. Of passing interest
are the biographies of Malawi cabinet ministers up to the mid-1970s contained in
Afrika Biografien (Africa Biographies) (Bonn, Germany: Friedrich-Ebert Stiftung,

1972). The latter biographies were issued in loose-leaf form, both in an English and a German version, whenever cabinet changes took place. Other early sources of biographical information are: *Dictionary of African biography* (London: Methuen, 1971); and John Dicke, Alan Rake *Who's Who in Africa* (London: African Buyer and Trader, 1973).

505 **The Rhodesias and Nyasaland: a guide to official publications.**
Audrey A. Walker. Washington, DC: Library of Congress, 1965. 285p.
This reference work, published by the African section of the Library of Congress, is a useful bibliography, based on the library's very extensive holdings, of colonial-era official documentation by the colonial government of what were to become Zambia, Zimbabwe and Nyasaland.

506 **Southern Africa annual review.**
Edited by Christopher Pycroft, Barry Munslow, Mark Adams.
London: Hans Zell, 1990. 340p.
This work, an annual usually published three years in arrears, contains extracts from various newspapers, weeklies and radio broadcasts relating to the entire region of Southern Africa. The 1990 volume includes material from 1987/88.

507 **A study of indigenous and international non-governmental organizations working in Malawi.**
Linda S. Howey. Lilongwe: USAID, 1989. 67p.
A listing and description of all NGOs in Malawi.

508 **University of Malawi publications: a guide.**
Fassil Aradoom. Washington, DC: Library of Congress, 1979. 41p.
This work is a handy guide, and not as outdated as its date might suggest, to the publications issued by the various departments and research centres at the University of Malawi. Though the specific listings of works published in Malawi, based on the Library of Congress extensive holdings, are obviously out of date, the fact that most departments publish ongoing series of works, allows the reader to be appraised of sources of documentation at the university.

Africa today.
See item no. 2.

Africa.
See item no. 3.

Malawi in maps.
See item no. 20.

Malawi: official standard names.
See item no. 22.

National atlas of Malawi.
See item no. 26.

Notes on the climate of Malawi.
See item no. 27.

Short history and annotated bibliography on soil and water conservation in Malawi.
See item no. 28.

Draft environmental profile of Malawi.
See item no. 32.

Note on the underground water resources of the Protectorate.
See item no. 35.

African cichlids of Lakes Malawi and Tanganyika.
See item no. 36.

The amphibians of Malawi.
See item no. 37.

Dictionary of plant names in Malawi.
See item no. 41.

First checklist of the herbaceous flora of Malawi.
See item no. 45.

Malawi's national parks and game reserves.
See item no. 50.

Mammals of Malawi.
See item no. 51.

Preliminary annotated list of Malawi forest insects.
See item no. 54.

Preliminary annotated list of some edible fungi.
See item no. 55.

Ten (or so) primates of Malawi.
See item no. 57.

Trees of Malawi.
See item no. 58.

The useful plants of Malawi.
See item no. 59.

David Livingstone: a catalogue of documents.
See item no. 78.

Nyasaland mails and stamps.
See item no. 111.

An annotated list of independent churches in Malawi, 1900-1981.
See item no. 135.

Provisional annotated chronological list of witch-finding movements in Malawi, 1850-1980.
See item no. 158.

Religion in Malawi.
See item no. 159.

Population and housing census, 1987.
See item no. 174.

Industrial and trade directory.
See item no. 376.

Inventory of designated roads in Malawi.
See item no. 386.

Oral literature research in Malawi: a survey and a bibliography.
See item no. 416.

Directory of Malawi libraries.
See item no. 440.

An inventory of S&T library facilities available in Malawi.
See item no. 441.

Printing presses and publishing in Malawi.
See item no. 449.

Indexes

There follow three indexes: authors, titles, and subjects. Title entries are italicized and refer either to the main titles, or to other works cited in the annotations. The numbers refer to bibliographical entries and not to pages.

Index of Authors

Index of Titles

173

Index of Subjects

development policies 336, 339, 354
dictionaries 395-7, 401-3
diplomatic representatives 2
Domingo, Charles 148
drought 79

E

ecology and environment 17, 30-5, 79, 83
economy 2-4, 99, 185, 256, 277, 295, 305-40
education 242-53, 319, 468
EEC 298
electricity 378
energy 33, 378-9
estates 120, 125-6, 128-30, 188, 206, 325, 350
ethnicity 80, 257
ethnomedicine *see* herbalists
expeditions *see* travel

F

family formation 223
family law 283
famine 83
fertilizers 355
fish 36, 48, 312, 320, 349
flora and fauna 16, 31-2, 36-60, 157
food production 196, 205, 219, 313
food supply 209, 224, 342, 357
forced labour 86
foreign relations 295-304
forests 31, 39, 43-4, 58
fossils 68
fungi 55

G

game reserves *see* national parks

gazetteers 22, 26, 39
gender issues 191-207
geography and geology 3, 17-29, 94
government 2, 4
grasslands 46
group lending 366

H

health issues 99, 195, 201, 219, 224, 227-41, 427
herbalists 229, 231, 233, 235
history 2-4, 67, 69-133
housing 212-13, 217-18
housing census 174

I

income distribution 307, 369
income generation 196, 198
illiteracy 243
independent churches 135
Indians 221
industry 319, 330, 343, 373-83
informal sector 213, 314-15, 319, 382
innovation 199
insects 54
interest groups 84
Iron Age 63-5
Islam 92, 145, 152
Italians 80

J

Jehovah Witnesses 170
job creation 189
Johnson, William 154
Johnston, Sir Harry 70
journals *see* newspapers
Jumba dynasty 92, 124, 145
juvenile literature 1

K

Kariba dam 190
Karonga 90
King's African Rifles 89, 127
Kirk, John 105
Kota Kota 21, 92, 145, 155

L

labour 120, 125-6, 180-90, 316, 319
Lake Malawi 29, 36, 47-8, 79, 117
Lambya kingdom 81
land issues 94, 120, 126, 184, 284, 286-9, 294, 316, 319, 343, 348, 361
land survey 24
languages 394-403
legal codes 279-91
leprosy 237
libraries 439-44
Lilongwe 121, 208-18, 315
linguistics 395-403
literature 404-22, 473, 476, 501
Livingstone, David 78, 95-6, 105, 166
Livingstonia Mission 115, 143
local government 207, 273
Lomwe 107, 121, 188, 350
low-income housing 211

M

Madagascar 307, 327
magic 167
maize 357
malnutrition 202, 219
mammals 38, 51
management 380, 383
Mang'anja 141
maps 20, 24, 26
marriage 176, 283, 290
martyr cults 150, 165

U

ungulates 42
Universities' Mission 96,
142, 147, 153-4,
168
uprisings 91, 100,
101
urbanization 122, 208-18,
220

V

vegetation 20, 41, 46, 60,
66
Viphya mill 330

W

Watchtower Society 102,
170
water resources 28-9, 35,
367
welfare associations
143
wildlife 32
witch-finding
158
women 191-207, 220, 223,
245, 266
women farmers
204-5
World Bank 311, 326,
337, 363

Y

Yao 114, 131, 136, 145,
152, 177, 179, 397, 399
Young, C. 77, 153

Z

Zambezi 105
Zambia 85, 119, 124, 143,
181, 190, 214, 221,
256, 322, 343, 377
Zimbabwe 181, 214, 222,
301, 377
Zomba 16, 21, 122, 332
Zululand 85

Map of Malawi

This map shows the more important towns and other features.

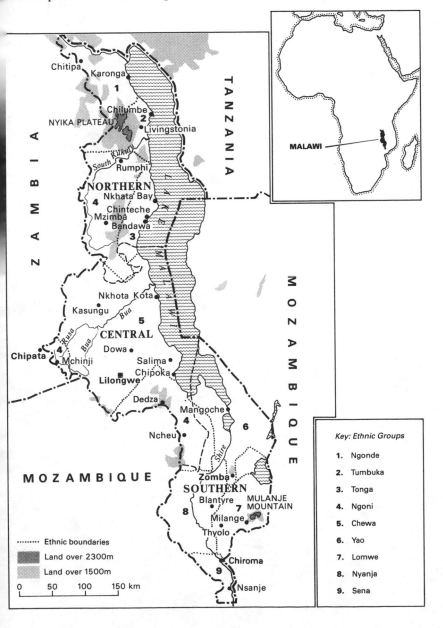

Key: Ethnic Groups

1. Ngonde
2. Tumbuka
3. Tonga
4. Ngoni
5. Chewa
6. Yao
7. Lomwe
8. Nyanja
9. Sena

········ Ethnic boundaries

Land over 2300m

Land over 1500m

0   50   100   150 km

ALSO FROM CLIO PRESS

INTERNATIONAL ORGANIZATIONS SERIES

Each volume in the International Organizations Series is either devoted to one specific organization, or to a number of different organizations operating in a particular region, or engaged in a specific field of activity. The scope of the series is wide-ranging and includes intergovernmental organizations, international non-governmental organizations, and national bodies dealing with international issues. The series is aimed mainly at the English-speaker and each volume provides a selective, annotated, critical bibliography of the organization, or organizations, concerned. The bibliographies cover books, articles, pamphlets, directories, databases and theses and, wherever possible, attention is focused on material about the organizations rather than on the organizations' own publications. Notwithstanding this, the most important official publications, and guides to those publications, will be included. The views expressed in individual volumes, however, are not necessarily those of the publishers.

VOLUMES IN THE SERIES

1   *European Communities*,
    John Paxton
2   *Arab Regional Organizations*,
    Frank A. Clements
3   *Comecon: The Rise and Fall of an
    International Socialist
    Organization*, Jenny Brine
4   *International Monetary Fund*,
    Anne C. M. Salda
5   *The Commonwealth*, Patricia M.
    Larby and Harry Hannam

6   *The French Secret Services*, Martyn
    Cornick and Peter Morris
7   *Organization of African Unity*,
    Gordon Harris
8   *North Atlantic Treaty Organization*,
    Phil Williams
9   *World Bank*, Anne C. M. Salda
10 *United Nations System*, Joseph P.
    Baratta

TITLES IN PREPARATION

British Secret Services, Philip H. J.
    Davies
Israeli Secret Services, Frank A.
    Clements

Organization of American States, David
    Sheinin